Fifth Generation Management
REVISED EDITION

CO-CREATING THROUGH VIRTUAL ENTERPRISING, DYNAMIC

TEAMING, AND KNOWLEDGE NETWORKING

Charles M. Savage

Butterworth-Heinemann
Boston Oxford Melbourne Singapore Toronto Munich New Delhi Tokyo

Library of Congress Cataloging-in-Publication Data
Savage, Charles M.
    5th generation management : co-creating through virtual enterprising, dynamic
        teaming, and knowledge networking / Charles M. Savage. – Rev. ed.
    p.   cm.
    Rev. ed. of: Fifth generation management / Charles M. Savage. c1990.
    Includes bibliographical references and index.
    ISBN 0-7506-9701-6 (pbk.)
    1. Industrial management.   2. Organization.   I. Savage, Charles M. Fifth generation
        management.   II. Title.
HD31.S322   1996
658.4'02–dc20   95-46034
                                                           CIP

British Library Cataloguing-in-Publication Data
A catalogue record for this book is available from the British Library.

The publisher offers discounts on bulk orders of this book.
For information, please write:

Manager of Special Sales
Butterworth-Heinemann
313 Washington Street
Newton, MA 02158-1626
617 928-2628
Fax: 617 928-2620
Email: wmb@bh.com
Web site: http://www.bh.com/bh/

10 9 8 7 6 5 4 3 2

Printed in the United States of America

HD
31
.532
/996

CONTENTS

FOREWORD BY TOM PETERS

Destroy all organization charts! Walk the talk! So easy to say . . .
I do, all the time. But many organizations have a congenital blockage about destroying the comfortable.

In *Fifth Generation Management*, CEO Frank Giardelli of Custom Products and Services, Inc., destroys his organization's chart.
For him, the walk is not talk, but probing dialogue. He does not
"communicate," he conducts a remarkable conversation. It is
simple, straightforward, and honest. His colleagues are not just
empowered, they are energized.

Instead of talking about walking the talk, perhaps we should
start saying, "Dance the dialogue!" This strategic dialogue, as
Sherrin Bennett and Juanita Brown call it, is what we need in
executive suites around the globe.[1] Rather than just looking at
numbers for strategic planning purposes, we need to reflect on the
infrastructure of meaning, models, and metaphors that undergird
our organizations and turn them into vibrant communities.

Charles Savage provides a remarkable example of this strategic
dialogue, as Frank Giardelli and his colleagues let go, somewhat
fearfully, of the tried and true of their steeply hierarchical organization. Like many of us, the skeptic Gregory Kasmirian does not
give in easily. Marjorie Callahan wisely captures their old and new
mental models on a flip chart, as they indeed dance their way
through a remarkable dialogue.

Through their explorations, we feel the curse of the "A," "B," "C" triad, the archetypal metaphor of the hierarchy. The dynamics of the triad blind B to discovering and building upon the creative talents and capabilities of C. It breeds suspicion and distrust, the *real* cost drivers in our companies.

Their dialogue also brings out the importance of the "customers' customers." Through a simple set of four overlapping circles and two words, "capabilities" and "aspirations," Savage redefines the *value chain* into a *valuing cluster* that inspires strategic dialogue not only within but between companies.

Our companies are no longer just in the one-at-a-time transaction business; more often they are co-creators along with other members of the "valuing cluster." We call this mass customization, and the trick is that we do not just customize *for*, but *with* our customers to meet the aspirations of *their* customers. Boeing customized the 777 *with* United, Japan Airlines, and others. Titeflex in Springfield, Massachusetts, customizes flexible piping *with* its customers in a matter of hours, because it has built a highly agile infrastructure. It knows how to listen to and dialogue with its customers to make them more successful with their customers.

It is not our customers' needs, but their aspirations that really count. It is not their problems (weaknesses), but their capabilities (strengths) that should be the focus of our continuous dialogue. As they feel we value them, their trust and openness will increase, and together we can build upon one another's strengths to co-create a profitable and innovative future.

The key to this book is Savage's simple yet forceful exploration of work and human time. Work is dialogue . . . a creative dialogue where we not only create products and services, but co-create one another. This only makes sense if we realize that it is *meaning* and not just *satisfaction* that really matters. In human time, the underlying patterns and resources of the past and future provide the canvas upon which to discover the meaning that inspires our innovation and co-creativity.

In 1991 I named *Fifth Generation Management* my business book of the year. I find that the new subtitle of this revised edition, *Co-creating Through Virtual Enterprising, Dynamic Teaming, and Knowledge Networking*, captures exceptionally well the shift in focus over the last five years from "integration" within a single company to "synergy" and "collaboration" within and between companies. Our challenge is not to "get it right" so we can put the organization on automatic pilot, but to participate in the drama of co-creation with our colleague companies. It is confusing, it is messy, but in the swirl of possibilities, dancing the dialogue is incredibly exciting and revitalizing.

PREFACE TO THE FIRST EDITION

The ecology of the world business environment is changing dramatically. Gone are the days of the comfortable protected market niches. And gone are the days of geographic isolation.

Change is everywhere. Europe is putting itself together under the 1992 "single market" banner in ways it has not known since Charlemagne. Japan is opening itself to more foreign products. The Pacific Rim's economic power grows. The Soviet Union and Eastern Europe are repositioning themselves in the family of nations. And Africa, Latin America, Australia, China, India, the Middle East, and other nations are striving for greater involvement in the world economy.

Change in technology is also everywhere. Steam energy is changing to computer power as the main driver of economic life. Telephone connectivity is evolving into combined voice and data links. And isolated companies are initiating multiple strategic alliances with the aid of local and wide-area networking.

Nowhere is change going to be more dramatic than in the way we manage and lead our enterprises in the 1990s and beyond. The logic of computers and networking makes obsolete many of the deeply cherished notions of the past.

Yet just as long distance runners sometimes "hit the wall" of their capabilities and endurance, many companies are hitting the organizational wall, or so it seems. They have trouble absorbing more computer-based technology. The reasons for this are often unclear. Could it be that we are putting fifth-generation technology in second-generation organizations? Could it be that we really are not hitting the wall, but instead are squeezed against a bottleneck? We long to break free of our cramped quarters, confining organizational structures, and shallow notions about management and organization.

Throughout the industrial era it has been possible for the organization to absorb each new wave of mechanical technology. Yet as wave after wave of computer technology beats against our traditional ways of doing things, we find ourselves in the backwaters of confusion and uncertainty. How are we to understand what is going on?

Despite the promise of the new computer technology, flexibility and adaptability remain out of our grasp because of continual turf battles, provincial politics, and rigid control systems. Our confusingly complex organizations have more antibodies than we can cope with. What should we do?

Many are saying the answer is "integration." Put in computers, more computers, and still more computers, then network them together. The literature is full of references to computer-integrated manufacturing (CIM) and computer-integrated enterprise (CIE). Why is enterprise integration turning out to be more of a challenge than most people expected?

Could it be that integration is much more than just a technological undertaking? People are finding that integration impacts the very structure of our organizations. However, like the immune system of the human body, our organizations resist the imposition of new modes of operation, primarily because they threaten established expectations and balances of power. Many organizations are actually held together by an intricate web of accommodations and IOUs.

Then why bother about integration and networking?

Integration is essential if companies are to become more responsive and agile in dealing with the complexity of ever-changing global markets. Networking is necessary if we hope to work more in parallel across the various functions, such as marketing, sales, engineering, manufacturing, finance, and service. And both integration and networking are preconditions if we wish to manage our multiple strategic alliances with suppliers, partners, and customers.

We certainly do not lack a vision of what we would like to do. However, we are locked in a constellation of assumptions, principles, and values, our inheritance from the industrial era, that hobble our efforts and keep us bottled up in traditional modes of behavior.

Different companies use different metaphors to describe this sense of confinement: stovepipes, silos, turf, tree hugging, functional blinders, and empires. Often engineering and manufacturing do not want to leave their warm and cozy stovepipes and talk with one another. Finance is often encased in its own silo, insensitive to the pressures on the rest of the enterprise. Many departments jealously defend their turf, their hard-won prerogatives. When the winds of change blow, functions usually cling to their trees for protection. Functional blinders cause rework, because one function does not understand another's constraints. Little empires exist all over most companies.

As I have worked with companies over the years, it has become clear that our steep hierarchies, the legacy of the industrial era, are incapable of effectively absorbing and using the computer and networking technology now available. The reason is relatively simple: the space is too confining and people are too bottled in. It is small wonder that many companies are disappointed in their investments in computer-integrating systems.

It makes little sense to put vast amounts of money into technology with only a pittance for our people and organizations. Yet this is exactly what we are doing.

In some people's minds, CIM and CIE suggest that we are headed toward "paperless" and "peopleless" factories. These people argue that automation, combined with computers and a few professionals, will make it possible for top executives to sit in their "command and control centers" and direct the future of the firm. After all, the hardware and software will have been connected together in one "automated" and "integrated" whole, from boardroom to shop floor. This vision of CIM is a dead end because it leaves people out of the equation, and people are what give an organization its flexibility and creativity.

I am convinced that if we hope to achieve effective integration, we must make the transition from steep hierarchies to flatter networking organizations: from second-generation to fifth-generation management. To be sure, there will always be some hierarchy in our enterprises. However, the mode of operation in human networking enterprises is qualitatively different from what we have known in traditional industrial-era hierarchies. Rather than focusing on the computer and manufacturing, we need to develop a new understanding about the requirements of management for the next century.

PREFACE TO THE REVISED EDITION

It has been six years since we published *Fifth Generation Management*. A lot has changed since then, and yet so very much is still the same. In this updated and revised edition, we have completely rewritten the first five chapters, the story of a president who casts aside his traditional organization chart. We have added references to some new and exciting books in Chapter 7, books that echo the themes of this book. And we have made appropriate changes throughout the rest of the book.

The subtitle is new: *Co-creating through Virtual Enterprising, Dynamic Teaming, and Knowledge Networking*. This replaces the former subtitle, *Integrating Enterprises through Human Networking*. It captures more effectively our understanding of the new business environment. Instead of just selling to our customers, we are co-creating with them new products and services. When Microsoft involves thousands in its beta testing of Windows 95, it is involving them in a co-creative process. Virtual Enterprising is the process of combining the talents and capabilities of many companies to produce a product or service, much as Boeing combined the talents, knowledge, and experience of not only its subcontractors but also United and Japan Airlines in the production of the 777. Dynamic Teaming is the process of teaming and reteaming resources both within a company and between companies to seize and deliver on concrete market opportunities. And Knowledge Networking is the process of combining and re-combining one another's knowledge, experiences, talents, skills, capabilities, and aspirations in ever-changing, profitable patterns. This requires, among other things, a change in the way we value one another's knowledge. Typically the industrial era has bred a culture of devaluing that has made our knowledge assets less accessible to one another.

In four years we will all experience a new millennium. What we experience will be our own creation as much as anything else, for good or evil. Over the past millennia we have nurtured ourselves and built wealth through the use of land, labor, and capital. We have benefited by the abundant resources of nature, both above and below ground. In fact, during the industrial era, the last two hundred years, we have been subsidized by the riches of nature, be they oil, bauxite, or ferrous oxide. We have built machinery, cars, ships, planes, and buildings; ladders, cans, and silverware; and writing pads, pens, and stamps.

In the latter half of this century the ecology movement has taught us that these resources are more limited than we thought. Our waste products not only clutter the landscape, but the micro-garbage, the chemical toxins, cause cancer and other health problems.

We are quickly realizing that land, labor, and capital are not enough to build the future on. We need a new resource in addition to these three. What could it be?

For centuries the riches of nature lay buried below the earth's surface. Could it be that the new source of wealth is already within us, but that we do not see it? Could it be that our attitudes and assumptions keep it hidden?

Could it be that the ancient Greeks' notion that "work is pun-ishment," that Aristotle's notion of clock time, that Descartes's notion of the split between the thinker and objects, and that Frederick Winslow Taylor's split between "planning and doing" all conspire to keep the fourth source of wealth hidden?

Could it be that we have learned to mine below the surface of the earth, but that we do not know how to mine the human mind?

Could it be that *knowledge and knowledging*, taken together, are the fourth source of wealth, along with land, labor, and capital?

It is not just what we know, but how we combine and recombine what we know (knowledging) that makes knowledge valuable. It is the *substance* (knowledge, capabilities, skills, experience, aspirations, etc.) and the *process* (thinking, feeling, seeing, listening, calculating, learning, integrating, innovating, creating, anticipating, etc.), that, when combined, give us this new source of wealth.

Some will argue that this is nothing new, and in some ways this is true. We already think, discuss, plan, record, analyze, innovate, and create. Could we do them better? Absolutely. Preliminary studies done around the world indicate that we are leveraging from five to fifteen percent of our knowledge potential in our organizations.

We have developed an elaborate language for describing the transformation of raw materials into finished products, but we hardly know how to talk about the transformation of raw ideas into finished products and services. We can tell how effectively we are turning our inventory, but we hardly have a clue as to how well or poorly we turn our knowledge. Companies have an opportunity to start to excel in developing new ideas and weaving them together. This challenges us to continually envision the possible, to continually sort out our knowledge, capabilities, experience, and learnings, and to act in a timely manner. These three elements, envisioning, knowledging, and taking decisive action, are the three themes which underlie this book.

The heart of the book is in the exploration of "work as dialogue" and "human time and timing" in Chapter 10. Work is an expressive and creative dialogue and human time is the frame in which we discover meaning and significant patterns. Certainly as we take more seriously knowledge assets and intellectual capital we will need to fundamentally rethink the nature of work and the ways we relate to the past, present, and future.

Some companies are leading the way. Dow Chemical in the United States, Skandia in Sweden, the Canadian Imperial Bank of Commerce in Canada, Sharp in Japan, and Mettler-Toledo in Germany have all realized, in their own ways, the value of knowledge, intellectual capital, and collaborative intelligence. Dow has an innovative world-wide project to sort through its patent portfolio. Skandia is a leader in accounting for intellectual capital. CIBC has set up a group that focuses on lending against "knowledge assets."

Sharp has developed an easily sharable knowledge base. And Mettler-Toledo effectively uses the knowledge and skills of its customers to jointly develop new products.

Our future is not given, but is up to us to create together with one another, as individuals, companies, and countries. If we can indeed realize that we co-create through virtual enterprising, dynamic teaming, and knowledge networking, we can begin to lay the foundation for the next economy. Everyone is needed, because the simple truth is that it will be an economy that will thrive as we learn to value and take one another seriously. Please join in and help build this foundation for our future. If you would like to explore the themes of this book, please join us for a lively dialogue on the Internet's World Wide Web at: http://vision-nest.com/ BTBookCafe.

ACKNOWLEDGMENTS

The reception of the first edition of *Fifth Generation Management* in English, Japanese and Korean far exceeded our expectations. It has lead to work and dialogue with people in India, Japan, Turkey, Italy, Sweden, Germany, Korea, Portugal, Canada and the United States about new ways to organize and team together. I was honored when Tom Peters selected this as his business book of 1991, and I am indebted to him for writing the foreword for this revised edition.

In many respects, the writing of this book has been a collaborative effort, enriched by many colleagues, past and present, too numerous to list individually. Nevertheless, my sincere thanks for your support and insights. I have also valued the comments and ideas of many readers.

This particular project was initiated by Jack Conaway at Digital Equipment Corporation. Initially he wanted a book on Computer Integrated Management (CIM). It grew in scope to include the human element in the first edition, and in this second edition I have gone beyond the concept of "integration" to explore the synergy and creative energies which can develop among and between companies.

In helping to shape the first edition, I am particularly indebted to Jan Hopland, Warren Shrensker, Larry Gould, Tony Friscia, Tom

Blakely, George Hess, Joe Hurley, Dan Infante, Dan Appleton, Wayne Snodgrass, Kazuto Togino, Dan Shunk, Rolf Lindholm, Debra Rogers, Gerhard Friedrich, Chris Criswell and Robert Hall. Early on I also fell in love with a software program developed by an Australian, John Galloway, called Netmap. Figure 12.2 somewhat approximates what can be done with Netmap. John's colleagues Bob Archibald, Rob Beckman and Leslie Berkes, had helped over the years to understand the power of Netmap.

Once this book was first published, I set out to discover, together with colleagues at Digital Equipment and elsewhere, ways the ideas can be concretely implemented in companies. Joan Lancourt, Jocelyn Scarborough, Mike Applebee, Bob St.Cyr, Charleen O'Brien and Bruce MacFadden have all been inspirations. Jocelyn Scarborough and I first tried out the Knowledge Networking process with the top leadership team at Los Alamos National Laboratory, and it worked beautifully. Lee Hebert, Manager of Monsanto's plant in Pensacola, Florida successfully used, in part, the thoughts of the book to redesign his entire operation into twenty teams in a very flat hierarchy. Jessica Lipnack and Jeff Stamps helped me better understand the dynamics of networking and Jeff introduced me to the concept of Holonics. Arun Gairola, Matthias Bellmann, Gösta Lundqvist, Thommy Berglund, Karl Kommissari, Alf Zeumer, Jürgen Schlien, Gerd-Georg Kiessel of ABB have been colleagues and partners in finding new ways to engage customers and their customers. Bill Lacy and Debbie Twadell of MGIC Investments have had the courage and vision to transform their company into a dynamic teaming model. Norm Wright at Martin Lockheed has both understood and deepened this work. And Lars Kolind of Oticon has had the courage to find his own way into the Knowledge Era.

I have found tremendous inspiration in the work of Hans-Jürgen Warnecke and his colleagues, including the team headed by Wildried Sihn, of the Fraunhofer Institute in Germany. Their work on "fractal enterprises," complements the work of Steve Goldman, Roger Nagel, Kenneth Preiss, and Rick Dove on "agility" at Lehigh University. In Japan, Ikujiro Nonaka has Ibeen a wellspring of new insights. These efforts offer a new intellectual framework for understanding manufacturing and service companies.

As I have developed this revised edition of *Fifth Generation Management*, I am indebted to Brenda Reicheldorfer, Jack Spurgeon, Iain Duffin, Ron Wade, Lars Bruzelius, Beth Reuthe, Per-Hugo Skärvad, Jeff Smoller, Hubert St.Onge, Michael Staunton, Leif Edvinsson, Kurt Vikersjoe, Jan-Erik Johanson, Jan Lapidoth, Klaus Tschira, Michael McMaster, Paul Kidd, Warner Burckhardt, Karl-Erik Sveiby, Sally-Ann Moore, Sven Atterhed, Jackson Grayson, and Gen. Billy Thomas for their thoughts, comments and suggestions. Gen. Thomas helped me understand that parts of the military are way ahead of industry in their understanding of virtual enterprising and dynamic teaming. Brian Joiner, author of *Fourth Generation Management*, graciously shared the high jumping metaphor.

Karen Speerstra, Stephanie Aronson, Maura Kelly and John Dixon of Butterworth-Heinemann have been a delight to work with. Sherrin Bennett has skillfully rendered the graphics of Part One. George Por, a colleague and mentor, is helping to make it possible to put portions of this book onto the World Wide Web so we can experience the dialogue of discovery first hand after publication.

Dan Burrus, author of the best selling *Technotrends*, has ably captured the spirit of this revised edition in his Afterword. His passion and vision will help us more readily understand and move into the Knowledge Era.

Finally, those closest to us contribute the most, even without our being aware of it. Without the warmth and stability of a home, the lonely isolation of thought can be unbearable. Carl and Sophia's probing minds challenged me to look more deeply at our patterns of learning and growth. In addition, Carl found numerous ways to improve this text. Lena's impatience with the superficial caused me to understand how important it is to be honest and open with one another at home and work. And my parents, Beatrice and Roy, have been continual sources of support over the years.

To Lena, Carl, and Sophia

 PART ONE

Five Days that Change the Enterprise

CHAPTER

1

MONDAY

A Troubled President

One Monday morning, Frank Giardelli, CEO of Custom Products and Services, Inc., a division of a large manufacturing and service company, arrives at his regularly scheduled staff meeting. Already present are the vice presidents of the functional departments: Wesley Schroeder, engineering; Vincent Gutierrez, manufacturing; Marjorie Callahan, finance; Carol Soo, sales and marketing; Gregory Kasmirian, service; and Alan Tanaka, human resources. Their casual conversation goes on as he enters the boardroom.

He stands silently in front of them, waiting. The room grows quiet as, one by one, they notice that he is holding the familiar organizational chart. They cannot quite read their names on it, but each knows where his or her name is written.

Now they gaze at him, at the chart in his hands. The tension softly grows.

"Somebody ask me what's on my mind," says Frank.

"What's on your mind, Frank?" asks Gregory Kasmirian, VP of service, trying to sound casual.

"I'm glad you asked. This morning I found three major capital requests in my in box." He lays the chart on the table, walks to the flip chart, and picks up a marker.

"Manufacturing wants $175,000 for a shop-floor scheduling system." On the flip chart he writes "175."

"Information systems wants $80,000 for consulting and software to build a Home Page and get our company up on the World Wide Web of the Internet. Included is the salary for a webmaster and the building of a corporate-wide web for internal use." Below the first number he writes "80."

"And engineering wants state-of-the-art workstations and networking capabilities for passing CAD files between ourselves, and our suppliers and customers—half a million dollars' worth, as a matter of fact." He writes "500" and draws a horizontal line beneath the three figures.

Everyone silently mouths the words "seven fifty-five," but Frank turns back to the staff without writing anything further.

"Now, as you know, advanced information systems is what we're all about. I've asked each of you not to be shy, to let me know what you need if you're going to do your job the way it ought to be done. At least once a week for the past ten years, I've said I don't want this company to take a back seat to anyone technologically, and I've asked you all to help us get to the twenty-first century ahead of the competition. Certainly, establishing a presence on the Internet and developing the ability to engage in electronic commerce are key building blocks, but by themselves they are not enough.

"And you've done all I've asked. So far, so good."

The Numbers Do Not Add Up

Turning back to the flip chart, Frank draws a question mark beneath the line.

The vice presidents' attention shifts from the flip chart to his face. He continues.

"But this just doesn't add up. Just like most of the information systems budget requests over the last five years, it bothers me. And I don't know why.

"First of all, Vincent, I don't understand why that MRP II (Manufacturing Resource Planning) package that cost us a million and a half—not to mention countless hours of training—isn't up to the job. But you're telling me it can't control your discrete hour-to-hour scheduling needs."

Vincent Gutierrez, VP of manufacturing, shifts uneasily in his chair.

"Wesley, you tell me engineering has to have these new workstations so they can enhance their true solid geometry and a form-and feature-based CAD system. You also want to send your digital files directly to manufacturing and to our manufacturing suppliers and customers, and that'll mean more money for equipment so that manufacturing can read your files.

"In addition," he continues, "MIS's budget is already going through the roof. Four-fifths of it's for maintenance. It's eating up

our resources trying to jury-rig all our inflexible applications to meet user demands that keep changing."

Sleepless Nights

Frank continues, "There's something else that doesn't add up, and it goes beyond these numbers. This 'something' has given me many sleepless nights.

"For all our good investments in the past, for all our good efforts and for all our good people . . . *why, why, why do we seem to be so slow in responding to the market?*

"Why do we have such a hard time mobilizing our resources when opportunities spring up?

"Why do we seem to be so rigid and inflexible?"

Wesley Schroeder, VP of engineering, smiles. "You know, Frank, it's not surprising; people don't know how to work together. When's the last time we offered 'team-building' training? It's essential if we're to move to an Integrated Product Development Process, using concurrent engineering."

Frank does not smile; the pain is too deep. "Wesley, I wish it were that easy. We have been working with teams for some time under our Total Quality Management program. They've helped, but there's something more. . . ."

Vincent Gutierrez sees his chance. "You know, Frank, if we can complete our work and qualify for ISO 9000, we will have come a long way toward straightening out our processes. In addition, we're almost finished re-engineering our product development and order processing activities. Soon we'll be an industry-recognized benchmark site for the 'art-to-part' and 'order-to-delivery' processes. I can just see the flocks of journalists we'll have to turn away when word gets out."

Marjorie Callahan, VP of finance, notices that Frank's face is not lightening up. She wonders whether Frank is bothered by all the layoffs that are a fallout from the re-engineering. She knows that under Frank's tough exterior is a person who cares a lot for his people.

"I wonder," reflects Alan Tanaka, VP of human resources, "if I've been too slow in updating our reward systems. All our surveys show people are dissatisfied by the way they're rewarded. Frankly, it's tough to know what to do."

Frank looks at Wesley, Vincent, Marjorie, Alan, and the others, catching them by surprise with his comment. "Have you been walking the halls and the shop floors lately? Have you noticed, as I have, that there is relatively little laughter these days?"

"This is a business, and people are serious about their work," responds Gregory Kasmirian. "I'd expect laughter at a party, but at work . . . hardly."

Marjorie has been quiet, listening, not to the words, but to what's below the words. "Frank, I understand what you mean about the information systems capital expenditures, and I know you support our efforts in quality and re-engineering, but your comment about laughter caught me. You're right, there is little laughter, much less than when I first joined the company eight years ago. I wonder . . . laughter . . . it occurs at the intersection of the expected and the unexpected. Are we drowning in the expected? Has routine taken over this place?"

She continues, "As Carol will agree, the market is full of surprises. Our customers are always up to something new. Our MIS director has just given me a crash course in the Internet and I noticed that three of our competitors already have Home Pages and the ability to sell directly through the Internet."

Carol Soo, VP of sales and marketing, quietly smiles. "Our competitors are moving on the Web, but look at us. Sometimes I wonder who we serve, our bosses or our customers? It seems the rules of business have just undergone a major revision and we've hardly noticed. We're still worried about departmental politics when other companies are reaching out to their customers in new and innovative ways."

"Carol, you're right," responds Frank. "We spend so much time looking up and down that we hardly look out at the rough and tumble excitement of the market. We expect your people, Carol, those in sales and marketing, to be in touch with the outside, but when they bring new ideas back inside, we hardly listen . . . or even laugh.

"In fact," he continues, as he points to the organizational chart, "people have put walls around both their boxes and their departments that give them comfort and shelter, but at what price?

"At one point in time I looked at our organization chart with awe. It showed everything so orderly and neat. It gave a sense of accountability. It motivated people to want to climb the ladder. We knew who to go to for what.

"Recently, I have been having second thoughts," continues Frank. "It started with the tremendous flood of literature on the 'learning organization,' inspired by the work of Peter Senge. Why should people be so excited about learning? Then I realized that our existing hierarchical organizations have been designed not to learn. I then thought of all we've spent on outside consultants to help us communicate our thinking. Then I realized that our company is designed not to communicate. There is too much incentive to manage the news. And then I looked at our yearly Quality surveys that touch on people's attitudes, and realized how frustrated people are with the lack of effective decisions. Are we also designed not to make decisions? Learning . . . communicating . . . deciding . . . all critical, yet these three attributes do not come easy. Why?"

"I've been wondering that too," notes Vincent. "Why is it?"

Frank looks at Vincent and says, "Funny thing—I have a feeling the very way we describe ourselves to ourselves has something to do with our problem. I was recently reading in a CEO magazine the story of Eastman Chemical and how they spent a year working to discover their core competencies. Once they had done this, they found they had outgrown their hierarchical organizational chart, and substituted instead what they call their circular 'pizza' chart, a large round circle with smaller circles nested in it."

Torn in Half!

As if to drive his point home, Frank lifts their organizational chart and slowly tears it in half. "I'm calling an end to this rigid organizational structure." He tosses the chart in the basket near by.

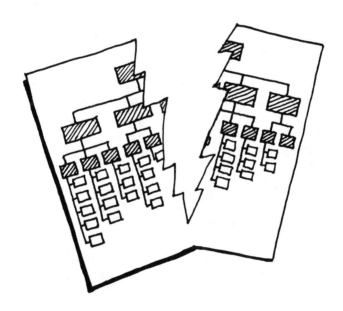

Looks of discomfort spread across the room. Laughter is on no one's mind. Frank notices the looks on their faces. There is two minutes of silence, which seems like two hours to some. Even though there are no words, the question is the same: "What does this mean for my job?"

For people grown used to the expected, this unexpected turn of events is shocking.

Wesley mumbles, "What did you just do, Frank? Why did you tear our organizational chart in half? What do I tell my people?"

Vincent joins Wesley. "Yes, and who do our customers talk to when they have problems?"

"Now you really have me confused," protests Alan. "I don't even know how to design a reward system that's not hierarchical. Who will do the reviews? We will have anarchy from the executive suites to the shop floor!"

Frank looks slowly around the room. "Perhaps it was an impulse and perhaps I will regret it, but there is something about the chart that doesn't strike me as true to life. Listening . . . learning . . . communicating . . . and deciding . . . they get lost in the ownership questions, the "hierarchy of importance" questions, the turf questions, the job definition questions, the recognition questions. . . . What if we eliminate this turf-based model? Many companies have already been flattening their hierarchy. A few have been finding new ways to present their hierarchies, such as Eastman Chemical.

"I see your worried faces. You are not losing your jobs . . . but maybe you are. Wait, let me state that again: your salaries will continue. The hierarchical organizational chart is based on narrowly defined rectangular 'job' boxes knitted together with thin horizontal and vertical lines. But what I want are people with robust capabilities that can weave themselves together in ever-changing patterns, depending on concrete market opportunities."

Silence . . . everyone hears the loud sound of silence!

Frank continues, "I'd like your help this week. It's going to be hard work, but we must do this for the health and continued growth of the company. I would like your help in rethinking the way we operate in this company. I'd like you to clear your calendars for the week and be ready to spend the time together to help me put a dynamic new foundation under Custom Products and Services, Inc."

They all think of the busy week ahead, all they have scheduled, and then gradually they realize that something more important has come up.

Marjorie comments, "I have a friend at General Electric. They have been working on transforming their organization for the last fourteen years. How can we expect to do something in one week?"

"We probably can't, Marjorie," responds Frank. "But I have a suspicion, and it is only a suspicion, that our attitudes have a lot to do with our lumbering slowness and our inability to master continuous change.

"Have you ever noticed how hard it is to mobilize a team from different parts of the company? People don't know where to get the talent needed for the opportunity. Why is this?"

Wesley, uncertain if this is the right answer, nevertheless makes a try: "Could it have something to do with the way we think of ourselves and our relationships, as defined by that piece of paper you just tore in half?"

Frank smiles faintly.

Beyond the Scissors Kick

Something is happening in Wesley; he seems to be seeing some connection. "I'm not sure if I have it right, but let me try.

"Our discussion reminds me of my high school track days. I was one of our star high jumpers, a real master of the Western roll. Previous jumpers had used the scissors kick, but with the Western roll, we were able to scale new heights. Then we heard of this guy from Oregon who ran fast towards the jumping pit, turned slightly so his back was facing it, and as he jumped backwards and headfirst, he kicked his feet high as he sailed over the bar. We laughed, envisioning the concussion every time he landed on his head. Our laughter stopped after he won the 1968 Mexico City games with a jump of 7' 4 1/2" [2.24 meters]. Now nearly all the world-record holders do the Fosbury Flop, and have pushed the present world record over 8' [2.44 meters]. The interesting thing is that Dick Fosbury discovered how to more effectively use natural momentum and the body's center of gravity to reach these new heights. Frank, it seems to me that your sleepless nights may be caused because we are stuck on the scissors kick, when the rest of the industry is moving to the Western roll and a few have caught on to the Fosbury Flop."

Frank, listening carefully, wonders, "What changed in high jumping in the transitions between the scissors kick, the Western roll, and the Fosbury Flop? Did anything physical change, like the nature of the bar or poles holding it?"

"The only outward change has been more padding upon landing," responds Wesley. "But I suspect you are getting at something else, aren't you?"

"Yes. If I understand what you're saying, the physical conditions remained essentially the same; the real change came in the jumpers' mindset. Their understanding of the best way to jump changed, and with those changes they were able to scale new heights, and to use more natural methods, were they not?" asks Frank.

"Frank and Wesley, are you suggesting that we may need a mindset change?" asks Carol. "It reminds me of the shifting nature of mass communication. First we experienced 'broadcasting' by the networks, then with cable we have had access to what might be called 'narrowcasting,' the marketing of more specific information to clearly definable groups. And with the Internet and its World Wide Web capabilities, we now have 'cybercasting.' Only a few could do broadcasting because of the tremendous expense involved, more could provide narrowcasting, and now virtually every company can set up its own Home Page and make available interactively products, services, and other information on the Internet.

"Frank," she continues, "if our traditional hierarchical organization is like the scissors kick, or broadcasting, then you are right in challenging us to reconsider our mindset. How do we use our natural abilities and build upon our organization's center of gravity? Perhaps the concepts of 'lines and boxes' and 'jobs' are artifacts of the past, as William Bridges suggested in an article I recently read in *Fortune*. This begins to make sense, but I still feel very uncomfortable, because I don't know what really takes its place. I don't have the confidence that we can do the business equivalent of the Fosbury Flop or cybercasting."

Gregory, silent until now, asks, "Run that by me again . . . by tossing out the organizational chart, we're letting go of the scissors kick and learning to jump in new ways at customer opportunities?

We don't jump for our bosses, but instead, we jump at opportunities? Frankly, it makes me a little jumpy!"

Laughter . . . finally some laughter.

Gregory looks around the room, continuing, "It's one thing to refer to high jumping, but organizations are much more complex. The hierarchical model has stood the test of time. It has worked well. The church and the military couldn't live without it. Many businesses have done very very well with their hierarchies, so what's all this about Fosbury Flops . . . are we about to experience our own flop?"

The Military Understands Already

Wesley grimaces. Thinking back to his own military days, he responds, "You know, Gregory, when people think of the military, they think of its hierarchy, but there's more to the story. As a former colonel I can well appreciate the bureaucratic and hierarchical model most have of the army. The fact is that that might be the situation during peace, but under war conditions, you would be surprised how fluid and flexible things are. It's this fluidity and agility that we need in our company. And as far as the church is concerned, it typically has fewer levels than in an average corporation. As you well know, it's too easy to trade in simplistic stereotypes."

Everyone listens as Wesley continues his impassioned remarks. "Why does the military continuously train to achieve fluidity and flexibility? We must be able to operate in an ever-changing environment, often referred to as the 'fog of war.' We practice a very fluid teaming concept called 'combined arms task forces,' because training and war require the continuous creation of new and different task forces, or 'teams.' Individual soldiers often find themselves on different teams virtually every day, and sometimes as often as three or four times a day. Military training is designed to create the mindset for 'teaming,' which is so critical for combat. Why can't we do this in commerce?"

He continues, "Gregory, if you sense a tone of defensiveness, it's there. You just hit a couple of my hot buttons. And as far as the Fosbury Flop is concerned, it's anything but a flop. It's a way to do the near impossible, and this is what I think Frank is asking us to do."

"Wesley, I'm listening," responds Gregory. "Up until today my world has been so easy and comfortable. I'm going to have to do some rethinking. Thanks for helping me redefine my understanding of the military. It sounds like they're ahead of much of industry in their thinking and execution."

Carol springs to her feet. "Remember how we used to say 'customers beware'? Now we need to 'be aware of customers,' their interests, capabilities, and aspirations. From what you say, Wesley, the military certainly has to be aware of their 'customers.' This is truly a mindset change, and yet it is so much more natural. I certainly was not a high school high jumper, but if I've understood your story, Wesley, this shift is as big as the shift to the Fosbury Flop and will take as much practice to be successful."

Frank looks up at the clock. Several intense hours have passed. He senses the need to give his colleagues some time to think.

"Let's get together tomorrow morning at 8:30 and pick up our discussion," Frank suggests. "I know how word spreads around this place, so take the opportunity to talk to your own colleagues. Invite their ideas and suggestions. If we're going to deal with mindset changes, it's best it be out in the open even though some may get very confused.

"I'd like to spend tomorrow developing an understanding of how we might better interact with our multiple markets. From each of your perspectives, what would increase our responsiveness to our customers? How can we enhance their capabilities, helping them as well as ourselves? How can we find new heights of effectiveness?"

There is uncertainty as they quietly file out of the room.

CHAPTER

2

TUESDAY

Boring Numbers

Even before 8:30 they all have their coffee and are in place, everyone except Carol. She comes briskly into the room five minutes late, looking a bit bedraggled.

Even before Frank has a chance to say something, Carol is in front of the room. "My team and I have spent a good part of the night developing a set of profiles of our customers. I'd like to share our overheads with you as background to our session," says Carol. This is her chance to "educate" her colleagues.

After about 20 minutes of endless overheads showing product breakdown by customer type, Wesley asks Carol, "This is a wonderful summary of what we were just through in our strategic planning exercise two months ago, but I don't see how this relates

to Frank's question of yesterday, 'Why are we so slow when opportunities are staring us in the face?'"

"Well, as I was saying . . . hmmm, maybe you're right," responds
Carol. "These slides . . . well, they may be boring. But why?"

"Yeah, I'm glad you said that, Carol," jumps in Gregory. "I'm
getting restless just looking at numbers. Yet these are the numbers
that tell us how we're doing in the market, and they're the numbers upon which our collective bonus will be based, so I guess they
are important."

"I work with numbers all day, every day," adds Marjorie, "and I
agree with Gregory that these are important, but there's something
missing. It may seem strange, but these numbers simply capture
the past and potential transactions with our customers. Carol, I'm
beginning to wonder whether you didn't give us this boring presentation to make a point."

Carol gives a faint smile, and muses, "Perhaps, perhaps
. . . You're right, as we pulled together these reams of numbers, I
realized how much we are focused on *transactions*. Of course
they're important, because, as Marjorie knows, without a transaction, it's impossible to invoice. Yet we also realized that these
numbers tell us 'who' buys what, but not 'why' they buy what
they do.

"Early this morning," she continues, "as we were putting the
finishing touches on our slides, one of my colleagues in marketing
started to ponder the 'why' of the customer. It led us to a fascinating discussion about where we start in our interaction with our
customers. Two people on our staff immediately said it was a no-
brainer; we obviously start with the customer's needs or the
customer's problems. For some reason I wasn't satisfied with this.

"I began to wonder about the 'why' questions. Why are our
customers buying our products and services? What are they trying
to do with their customers? Do we ever get into the minds of our
customers?"

Wesley shifts in his chair. "Carol, I'm not very skilled in marketing, but I and some of my people have sometimes been with
your sales people on important initiatives. Typically we're responding to a request for proposal or other detailed statement of
work that lays out the customer's needs. And you are so right—we
seem to always want to hone in on the customer's problems, for

after all we are THE solutions specialists. It's funny how we can so readily solve our customers' problems, but we flounder endlessly in our own problems; another 'why' for us, right, Carol?"

Beyond Transactions

Marjorie looks at Carol, then to the other colleagues. "We started this morning with a dry set of slides. I agree that transactions are what pay our bills, but Carol's 'why' questions have some relevance.

"Frank and Wesley, perhaps our high jumping technique is stuck at the level of the scissors kick. We should be changing our technique and focusing on something more. 'Why' do our customers do what they do?

"Many of them have their own customers, and typically they're trying to delight those customers. They are driven by some vision, some understanding of their own market. They have aspirations they're trying to fulfill. How are they going to realize these aspirations? Perhaps there's something beyond just seeing customers in terms of transactions. Do we listen? Do we listen to our customers' aspirations? Have we captured these aspirations on any overhead slides?"

Carol lights up. "Thanks, Marjorie, you said it much better than I could. I've felt uneasy for a long time, but didn't know how to break out of the old mindset. Marketing has superb skills at telling, but you're right, we are not very effective listeners. And the only way to discover our customers' aspirations is to do some heavy-duty listening."

Frank, sitting pensively, comments, "Thank you for taking the initiative with our meeting this morning. It's interesting that we didn't get hooked by the numbers, but instead shifted the discussion to another level. I wonder if there's some connection between the little laughter and the boring market statistics?"

"How so?" asks Gregory, who is a bit lost.

"Gregory, what's your service strategy? Is it a 'break-fix' approach, or do you anticipate potential service problems and act in a proactive manner?" asks Frank.

"We used to be a 'if-it-ain't-broke-don't-fix-it' type of shop, but then we realized how much we get jerked around by our customers. So we've been looking at the patterns of failures and have begun to do two things: we confront engineering with their sloppy work when necessary, and we meet our customers and teach them how to repair some of the problems we can anticipate. They're happy because they don't have to wait the four to six hours for a service technician, and we're happy because we can plan our resources more effectively," explains Gregory.

"That's interesting; you're actively looking for patterns," comments Frank. "And you're noticing how it's helping you in your service business. These patterns have always been there, but in the past we just never took the time to discover them. Carol and Marjorie have been exploring ways we can move beyond just looking at transactions, and instead learn to discover the patterns in our customers' aspirations. Gregory, do you think that your approach in service can apply to the way we interact with our customers from a marketing perspective?"

A big smile—Gregory gets it. "Bingo, I see the connection now. And Wesley's discussion of high jumping is also becoming clearer. Sorry, Wesley, for being an ol' stuck-in-the-mud type of person.

"As you were saying, Frank," he continues, "if we think in the 'break-fix' way, we'll never reach new heights of excellence. The shift in attitudes is what it takes to learn to listen and interact differently with our customers. This listening will help reveal the key patterns of problems so we can take proactive action with our customers. Wesley, I'm beginning to like high jumping!"

"This all seems to be making sense to you all, but I like to think in pictures. I am a concrete sort of guy," says Vincent. "Can someone draw me a picture of what we've been discussing?"

Everyone looks around the room. There's not an artist to be found. Marjorie stands up, recognizing the lack of talent in the graphic arts area, and volunteers to draw on a flip chart.

Beyond the Value Chain

"The traditional 'value-chain' model is often pictured as a series of horizontal boxes," explains Carol. "Marjorie, can you note this on the flip chart?"

Marjorie draws the model. "Is this what you had in mind, Carol?"

"Yes, and you have captured nicely the focus on *transactions,* and the way this model is driven by *customer needs,*" responds Carol.

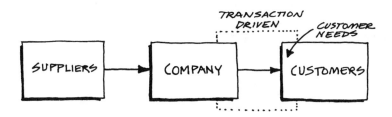

Wesley sees his chance to show off a bit. "We've done extensive training within engineering to identify customer needs and turn them into concrete engineering specifications. All my engineers have been trained in the techniques of the 'House of Quality,' a rigorous process of defining, testing, and detailing engineering specifications that respond to our customers' needs. We then create 'integrated product development teams' that involve design, testing, manufacturing, product support, service, and whoever else is needed, to ensure the manufacturability and serviceability of our products through their life cycle."

Vincent and Gregory are nodding their heads. Gregory adds, "This has made a big difference, because we're able to get the engineers to design in our service concerns. This is especially important as we're discovering the patterns of service problems."

"This is the way it works," notes Vincent, "but we're still bothered by engineering's arrogance. Even though we're supposed to be working together on these teams, we still feel the heavy hand of the engineers and frankly they're still not listening as well as they should to learn from our experience and knowledge." As Vincent says this, he cannot help but wonder if he is not again playing the power game, trying to score points with Frank.

Aspirations and Opportunities

Carol is focusing on the value-chain model. "Marjorie, you know what strikes me with this model is that it's hard for the company, our company, to see beyond our customers. Like driving behind a big truck, it's hard to see what's down the road. We've noticed that if we wait for customers to articulate their needs, it's often too late. Could you extend this model to the right, adding our customers' customers? And could you somehow indicate where the aspirations of our customers are?"

Marjorie adds another box and notes the area of aspirations and opportunities.

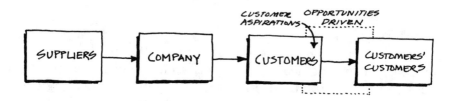

"Wait a minute, Marjorie and Carol, our engineering efforts don't focus so far upstream as to include our customers' aspirations. They're not concrete enough. We need concrete specifications that we can put directly into our CAD systems. How is it possible to sketch an aspiration, something that's so vague and ambiguous?" asks Wesley.

If Wesley is Mr. concrete, with a small "c," then Vincent is Mr. Concrete with a big "C." Therefore, his colleagues weren't quite ready for Vincent's comment. "Could we find some significant patterns in the aspirations of our customers? I wonder if our customers know what's really possible without knowing how we can help turn their dreams into specific products and services?"

"Say that again, Vincent," exclaims Marjorie. "Are you saying that by carefully listening to the aspirations of our customers we can find patterns? Moreover, in our interaction, we can help our customers crystallize their thinking about what's possible?"

Alan, who has been so very quiet that most of them had forgotten he was in the room, because he did not know how to engage in the business discussion, finally says, "Vincent, you know how we've been stressing 'employee empowerment'? Well, I wonder if we could talk about 'customer empowerment'?"

Emboldening Customers and Strengthening Their Capabilities

"That's an interesting way to put it, Alan, because many of our customers don't have a clue as to how they can ever realize their aspirations. Often they don't know what kinds of resources are available outside their companies, and therefore it's hard for them to know what concrete steps they could take to seize on a market opportunity with their customers. Perhaps it's not just empowerment, but a process of emboldenment, helping our customers to become bolder in their aspirations," responds Vincent.

"As you, Vincent and Alan, have been reflecting on aspirations, I've been thinking of our typical sales training courses," adds Carol. "We teach our people to identify customer needs and to identify customer problems, so we can provide our solutions. But we haven't been training our people to listen for aspirations or to understand the patterns of opportunities arising between our customers and their customers. You're stretching my thinking, but why not?"

"And you're stretching mine as well," interjects Wesley. "In the past, engineering has teamed up with sales, better than in most companies, to identify needs and quickly engineer products. But how do we engineer aspirations?"

Marjorie's face lights up. "You know, Wesley and Carol, when we think in terms of transactions, we're constantly looking at the customers from behind our products and services. But when we start to look at customer aspirations, then we need to think more about capabilities and competencies."

"What do you mean?" asks Wesley. "I know there's more talk today about core competencies, but I've never really understood what's flame and what's smoke. What competencies and whose capabilities?"

Marjorie continues, "Wesley, think about what Vincent is saying. Do our customers buy our products, or do they buy our capabilities and competencies?"

"Of course they buy our products," quickly responds Wesley.

"Wait a minute—don't our products evolve over time, Wesley? When a customer buys from us, isn't he or she buying a relationship, not just a specific product? Sure, I know that in many instances, depending on the product or service, it's a one-time transaction, but with the increased interest in quality and supplier relationships, companies are also buying quality relationships. Therefore, they want to believe that they can benefit from succeeding generations of products, don't they?" responds Marjorie.

"Sure . . . that's true," admits Wesley. "But how do our customers know our competencies when we haven't really understood them ourselves? We've been so busy trying to re-engineer discrete processes that we haven't taken the time to sort our overall competencies."

"Alan, you've put your finger on a more important reward system, the system by which our customers reward us for our competencies," comments Frank.

"How can we use our competencies well if we don't know the competencies of our customers?" asks Marjorie. "Our sales strategy has been to look for the needs, the problems, and the weaknesses of our customers, so we can plug the breach with our wonderful products and services. How good are we at looking for their strengths, their core competencies and capabilities? Is this what you were suggesting, Alan, as you talked about emboldening our customers?"

Redefining STAFF and LINE

"Yes, I think so, but I'm not sure; this is a new area for me," answers Alan. "The reason I feel uncomfortable is that we in HR have always just looked at our own people and our jobs. Our challenge has been to get the right people in the right boxes, or jobs, and then try to motivate them. But if we're going to stretch our model, looking at ways to strengthen our customers' capabilities with our own capabilities, then we're going to need another model. Our existing self-understanding is much too narrow. Now I'm beginning to understand why so many people want to avoid HR—they don't see our business relevance."

Having torn the organizational hierarchy in half yesterday, Frank is in a more pensive mood today. "Alan, perhaps we have set you up. Typically, HR is part of the staff, not part of the line. The line is where the action is, and yet we need help in competency development. Do we have it wrong when we distinguish between STAFF and LINE? What if you thought of yourselves as part of the line? How would you think differently?"

"My head is spinning," admits Alan, "but I'm beginning to get a glimpse of what might be. Instead of looking just at jobs, the jobs within the four walls of our organization, what if we look for relevant competencies, competencies in-house, but also competencies of our supplier and customer organizations?"

"Once we've defined competencies, what do we do with them?" asks Gregory.

Vincent steps in. "Gregory, just having competencies doesn't do anything for us, unless we can organize them. But how and why would we organize them in one way and not another?"

Seeding Opportunities

"That's it," interjects Carol. "We need something around which to team competencies: ours, our suppliers', and our customers'. Can the opportunities we discover through this new focus on the interaction between our customers and their customers provide the grains of sand, the irritant, around which we coalesce competencies?"

"What a different model!" notes Wesley. "The irritant, the grain of sand, is the opportunity, something concrete and substantial. Just as an oyster produces a pearl from the irritant, couldn't we produce our next generation of products and services from these opportunities? But what will keep us from jumping all over the place, following any and all opportunities, real or imaginary? I can see our effort quickly becoming so diffused that we lose focus and momentum.

"How do we identify and communicate these opportunities?"

"'Communication' is an interesting word," reflects Marjorie. "We hear it all the time, but what does it really mean? Usually it means 'telling.' It's a fancy word to use when we want to tell others they should do something. Frankly, it sounds hollow. As I think about it, what we need is 'conversation' and 'dialogue.' We 'communicate' all the time at staff meetings. We sit around a big horseshoe table and talk. We say what's on our minds. Then the next person has the floor and they say what is on their mind, hardly having heard our remarks, and so it goes, talking past one another. Is that communication?"

"Marjorie, you're making me feel uncomfortable again," notes Gregory. "'Communication,' 'conversation,' 'discussion,' and 'dialogue'... aren't they all the same?... Maybe not, come to think of it. A good dialogue is a give and take where we enrich one another's thinking. Too often I get a headache from too much communication, too much discussion. 'Discussion' seems to come from the same root word as 'percussion' or 'concussion,' as Peter Senge likes to say. Is this what you're saying, Marjorie?"

"Yes," responds Marjorie. "Often we think in terms of communication, because we want discipline and order in our organization. But frankly, dialogue requires much more discipline, because we have to listen and respond, not just tell."

Still at the flip chart, she adds, "It sounds like we're going to need much more discipline and rigor than we've had in our boxes and lines organization. We need the discipline of quality dialogues among and between our different functions, and we need the discipline of quality dialogues with our suppliers and customers. Without rigorously testing and retesting ideas, hunches, intuitions, and possibilities, we won't be able to sort out the wheat from the chaff. This is where HR could help in a significant way, in facilitating quality dialogues between all concerned. We need to tap people's learning, their experiences, their thoughts and feelings, and their knowledge and aspirations in new ways."

"But wait—dialogues can be endless, and they can wallow in silly feelings," comments Gregory somewhat skeptically. "Where is the crispness, where is the decisiveness, and where is the action in dialogue?"

"Gregory," responds Wesley, "think of our endless communications. Do they get decisive action? Not necessarily. Why not?

Could it be that too often we cancel one another out, rather than building on one another's insights? How are you finding the patterns in service? Does one person come up with all the answers, or are you able to pool everyone's thinking?"

The skeptic smiles. "Wesley, you and Marjorie are doing something to my head. At first I thought you were playing semantics, but I'm beginning to see why using the scissors kick only gets me so high," admits Gregory.

"See what you did yesterday, Frank, when you tore our organizational chart in half?" interjects Carol. "You released our thinking. We haven't had such an honest and open discussion, oops, I mean dialogue like this for as long as I can remember; is this what you had hoped for?"

Frank is touched; he has longed to move beyond petty game playing. "Yes—without comfortable boxes, what do we have? Nothing but our own wits, experiences, and visions. What if we could have dialogue like this with our suppliers and customers? Think of what we could discover!"

As Frank is talking, Marjorie is quietly drawing four large overlapping circles on the flip chart.

Frank looks at Marjorie and asks, "What do we have here?"

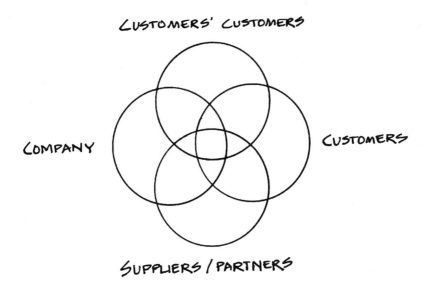

"I was struck by our value-chain model," responds Marjorie. "In a horizontal series of boxes, it isn't possible to directly see our customers' customers. But if we redraw them as overlapping circles, then it's possible to envision a quality dialogue with the three key elements of our world: our suppliers (and partners), our customers, and our customers' customers."

"Interesting," notes Alan. "This suggests that our organization, our company, is only a fourth of the picture. I'm going to have to rethink our human resource model, because it's becoming clear to me that our world has to include the people and the capabilities in all four circles. Interestingly enough, our traditional reward systems aren't much help with the employees in the other three circles. Perhaps we can find another approach."

Adding Value and Generating Value

Frank takes a hard look at Marjorie's model and, turning to the group, asks, "We've assumed that our mission is to add value to the raw materials we buy from our suppliers. Isn't this what the value chain is all about, a sequential set of steps where value is added along the way? I'm just beginning to see that in addition to this activity, our challenge may well be to 'generate value' at the overlaps between the participants in this picture. Is there a difference between adding value and generating value?

"What does it mean to 'generate value'?" he asks rhetorically. "How do we understand the aspirations of our customers' customers? By listening to them, we can better understand the demands they're placing on our customers, their suppliers. By valuing our customers' customers, we're able to help generate value for our customers. Secondly, by offering our customers tools to explain their products and services to their customers, we help them generate value. Often our customers and our suppliers need to interact. Instead of being a blockage, we can help to enhance the interaction between them, thus generating value.

"For example," he continues, "suppose we provide a variable control motor that goes into our customers' machine tools. By looking at their customers' aspirations, we can better size the characteristics of our product. We can then supply literature to our customers showing how our motor enhances their production.

This helps them sell their products. Our motors are controlled by complex microprocessor circuits. By including our suppliers in our discussions with our customers, we can be more responsive to rapid changes in the market. Finally, as we nurture our supply base, we are better able to offer a well-configured set of motor products for our customers. How do we see all these things?"

"It may sound silly," responds Gregory, "but we might see better through our ears than our eyes!"

Everyone looks around the room, then at Gregory. Now he's stretching the others' thinking.

"Seeing through our ears . . . say more," prompts Vincent.

"You guys won't believe this," smiles Gregory, "but things are beginning to make sense to me. Seeing is like doing the obvious, like the scissors kick. But with our eyes we see so little. Hearing is like the Fosbury Flop; we put ourselves in a different position and are able to pick up so much more. Aspirations are not yet concrete, so they cannot be seen. They can only be heard. If we don't know how to listen, we'll never see these aspirations. And it's these aspirations that become the dots to connect as we develop a pattern in the future. It's not communication, but dialogue, that reveals the possible."

Frank is smiling and scratching his head. "Gregory, where have you been all my life? I've just seen a part of you I never knew existed."

"Me too," says Gregory. "I thought I knew myself until you started us down this track, Frank. Now I'm beginning to understand things a little differently. Marjorie, earlier you started talking about a mindset change. Well, I guess I was so set in my mind that it was hard to begin to understand what you were suggesting. Now it's beginning to click."

"I'll say it is," says Marjorie, as she looks warmly at Gregory. "I'm still letting your words 'but with our eyes we see so little' roll around in my mind. In a few words you certainly said a lot."

She continues, "And I also must make a confession. When Frank first made the distinction between adding value and generating value, I was lost. It didn't make sense. As a finance person, I can calculate the steps in adding value to raw materials, but like Alan, I don't know where to begin in calculating the 'value generating' processes. But believe it or not, Gregory, you helped me to see, because I think I heard you. By careful listening, we see possibilities that we can develop into concrete products and services. I can see how this creates value for ourselves, as well as for our customers and suppliers. Listening and dialogue that happen at the overlap between our worlds: ours, our customers, their customers, and our suppliers—yes, we can generate value there. But how?"

Carol is inspired. "Marjorie, my sales and marketing world is standing upside down, but it feels good. Let me try out a thought . . . our company doesn't only process raw materials, we also process raw ideas."

"Yes, say more," responds Frank.

"If we go beyond the transaction model, if we begin to listen to our customers' aspirations, then these aspirations, these ideas, become as much of a raw resource as our raw materials," continues Carol. "Our challenge is to help turn these raw ideas, these dreams, these aspirations, and these plans, into something concrete, something against which we can invoice."

"But we can never do this if we only focus on aspirations and not transactions," comments Vincent, who has picked up Gregory's skeptic's role.

Smiling, Gregory responds, "Vincent, perhaps we're trapped in our ways of thinking. Too often we think in terms of 'either/or,' when we need to shift to a 'both/and' model. We need to pay attention to both transactions *and* aspirations. We need to process both raw materials *and* raw ideas. We need to both talk and listen. We need to both communicate and dialogue."

"That really helps, Gregory. It puts things in a much better perspective," says Frank. "I like what you've been saying."

Frank looks at Marjorie, who is still standing at the flip chart. "What have you drawn?"

"Frank, in addition to the traditional value chain that we extended to include our customers' customers, I've redrawn the model as four overlapping circles," responds Marjorie.

She continues, "Note that with the four circles, it's possible for our company to see in all three directions at once. We can indeed enter into dialogue with these three communities. We can listen for their aspirations. We can spot capabilities. We can begin to generate value at the overlaps. Let's call these four overlapping circles the 'valuing cluster.'

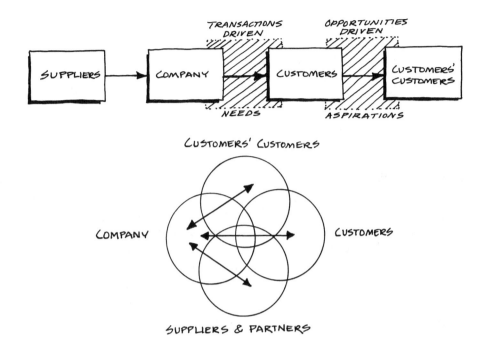

"I'm a little puzzled as to how we will do this in the concrete. I must say that it feels better, but as you know, I like concrete things, and this has a little vagueness. How do we make it work? Wesley and Vincent, can you help?"

"That's interesting, Marjorie. I guess you're looking at me as the engineer in the house," responds Wesley. "Typically, we take customer needs and figure out what basic materials we'll need to work with. We then engineer a product, thinking about the raw material characteristics. But you're right, we have to consider such things as manufacturability and serviceability, as well as the aesthetics of the product, how it will look. And now we're also having to design the product so it can be taken apart at the end of its life and disposed of in an environmentally responsible manner. There are certainly a lot more considerations to be accounted for than when I first began to work. Now this new model—when is it ever going to stop?"

"Wesley, how do you know the characteristics of your raw materials or component parts? How do you know how to work with our suppliers and other partners? It takes a lot of dialogue to get things right. And as I think of it now," adds Vincent, "we're very sensitive to our customers' expectations as to design characteristics. And without really thinking of it, we've also had a sense of what our customers are trying to do with their customers. Yes, that's it ..."

Transforming Both Raw Materials and Raw Ideas

Wesley wins an aha. "As we sort out everything, we're really weaving together a lot of ideas, insights, characteristics, capabilities, expectations, and aspirations and embodying them in our products and services. We're really working as much with raw ideas as raw materials or components. Yet we've always focused on the value-adding steps, not the value-generating dialogue that makes these steps possible."

"Does that mean, Wesley and Vincent, that the quality of interaction between all four circles is as important as the quality of our internal products and processes?" asks Marjorie.

"Now that you mention it, why yes," responds Wesley. "Hmmm, mindset, high jumping, World Wide Web, organizational chart ... perhaps there is a pony here. Perhaps we have been prisoner to a mindset, a paradigm, or a way of thinking, that has blinded us to some of the other things going on in our environment."

As Wesley is talking, Marjorie redraws the four circles with three lines, each with two arrowheads. "As I pointed out earlier, these lines represent the dialogues that are necessary for us to understand one another's capabilities and aspirations. Our challenge is to discover the patterns in these dialogues—what the opportunities are and how they fit together, much as we do to understand and fit together the patterns in DNA. This is something new for us, and it will tax our ability to listen carefully to our suppliers, customers, and customers' customers, as well as to ourselves. Can we do it?"

"Marjorie, that's very helpful," responds Frank. "Instead of being a value chain, it is a 'valuing cluster,' because as we actively value our suppliers, customers, and customers' customers we will

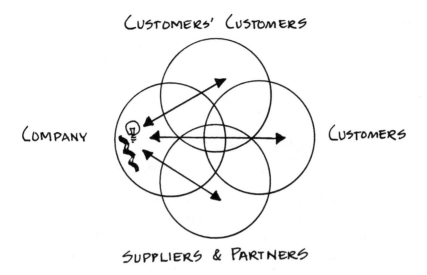

CUSTOMERS' CUSTOMERS

COMPANY   CUSTOMERS

SUPPLIERS & PARTNERS

find they are more open to dialoguing with us and will reveal more of their capabilities and aspirations. Yesterday you asked who we serve, our bosses or our customers? Well, this suggests that our challenge is not to serve but to dialogue, and this requires openness to the truth and a willingness to trust. I didn't see it yesterday, but I see it now. Respect for the truth and a trusting culture are absolutely essential to be effective in our business environment."

"Even though it looks a bit awkward, the Fosbury Flop is a more natural way of jumping, because it uses the natural momentum of the jumper more effectively. I begin to sense," says Wesley, "that by honestly decoding the patterns of our environment, we can be much more effective in leveraging not only our own capabilities, but those of our suppliers and customers. In the past our consultants have said we need a vision, but I now begin to see that we need the capacity to envision. There's a difference. Too often our vision has been nothing more than a statement of how we want to be seen. Does it buy us anything when we cannot see the others, their visions and aspirations? When we can see and listen to the others, we can begin to pick up on their momentum, can't we?"

"That's curious, but intriguing," notes Carol. "Instead of trying to market or sell our products and services, you are suggesting, Wesley, as I understand it, that we should be building on the momentum of our customers as they engage their customers. We certainly don't do this if we maintain a value-adding transactional model of business alone. I'm fascinated by the concept of market dialogue, although I'm not sure what it really means in the concrete. What's the seed of the dialogue?"

Finding and Growing Seeds of Opportunities

"Carol, it's right under our noses," says Marjorie. "The seeds are planted in the interaction between our customers and their customers. Like little acorns, these seeds have the potential to grow into significant businesses, if we can help cultivate their growth. But to even know that they're there takes special skill in listening and envisioning. Our raw materials are not just physical, they're also ideas that come from careful listening. Typically we've never looked this far out of the box."

Gregory, who until recently was the last to catch on, lights up. "You lost me for a minute, but I think I'm seeing the pattern. Through skillful dialogue with our suppliers, customers, and customers' customers, we discover one another's capabilities and as-

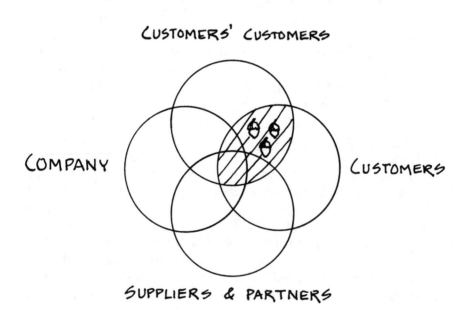

pirations. We also discover the seeds of business opportunities around which we can then cluster and team our capabilities. This becomes possible when we focus on opportunities and not just problems and needs. We then need skill in dynamically teaming capabilities across companies. Hmmm . . . I'm beginning to see why organizations dominated by boxes and lines are so slow . . . no, lethargic at best. Marjorie, how does the figure you have just drawn compare with the earlier figure, built upon extension to the value chain?"

Marjorie flips back to a previous drawing and adds some acorns to it. "You'll notice that they're essentially the same: one has four overlapping circles; this second is more linear. Both focus on the interaction between our customers and their customers to discover the seeds of opportunities. Traditionally, we've focused on our customers' needs. Now we need to also pay more attention to their aspirations. As we think about it, we have no real procedure to discover these opportunities or even to rank and prioritize them. Frankly, it's amazing, now that I think of it, how much we're missing."

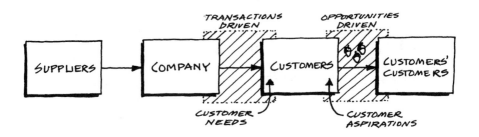

"Marjorie, you're absolutely right," responds Frank, "and we need to spend some time later this week devising a way to sniff out these opportunities and prioritize our efforts. In fact, I'm beginning to have second thoughts about how we've traditionally done our strategic planning, but let's take that up later."

"I also understand the message, Marjorie," adds Gregory, "but what about our bread-and-butter products, those that we make every day—where do they fit in?"

"That really brings us back to reality," notes Vincent. "We aren't always chasing new opportunities; 70 to 80 percent of our business is with the same old stuff. I agree with Gregory: how do our tried-and-true products fit into this model?

"Hmmm . . . perhaps I can answer my own questions," he continues. "I see from the way you've drawn the diagram that we aren't throwing out our transaction-based business; we're simply extending our model to also include a better understanding of the opportunities. It's so easy to feel attacked when some new idea comes up; it seems to threaten the way we've always done things."

Marjorie, looking at Vincent, says, "Isn't it easy to fall into the 'either/or' trap, as Gregory suggested? It is either your way or my way, it is either this or that. But I realize from your question that we are shifting our thinking to thinking in terms of 'both/and.' As Gregory said, we'll continue to do transaction sales based on customer needs, and we need to hone our skills in identifying opportunities at a very early stage. We'll still have sales catalogs with our standard products, but we'll also get good at growing seeds of opportunities so we can continually renew our product offerings."

Frank looks around the room and senses that everyone is on a high, a good time to break. "Let's break for the day and use your questions, Vincent and Gregory, to spark our dialogue tomorrow, picking up on Gregory and Marjorie's distinction between 'either/or' thinking and 'both/and' thinking.

"Oh, by the way, Vincent, no need to come armed with lots of view graphs; we saw what happened to Carol's presentation this morning. We've come a long way in our thinking today, realizing that we have not one but four circles to lead. Moreover, it looks like Alan and his department are going to have an increasingly significant role to play. I suspect the same holds true for the other staff functions, including finance, legal, information systems, training, quality, and facilities. I wouldn't be surprised if we find ways to reintegrate them all back into the line. Finally, as I said earlier, it feels good to be having such a substantive dialogue where everyone feels free to look the truth in the face and ask the tough questions. We are indeed making process. Let's see where we go tomorrow."

CHAPTER

3

WEDNESDAY

Either/Or-itis

There is an eagerness in the room, even though it is not quite 8:30. The sun is shining and the day is warm and comfortable. As Frank walks briskly into the room, Vincent spontaneously begins the discussion.

"Yesterday, you made a fascinating distinction, Marjorie," Vincent says. "I couldn't get it out of my mind: the distinction between 'either/or' and 'both/and' thinking. No wonder I tend to be so sensitive and defensive; I realize I've had a bad case of 'either/or-itis.'"

Laughter . . . and relief. Everyone recognizes the truth in Vincent's statement.

35

"Perhaps it comes with a manufacturing mindset. We want routine. We want long runs of the same products. We want consistency in processes. We want, as you said the first day, Marjorie, to enhance the 'expected' and eliminate the 'unexpected.' Anything that doesn't fit into our neat little world is called a 'problem.' In fact, problems are the bane of manufacturing, yet in a funny sort of way, we thrive on problems. I guess it brings out our macho side, now that I think of it."

He continues, "Now that I think of it, I have begun to think in terms of 'both/and.' I've been redefining our manufacturing processes so we can feel comfortable with the unexpected and the non-routine. We're learning to work in lots of one. We've broken our employees into teams, where each team is responsible for a whole product or product family. We're close to producing against orders, not just for inventory. We've had to do a lot of work with our suppliers to understand this process, but they're ready to deliver just in time. It was wonderful to turn off the lights on our high bay storage system because we no longer need it."

"Vincent, I didn't realize so much has been going on in manufacturing," notes Wesley, "but I have noticed it's easier for my engineers to get their prototypes through production. If you're developing this kind of capability, I can begin to see how we can create integrated product development teams that include our customers as active members."

Innovating with Our Customers[sm1]

"Interesting," exclaims Frank. "Does this mean that we could reposition our innovation program to include our customers? If we can innovate with them, then our products will be more robust and focused. This fits nicely into the figure that Marjorie drew at the end of the day. This is beginning to make more sense the more we talk, especially in light of the 'either/or' and 'both/and' distinctions. Marjorie, perhaps you could draw a long line across the paper. On one end put 'Expected' and 'Routine' and on the other 'Unexpected' and 'Non-routine'."

As Marjorie draws, Frank continues, "Notice how we've traditionally wanted to gravitate to either pole, conditioned by 'either/

or' thinking. But if we take a 'both/and' approach, it's so much easier to understand how we should deploy and manage our resources."

While Frank is talking, Marjorie draws the figure.

"There's real truth in this diagram, Frank," notes Vincent, "and I didn't really realize what we were doing until it was brought up yesterday. As I think of it now, the industrial era has lived in and for the routine and the expected. Our enemy, the non-routine, has always been the problem."

As Vincent is talking, Marjorie puts a box around the left end of the spectrum and labels it "Industrial Era."

Alan looks bewildered again. "Please help me. We can define jobs for the routine and expected tasks, but how do we develop job descriptions for the unexpected? We can reward people for what they're supposed to do if we know ahead of time, but how do we reward people for doing the unexpected? What criteria do we use?"

"Alan, when I tore the organizational chart in half on Monday, I didn't know what would happen," comments Frank. "For the first time in a long while, I did something for which I did not have a ready answer. I know this is tough and you feel under pressure, because you care so very much for HR, but perhaps the answer concerning our reward system will emerge as we better understand the new approach."

Boxes and Lines

"It's good advice, Frank," Carol says. "Perhaps we should take a little time to better understand how we've been influenced by industrial-era thinking. Frank, when you noted how hard it is for us to learn, communicate, and decide, it really struck home. That's so very true. So true that I was making some sketches for myself last evening. I sketched a very simple model of the hierarchy. Perhaps, Marjorie, you could create a figure with one box over two other boxes and label them 'A,' 'B,' and 'C.'"

Carol has hardly finished when Marjorie has the figure on the flip chart.

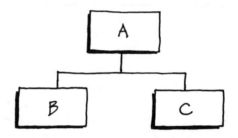

Carol continues, "As I've thought about this model, I've asked myself several questions. Let's explore them together. What are the strong relationships?"

Wesley thinks for a minute, then says, "Between A and B, and A and C."

All agree.

Carol asks, "What is the weak relationship?"

This time Gregory is ready. "I believe it's between B and C."

"These are the conclusions I came to also," responds Carol. "Does this strike you as being strange?"

Looks go back and forth; a couple of people grimace, trying to think of what Carol might be getting at.

Alan responds, "No, it isn't strange; in fact it's the cornerstone of our entire system. A is responsible and rewarded to make sure B does what he or she is assigned to do. That's why we work so hard on carefully defining each job, and making sure the proper supervisory skills are in place. Also, A usually sets up a competitive environment so both B and C are striving for recognition."

Marjorie thinks back to Frank's comment about how the company cannot learn, communicate, and decide. She looks at Alan, then the others, and says, "Alan, you're absolutely right; this is the way we usually think about these relationships, but now I see it in a new light. As I looked at the figure I asked myself, does B know C's capabilities? Does B care?"

She continues, "The answer to both of these questions is typically 'no.' Does A help B understand C's skills and talents? Typically not. And why not? Because A wants to use C to check on B and vice versa. What happens? What happens when something comes up that takes the skills and capabilities of more than one box?"

Vincent is beginning to catch the drift of Marjorie's remarks. "In those circumstances, things often fall through the white space between the boxes. If the challenge requires the combined talents of B and C then it often goes unmet, because A does not create that kind of collaborative relationship between B and C. As I think of it, these letters may be individual people, or they may be various functional departments, such as engineering and manufacturing. Even though we're working more closely with Wesley's engineers, I don't know how many times things have fallen between the cracks, and my people have to redline the engineering drawings to correct them."

Carol reenters the discussion. "You're catching on to some of the things I was thinking about last evening. First, given the model of the three boxes, there isn't really a learning relationship between B and C, much less between B, C, and A. B is looking for the weaknesses and the screw-ups of C, and vice versa, not C's talents, which he or she can build off of. A encourages this type of behavior because, supposedly, a competitive approach brings out the best in them. They, in essence, are devaluing one another's capabilities through inattention."

She continues, "Both B and C are very careful to control what A hears. They want to 'manage the news.' It isn't surprising that A is often ill-informed about what's going on in the organization. This model is not really designed to facilitate open communication either vertically or horizontally. And without a clear and honest picture of what's going on, decisions are hard to come by, or are not well informed. I know I'm probably overstating things, but by seeing these relationships stripped bare, we can better understand why Frank had the feelings he acted upon on Monday when he tore our organizational chart in half. Remember, Frank, you were frustrated because we are so slow to respond, and we don't have an organization that can easily learn, communicate, and decide."

"That's remarkable," exclaims Vincent. "What we have, in essence, is an organization based on structured distrust and a culture of devaluing. Ouch!"

"Run that by me again," says Gregory.

Distrust

Vincent sees Gregory struggling to keep up with the discussion. "A often fosters a relationship of distrust between B and C. If C knows B is looking for his or her weaknesses, he keeps not only his weaknesses hidden, but also many of his talents. This engenders distrust. Moreover, because they are looking for weaknesses in one another, they tend to devalue each other."

Marjorie suddenly sees something she hasn't seen before. "I have often wondered why, with so many highly paid professionals, we don't get more out of them. If their colleagues don't really see their talents, it's small wonder that these talents are not effectively used. This knowledge base, this talent pool, this resource of experience . . . it's not really being used effectively. This is a cost I've never calculated, and yet it's a real cost, the cost of underutilized assets, knowledge assets."

"Frank, could it be that this 'distrust' is the ballast that slows us down?" asks Marjorie.

"When you put it that way, why, yes, it certainly seems to be," responds Frank.

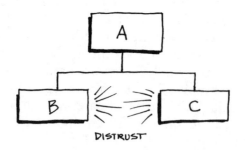

DISTRUST

Alan is staring at the flip chart. Slowly he turns his head towards his colleagues. "I haven't seen this before, but I see that our reward system has focused almost exclusively on what people do in their boxes; it doesn't really measure collaboration between boxes. In an innocent sort of way, have I colluded with this traditional approach to reinforce a distrusting environment?"

Carol looks at Alan, and after a pause, says, "That was a courageous thing to say, and a very honest and open statement. Thanks, Alan. Yes, I think it is true. But you are not to blame; this is the way we've all been thinking. We've all participated in this collusion, without really even knowing it."

Wesley is thinking back to his high jumping analogy. "Could it be that we have been caught by 'either/or' thinking as if there is nothing but the scissors jump? It seemed the most obvious way at one point in time. Is there another way to see the relationships between A, B, and C?"

Bigger than the Boxes

Wesley continues, "If what Marjorie and Alan are saying is true, we are not really using the richness of people's talents, either as individuals or as functional groups. We have resources we are seriously under-utilizing. It would be like Vincent only using his manufacturing equipment 30 percent of the time. I have always felt that our people are bigger than their boxes. They have more talents than fit the simplistic job descriptions. Come to think of it, it's not just our individual talents, but how we knit these talents together that gives us our core competencies. I'm beginning to understand what Tom Peters has been saying for a while."

Marjorie seems never to want to sit down. She is still at the flip chart, and this time she is adding something to the three boxes.

"Would we agree that our people are bigger than their boxes?" asks Marjorie. "And A's challenge is to help B and C combine their talents in ways that enhance the strength of the organization? In other words, A is a coach and mentor, whose challenge is to identify and combine talent creating a collaborative rather than competitive environment."

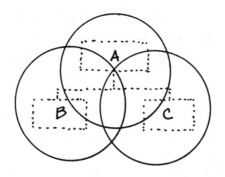

"Marjorie, do you realize that with this approach, there's likely to be more trust between B and C?" asks Wesley. "What has really changed, the relationships between the three, or A's attitude? By redefining A's role we are able to effect a significant change in the relationship between B and C. They learn, with A's coaching, to leverage one another's talents, one another's capabilities, one another's experience, and one another's aspirations. B and C are put in a relationship where they will learn to discover, value, and build off one another's abilities. This is a relationship of valuing."

"Fascinating . . . we've kept the hierarchy relationships, but have redefined them in a most intriguing way," notes Vincent. "Frank, perhaps the problem isn't with the traditional organizational chart, but instead with our understanding of how it operates. I'm beginning to believe there is something in Wesley's high jump analogy. By a shift of attitudes, we're able to build on the natural energy and talents of our people and our functions more effectively. With this shift, we may well be able to increase productivity and scale new heights of market performance. If we see this in relation to the scissors kick, the Western roll, and the Fosbury Flop, it's unlikely we will flop as we have been doing."

Laughter . . . Gregory shakes his head at Vincent's play on words.

Rethinking the Model

"Thanks," interjects Frank. "You've helped me to reinterpret our model. It makes sense. We're going to need some hierarchy, but I didn't know how to solve the challenge with the old way of thinking. I suspect that even Eastman Chemical, with their flat pizza organization, still very much has a hierarchy. What I sense is that the leading management group knows how to function as a team, and this has inspired the teaming process within the organization."

Carol, who started the discussion about the three-box model, looks excited. "You've understood what I was thinking last evening, only you've taken it further than I did. Now I just realized that there is also a connection to our discussion of 'either/or' and 'both/and' thinking. Notice that we can still have the hierarchy, but redefine its functioning in a more natural way. Alan, is it possible to rethink our reward strategy from this new perspective?"

"Well . . . er . . . perhaps . . . ," Alan fumbles for words. "Guess I'm a little dense—it takes a while for all this stuff to sink in. What we need isn't a reward system that keeps people captive to their boxes, but one that encourages and rewards collaboration. You know, I'm beginning to sense the artificiality of our traditional approach to rewards. It's been a very manipulative system, built on the idea that people do what is measured. That's true, but there is more to the truth."

Alan pauses, but no one interrupts. "Overlapping circles, people challenged to find and build off one another's talents, capabilities, and visions . . . I'm beginning to suspect that if we could create such a culture, the very act of valuing one another is a real reward. After all, we all want to be taken seriously by our colleagues. Yet how ironic—our existing model does just the opposite: it causes people to undermine, undercut, and demean one another's talents. It hasn't been a reward system, but a punishment system, masquerading in the name of a reward system. Ouch, it hurts when I think of it. No wonder I was so confused when we started this discussion; there was just so much I didn't see or understand."

Alan sees some smiles from his colleagues, accepting smiles. He begins to feel a part of this group in a way he never has, and it's nice.

Gregory, who is often the last to see a connection, turns to Marjorie. "Did you notice the similarity between the three overlapping circles you just drew and the four overlapping circles we were discussing yesterday? As an engineer myself, they remind me of what we call Venn diagrams, mathematical sets that show key relationships. What strikes me is that it's the relationship that's important, not the separation and the white space between the boxes. Come to think of it, this is why I liked the way you redrew the horizontal value chain as four overlapping circles in our discussion yesterday."

Both/And Thinking

"I'm not an engineer," notes Carol, "but it's clear to me that the overlapping circles really represent a 'both/and' approach rather than the 'either/or' mindset that has dominated our industrial era. We have a few minutes before we go to lunch; perhaps we can return to your drawing dealing with 'both/and' thinking, Marjorie."

Marjorie turns back to her earlier figure.

Carol turns to her colleagues and asks, "Can we add to this? What other contrasting poles do we notice?"

Everyone picks up the challenge and suggests contrasts for Marjorie to write on the flip chart.

As words are suggested, there is no discussion. Marjorie is busy writing, so busy that she doesn't have time to ask questions. After about fifteen minutes she steps back and looks at the flip chart.

INDUSTRIAL ERA

Routine	Non-routine
Known	Unknown
Linear	Non-linear
Bureaucratic	Non-bureaucratic
Hierarchical	Non-hierarchical
Pre-defined	Self-organizing
Jobs	Teaming capabilities
Control	Collaboration
Distrust	Trust
Problems	Opportunities
Discuss	Dialogue
Adding value	Generating value

"Quite a list of words," she notes. "What do they all mean? I can guess at some. We've already talked about the contrast between routine and non-routine. This reminds me of our comments about the expected and unexpected on Monday. I think I know what we mean by the contrasts between the known and the unknown and the bureaucratic and the non-bureaucratic, but I'm not sure about the difference between linear and non-linear; could someone help me?"

Wesley, who studied physics in college, and who has kept up with some of the latest developments in the field, responds, "'Linear' assumes a nice orderly progression, whereas a non-linear event jumps between states. When we heat water, it gets hotter and hotter in a linear manner, then it jumps states in a non-linear way, becoming steam. Perhaps I've been inspired by developments in chaos theory. We've discovered that a very small variation in an initial condition can cause significant changes later on. This is the so-called 'butterfly effect.' The beating of a butterfly's wings in Hong Kong can cause a thunderstorm in New York. I know it sounds far-fetched, but remember how a trader in Singapore made some decisions, by himself, that brought down a leading bank in the United Kingdom, Barings."

Wesley pauses. "I just discovered the connection between this phenomenon and our discussion of the seeds of opportunities. These seeds are small initial conditions, but if we can grow them with our customers, they could grow into very significant business for us. At first they are little seeds; then before we know it, they jump orbits and we are into a new business area, renewing our business."

Frank smiles.

"Thanks, Wesley, that makes good sense, especially from our sales and marketing perspective. It gives me some new ideas," says Carol. "Let's look at the next set of words. What do we mean by the 'predefined' and 'self-organizing' idea?"

Jobs and Capabilities

"Let me take a try at this one," volunteers Alan, who begins to speak with more confidence. "For a long time we've been using a 'predefined' approach to jobs. We try to figure out what has to be done, then find someone who can fill the slot, more or less. Our focus has been on the requirements of the job, not necessarily the capabilities of the people. We've also used this approach to define departmental charters. Our challenge has been to avoid overlap and redundancy. We've wanted clear assignments; then we can measure people's performance more effectively, or so the theory goes. But now I'm seeing in our HR literature more awareness that we need 'self-organizing' teams that are able to better adjust to one another's capabilities. Things are moving too swiftly to be able to predefine everything. The only way is to allow the organization to define itself as we go. This is also why, as I understand it now, there are second thoughts about the concept of 'jobs.' There's more appreciation for the need to master the processes of dynamically teaming capabilities, both within our company and between companies.

"Wow," exclaims Alan, "I've just seen something that's bothered me for a long while. I just gave you the impression that we're throwing out jobs and embracing dynamic teaming. But that's only partly true. I just realized how I've been a prisoner of 'either/or' thinking—either 'jobs' or 'teaming.' When we use 'both/and' thinking, we discover that we have both jobs and teaming, jobs for the routine and teaming for the non-routine. There'll always be those things that are routine, and we need well-defined jobs and processes to master them. And then there are those opportunities that take ever-changing sets of talents. If this is the case, then we'll need a reward system that recognizes both jobs and teaming, and anywhere between these two extremes."

"Nicely said, Alan," comments Frank. "In light of what you've just said, I begin to see the difference between control and collaboration. We were really touching on this one as we were discussing the three-box model. Instead of A controlling B and C, A's challenge is to coach and mentor his or her subordinates, creating a more collaborative relationship. This helps move the organization from a culture of distrust and devaluing to one of earned trust, where people feel that their integrity and talents are valued and appreciated."

Problems and Opportunities

Frank continues, "I now understand the distinction between 'problems' and 'opportunities.' We'll always have 'problems,' but if we see them from the perspective of 'opportunities,' then they can seed our learning. Moreover, as we are better able to recognize one another's capabilities, we'll enhance our skills in teaming the right competencies to seize concrete market opportunities. However, this requires quality dialogues with our customers and suppliers, and will lead to an ability to not only add value, but generate value as we work together. This makes some good sense, but I'm not quite sure what someone means about the distinction between 'satisfaction' and 'meaning.'"

"I put those words on the page myself," confesses Marjorie. "As I looked over the list I realized how in the industrial era we've focused on worker satisfaction and customer satisfaction. But satisfaction is very ethereal, here one minute and gone the next. It seems to me people want a sense of meaning, a feeling that what they're doing is significant. There's a deeper longing to be a part of a spirited organization, one that has a positive purpose. This is more than just having a vision. Do you know what I mean?"

Gregory picks up Marjorie's questions, to the surprise of everyone—or maybe not; they are all seeing a side of Gregory that they haven't experienced before. "Meaning, significance, patterns . . . they're somehow related. As we're looking at the patterns of warranty problems, we're discovering some very significant things, insights that we're sharing with engineering. It's been changing our relationship with engineering. Earlier they just thought of us as service grunts; now they're listening more to what we're finding. This is giving my people more of a sense of importance and meaning, and they like it."

Wesley looks up at the clock and notices it's past lunch time. He is amazed at how much energy there has been in their dialogue and how far they have come from Monday's gloom. Frank notices Wesley, and turns to the group and says, "Wesley has just noticed how quickly time flies when everyone is engaged. Let's break for lunch now and return tomorrow. Again we've covered a lot of territory today. We're making significant progress in rethinking our organizational model. The distinctions between 'either/or' and 'both/and' are extremely important.

"Moreover, we've seen the flaws in the traditional way of thinking of the hierarchy, but we've also discovered a way to both have the hierarchy, as coaches and mentors, and overcome its inherent weaknesses, a true example of 'both/and' thinking. Our discussions are pointing us to the importance of people's talents, knowledge, experience, and aspirations. These are really the first signs of our transition into the knowledge era, where we can use these talents. What strikes me is that the industrial era kept us captive to 'either/or' thinking, while the knowledge era opens up 'both/and' possibilities. It helps us to understand the need to be effective in the routine, for as Vincent reminded us yesterday, 70 to 80 percent of our volume is in tried-and-true items. It also gives us a way to reach out to our customers and together discover seeds of opportunities that we can grow together through innovative teaming. And with this new understanding, I am hoping we can become

KNOWLEDGE ERA
Both/And Thinking

INDUSTRIAL ERA
Either/Or Thinking

Routine	Non-routine
Known	Unknown
Linear	Non-linear
Bureaucratic	Non-bureaucratic
Hierarchical	Non-hierarchical
Predefined	Self-organizing
Jobs	Teaming capabilities
Control	Collaboration
Distrust	Trust
Problems	Opportunities
Discuss	Dialogue
Adding Value	Generating Value
Satisfaction	Meaning (significance)

much more agile, continually capturing our experience, improving dialogue, and mastering decisive action.

"Finally," concludes Frank, "Vincent, I hope you have overcome your 'either/or-itis' by now."

Laughter!

Marjorie is again enhancing their graphic as the others leave the room.

CHAPTER

4

THURSDAY

Excitement

Most are already in the room by 8:00. Frank arrives at 8:18, looks around, and suggests that they start. He senses some excitement, but can't quite figure out what's up.

"What's going on?" he quietly asks.

"Frank, remember what started this whole process? Your sleepless nights . . . your frustration with our lethargy . . . your feeling uneasy about a confining organizational chart . . . well, now several of us have had a sleepless night and we were comparing notes before you came into the room," says Marjorie.

"What's bothering you, then?" responds Frank.

Wesley jumps in. "It's not what's bothering us, it's what's exciting us! A couple of us were really struck by how we had been captive to 'either/or' thinking. It's so confrontational and assumes a winner and a loser. 'Both/and' opens up new ways to think of our resources. For example, I personally feel so much better because many of our routines work extremely well, even though they may be bureaucratic. At the same time our integrated product development teams are anything but bureaucratic. This will make it easier to shift back and forth. For example, once we've engineered a product family, we can mass customize it, combining both custom and routine capabilities.

"I drew myself a little diagram to capture these processes," he continues. He moves to the flip chart.

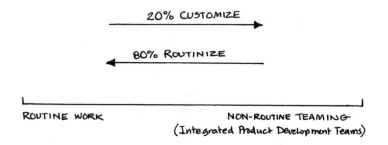

Wesley explains his thinking. "Using the 80/20 rule, I can use my IPD teams to capture our customers' aspirations, specifications, and needs in concrete drawings. Once we see the patterns, we can master the routines. At the same time, we can take some routine products and customize them for unique situations, thus giving us even more return from existing investments. It's exciting—I'm already seeing how I can help our company make more money."

"You know, Wesley," responds Carol, "you've just helped me solve the eternal marketer's dilemma: how do we continually adapt to ever-changing customer needs? Our sales people always want to give our customers what they want, even if it's not in the catalog, but they get beaten up by engineering and manufacturing for submitting 'strange' requests, as you call them. If my people can better understand our capabilities and if we can team more closely, we'll have a much more realistic understanding of the possible and the stretch."

She continues, "Marjorie's drawings of the four overlapping circles have given me a new view of our role in sales and marketing. Why keep turning over rocks looking for customer problems? Why keep asking them for their needs, especially when they're usually so inarticulate? I realize now that many customers are not terribly interested in just talking about their problems. They have more energy about what they are trying to do, just as we do. I can see now that it will be so much more exciting looking for aspirations, where we can grow new possibilities together. And if I can involve our colleagues in engineering, manufacturing, and service, then we can all win, including our suppliers and customers."

Realism Sets In

"I too feel your excitement," admits Frank. "We've gained some insight in our reflections together, we've had quality conversations, and we see new possibilities, but is this enough to build a solid future? I don't think so. We have a company of 2,760 employees, we sell to 215 major customers and many smaller ones, and we have a supplier base of from 47 to 98 companies, depending how we count it. It's one thing to feel good about a few new insights; it's something else to help our colleagues understand new ways of working on a daily basis."

Some of the morning's excitement seems to be lessening. They look at one another and think about the reality of their situation.

Marjorie ventures a comment. "You're right, Frank, it's one thing to have an exciting conversation among ourselves, but it's much more challenging to initiate a process that involves everyone in the company, so they too can benefit from these insights. Yet without a large systems change, where everyone is touched in some way, we'll never make it over the bar at new heights, to use Wesley's high jumping analogy. I've been doing some checking and it took Eastman Chemical's top management team eighteen months to think their way through their pizza organizational model, which they introduced in the early 1990s. They're still working on implementation within the organization. There are parts of the organization that still haven't caught on to the new mindset."

The ultrarealist, Gregory, nods. "I'm not sure how I would share our conversation with my 310 service technicians. They're a very practical bunch; many came out of the armed services, where they were top repair specialists."

"Gregory," interjects Marjorie, "earlier you said you were moving from a 'break-fix' model to one where you proactively look for warranty patterns and either beat up on our engineers to make necessary changes or prepare the customers to take corrective action themselves. What would it take for some of your technicians to sit down with our customers and jointly create a more comprehensive service strategy?"

"Marjorie, you must be reading my mind," smiles Gregory. "That's where we're headed. It's interesting too, because we're rethinking the way we do strategic planning. We still sit together among ourselves, figure out our vision, mission, strengths, weaknesses, threats, and opportunities, then factor in what we expect our competition might be doing, and voilà, our strategic plan. Too often this is like sitting in a bathtub, drinking our own bath water. Now I'm beginning to explore ways we can do our strategic planning together with selected customers, using the 80/20 rule. . . ."

Strategic Planning: A Dated Process

"Gregory, your thinking parallels mine," interrupts Frank. "Our traditional corporate planning process has functioned in the same way. After all, we all learned the same approach to strategic planning from the same books in the 70s and 80s. What a lame way of planning! I want to encourage you to reach out to our suppliers and customers and develop joint plans. In fact, and now perhaps I'm getting excited myself, we need to actively reach out in a variety of ways. Wesley and Vincent, how much time do your people in engineering and manufacturing spend with our customers and suppliers?"

Wesley thinks for a minute. "A little, but really not very much. I just don't have the resources to spare for that kind of work; we're all too busy."

"Certainly you're busy if you're trying to develop everything yourselves," chides Frank, "but if you were to better use our customers' ideas, experience, and aspirations, couldn't it help streamline our prototype development process?"

"Well . . . perhaps, but . . ." mumbles Wesley.

"Wesley, Wesley, do I detect a persistent case of the NIH (not invented here) syndrome?" says Frank with a smirk.

"Frank, why are you picking on me? You know engineers. They feel more comfortable sitting in front of their workstations than they do sitting across the table from a customer dressed in a coat and tie."

Laughter!

"Wesley, do you think the Internet and the World Wide Web with its multimedia sound and graphics will save your engineers from having to interact face to face with our customers?" Marjorie knows her question is provocative, but she understands that a company that hides behind technology, even the latest, is unable to pick up the subtle nuances of the market that are the early signs of the upcoming trends.

"Marjorie, you have a way with the truth that hurts, but thanks, you're right," admits Wesley. "Yesterday we talked about being able to pick up on the seeds of opportunities, or perhaps even to plant some ideas that can grow into significant opportunities. We'll have to become more interactive—our NIH, our not-invented-here, mindset keeps us from new sources of inspiration. What I don't see is how all this hangs together. As we evolve towards a new understanding, how does it come together? What will give us a sustainable competitive advantage?"

Sustainable Competitive Advantage

Vincent, who has been extraordinarily quiet, says, "Wesley, you have a knack for asking the right questions at the right time. 'What gives us a sustainable competitive advantage?' An excellent question. Some friends at ABB, Asea Brown Boveri, have worked out a most useful graphic on this topic.[1] Marjorie, could you draw five boxes in a stair-like fashion from the lower left to the upper right?

On the x-axis put 'Competitive Strength' and on the y-axis put 'Safeguard Against Imitation.'"

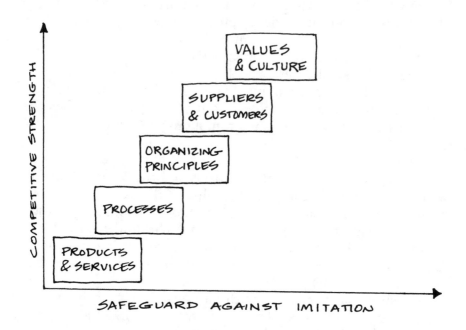

"As I've thought about this model, the wisdom is clear," notes Vincent. "Having excellent products and services gives us some advantage, but others can copy them directly or make similar items, so we're not buying that much. Well-engineered processes give us a little more strength and it's slightly harder for the competition to imitate us. Advanced organizing principles give us unique ways to reach and work with our customers and suppliers, and finally, if we can be innovative with our corporate values and culture, we have the most strength and that is the hardest to imitate. For example, Oticon, a hearing aid/hearing enhancement company in Denmark, with 1,200 employees world-wide, has developed such a unique culture that the president, Lars Kolind, is willing to invite Siemens and other competitors to visit, knowing that they cannot easily copy their culture. I have seen their facilities and they're a wonderful combination of high technology and high touch: high technology in that all paper is scanned in electronically and everyone works with groupware, and high touch in the way they discuss around the coffee pot, their equivalent of the water cooler."

"Vincent, you went pretty fast," remarks Gregory. "Could you slow down and run this one by me again? It seems important and I want to make sure I understand. Perhaps you could use your example for all five steps."

"Thanks, Gregory, you're right, it is important," responds Vincent. "Oticon was caught sleeping in the 1980s when hearing aids moved from the pocket to the ear. With miniaturization technologies, some companies pioneered the in-ear aid. Oticon needed to master this technology to stay current with the market, and they did. They were able to match their competitors' products. Kolind recognized the need not only for current products and processes, but that his company needed a cultural change. The fancy offices and big cars in the garage below gave people a false sense of security. He first moved the company out of comfortable but expensive quarters in downtown Copenhagen to a renovated two-story recycled office building beside an old Tuborg Beer plant just north of the city. He enlisted his information systems experts to help design open space where everyone could be connected by a robust local area network and a state-of-the-art groupware computer system. He envisioned a team-based operating environment where it's extremely easy to form and reform teams both electronically and physically around cutting-edge projects. Moreover, he used their information systems to connect over the Internet with the audiologists (their customers) who fitted their products for *their* customers, the end-users."

He continues, "If we apply the Oticon experience to the ABB model, we find they were able to quickly re-engineer in-ear miniaturized products. They build their processes around a robust information system. Organizationally, they've mastered the dynamic teaming and knowledge networking model. The company is led by a council of ten of the senior managers, each having responsibility for mentoring one or more projects. They are intimately connected with their customers, the audiologists, directly and over the Internet. And they have mastered a new culture that's built upon a responsible self-teaming and self-organizing approach. The co-workers (they don't use the word employee) have discovered the need to learn about one another's capabilities and aspirations, because this is essential in a teaming environment. They have no one person responsible for human resources; rather they have a part-time secretary who manages the records and two secretaries who handle the payroll of their 265-person head office."

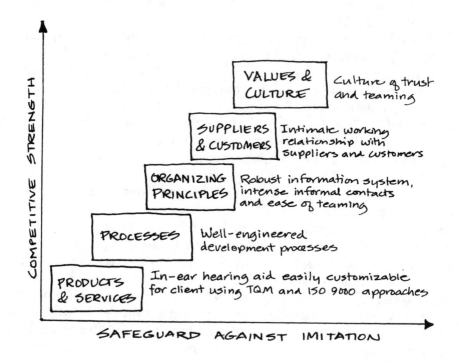

Vincent makes notes on Marjorie's chart, indicating the steps Oticon took at each level.

"Vincent, did Oticon approach each step sequentially?" asks Gregory.

"No, they worked on all five areas concurrently," responds Vincent. "Kolind realized that deeper change comes only through the interplay of a cultural change, new working partnerships with customers and suppliers, a robust teaming environment, well-engineered processes, and quality products and services. If any one of these elements is missing, the efforts will sputter to a halt. This has also been confirmed by some recent work in Germany at the Fraunhofer Institute."

Mastering the Basics

"Hmmm . . . perhaps that's why it's taken companies like GE and Xerox so very long to master their desired changes," remarks Marjorie. "If we just follow the management fad of the month we too will flounder in our own ways. I see your point, Vincent; we're going to have to involve not only our own people but also our customers and suppliers in our change efforts, and on several different levels. We'll need good supply management to ensure quality products and processes. We'll need excellence in logistics to get not only our products, but key information to and from our customers and their customers. We'll need a robust, open, and spirited culture that values one another's capabilities and aspirations, individually, functionally, and between companies. In short, we need to master the basics while being open to the unexpected. Let's do a little self-assessment in light of Vincent's story."

"I know how to get superior products, Vincent," notes Wesley. "It takes constant focus on quality. And we've been working to re-engineer several of our basic processes, as we discussed briefly two days ago. I'm not quite sure where we are on our organizing principles, as we are in the midst of thinking this one through. Customers, well, I think we're discovering the flesh and blood of our customers, their capabilities and aspirations. Finally, we've discovered that we've participated in a culture that often devalues one another and that is built mostly on distrust. This is not comfortable."

"This is fascinating," exclaims Frank. "Let's run through this one again. We've been focusing on Total Quality Management, ISO 9000, and the Baldrige Award to improve the quality of our products and services. We've really been making good progress in these areas. We've been re-engineering our 'art-to-part' and 'order-to-delivery' processes with good results. As far as organizational approach is concerned, we're still at sea with this one. As I impulsively tore the organizational chart on Monday, I realized that this still needs to be sorted out. But we're making significant progress if we think about Marjorie and Vincent's graphics. We understand that we need an organization that can enter into a quality dialogue with our suppliers, customers, and customers' customers, an organization that can spot the seeds of opportunities between our customers and their customers, and an organization that can enhance the capabilities of our customers so they can better meet their aspirations. It hasn't all come together, but the direction seems right."

He continues, "We also understand the fact that we need to excel not only with transaction-based relationships with our customers, but also through innovative alliances where we can more openly discover one another's capabilities and aspirations. This also feels right."

Frank pauses, thinking . . .

Culture of Valuing

"Frank, as you were talking," Marjorie notes, "I was thinking that it's the realm of 'values and culture' that influences all the other areas. Yesterday, we stumbled onto the fact that the hierarchical triad, A, B, and C, nurtures a distrust between B and C. As we thought about it, we recognized the widespread culture of devaluing in our company, and other companies like ours. As I thought about it last evening, I realized how easy it is to reinforce this process. We're continually looking for the weaknesses in each other to score some competitive advantage. We've certainly developed our skills well in this area.

"What also struck me," she continues, "is that we'll never be able to tap each other's talents unless we shift to a culture of valuing. It isn't just 'having values and culture' in the abstract that matters. What really matters is that you take me seriously and invest the time to know my strengths, my talents, my capabilities, and my aspirations, and what I want to do with these competencies. Likewise, it's up to me to invest the time to get to know your strengths. Vincent, thanks for sharing the ABB model; it really clarifies nicely the interrelationships between all five elements. And they all do interrelate."

"Marjorie, that does put a lot together," responds Frank. "If we've had a culture of devaluing, it's no wonder we haven't been good at learning, communicating, or deciding, much less teaming. I begin to see how subtle and insidious the culture of devaluing is. It's such a part of the woodwork of our thinking that we don't even see its consequences. As I think of it, the industrial era was built on Adam Smith's 'pin-making factory' model. Long processes were divided into little steps so it would be easy to train people and so they could use the dexterity of their hands. The industrial era was designed to arrange hands, not to build on the content of heads. I guess we have to actively unlearn some of the underlying assumptions of the industrial era."

"You're right, Frank," adds Carol. "As you've been talking, I've seen a new context for understanding sales and marketing. We are not one-way talkers, but we need to be very active listeners. I wonder if I should rename the marketing department the 'listening department'? Maybe I'll do it informally, because it's the raw ideas of our customers, their aspirations, that can become the wonderful challenges for our engineers. Instead of having to cook up the next product idea, if we work more closely between sales, marketing, engineering, manufacturing, and service, through strategic dialogue, we can build on the seeds of opportunities that others sow, or those that we sow. It's those little initiation conditions that can potentially blossom into unexpected winners. Wesley and Vincent, are you ready?"

"Wait a minute," interjects Alan. "Now I feel left out again. For a while I thought there was room in the line for us staff folk."

Designing a New Approach to Rewards

Alan continues, "But why should I ask for permission? Maybe that's a sign of the inferiority feeling on the part of staff. That's silly! Count me in too, because you're going to need help in redefining our organizational relationships, our reward systems, our learning approaches, and our ability to leverage one another's knowledge and experience.

"I've been pretty quiet, as you may have noticed," says Alan, "but I've been following the dialogue and I now see why designing reward systems is such a bear. Typically we reward someone for doing what we want them to do. They're expected to dance to our tune, even if we only give them a fragment of it. This approach is hopelessly shortsighted when it comes to robust teaming. A culture of teaming requires all the team members to be capable of discovering one another's talents, and using these talents. In a real sense, good teaming is a reward in and of itself.

"This is not understood. Too often individuals are afraid they'll have to give up their individuality to be part of the team. They'll have to submit to the mini-hierarchy that asserts itself on the team, however informally. They'll be subject to the very same vagaries as in the formal hierarchy. This is certainly not comfortable and it's no wonder many resist openly or quietly a move to a team-based culture. Thanks to our discussion of the difference between 'either/or' and 'both/and' thinking, I now see that good teaming can bring out the very best of the individual. Instead of being the 'individual vs. the team,' we can develop a model where the individual excels because of the dynamics of teaming, based on a culture of valuing. As you and I work together, we discover one another's talents and capabilities, talents I myself might not have fully appreciated. We are certainly experiencing this together this week, but you and I know it is not a part of our company culture. What can we do to help our colleagues throughout the company learn to value and build off of one another's talents?"

"Good question, Alan. I wonder," remarks Wesley, "if we could do a couple of things. First, each of us is responsible for our departments—at least if we choose to continue to have departments—one never quite knows now that Frank's torn the chart in half. But let's suppose we stop perpetuating the narrow-minded side of the A, B, and C triad. Instead, let's become active in continually challenging our people to discover one another's strengths. This is certainly a mindshift on our parts, but can we do it?"

Wesley looks around the room and senses agreement. He continues, "Second, we need to more systematically allow our co-workers to experience the process of identifying one another's capabilities and aspirations. Perhaps, Alan, you could devise a process through which we could put everyone."

"I'd be glad to give it a try, but I would like all of you to actively participate. It would be nice to have a process we can do in-house, where we as a staff can work in teams to facilitate it, rather than bringing in someone from the outside. I'll give it some thought."

Work Is Conversation

Carol looks at Alan. "As you've been talking, Alan, I've been thinking about the nature of work. We have seen work in terms of jobs. People give up their time to do their job, and they then get rewarded for their efforts through their wages, bonus, or other rewards. This is so simplistic. There's so much more to work. During this week, have we been playing the roles of our jobs? Not really. Have we even been working? Well, yes . . . perhaps work is a conversation, a real conversation, with its give and take. In our typical meetings, someone will say something, then someone else will speak, hardly making reference to the last speaker. This hasn't been happening this week. Why not?"

Wesley thinks out loud. "It's a funny thing, Carol, but I feel safe. I feel what I say will be taken seriously. And the irony is that we probably wouldn't have gotten to this point if Frank hadn't cast the shadow of uncertainty over us by tearing up the organizational chart. We aren't playing roles. We're open and honest with one another. I usually don't get into the feeling stuff, but frankly it feels so much nicer. I get tired of always having to play the analytical role of the engineer."

"Carol, did you use the phrase, 'work is conversation?'" asks Vincent. "What does that mean? In manufacturing we think work is changing the shape of something physical, refining, bending, cutting, grinding . . . or perhaps changing its location, moving, stacking, retrieving. That has little to do with conversation; in fact there's so much noise in the plant that many conversations occur at the tops of our voices."

Carol turns to Vincent. "Earlier we were talking about the need to enter into dialogue with our customers, to understand their capabilities and aspirations. Remember? This isn't transforming something physical or changing the location of a product. What is it? Is it work? Or something else?"

A bit perplexed, Vincent responds, "Well, I guess it is work, especially if we are doing it on company time."

"Does that mean that work is what we are getting paid to do?" asks Carol.

"Yes, that's also how we think of it," replies Vincent.

"But that doesn't tell us what work really is at its core. As I think back over this week, we've certainly been working, but we haven't transformed a single piece of matter, except for the flip chart Marjorie's been writing on. True, we are still being paid. But there is something more going on. We've been producing sentences, ideas, thoughts, feelings, intuitions. We've been shaping, molding, and refining these ideas. Your response to my comment is important to me, because it shapes what I'll say next. I don't know what's coming next until I hear you. Our time together hasn't been a series of monologues, but instead it's been rich dialogues. Our conversations and dialogues have been work. Our conversations and dialogues have been the anvils upon which we're hammering out new mindsets, new understandings of how to operate." Carol wants to continue but Gregory cannot hold back.

Strategic Dialogue Process

"Earlier I indicated the way I'm changing my strategic planning process. I now see it more as a strategic dialogue process. Without entering into an active conversation with our customers, without really listening closely to their aspirations, I won't be able to respond adequately. What are we getting from our customers? It's certainly not raw materials. Hmmm . . . raw ideas?" Gregory pauses.

"Gregory and Vincent, I'm beginning to see what Alan and Carol have been getting at," adds Marjorie. "Typically we think we work with matter, but we also work with ideas. Work is the expression of ideas. These ideas then shape how we handle our raw materials. In essence, we're embedding our ideas, our experience, our insights into the engineering drawings, the process controls, and the materials chosen. Each product or service embodies a whole bunch of ideas that have been shaped over time. So work is much more than what we get paid for. Work is a process of giving form to something, be it a piece of steel, a writing pad, or a statement uttered. As we respond to the expressions of one another in these activities, we either help enhance the ideas, the form, the shape, or we dent, demean, or destroy them."

"Marjorie," interrupts Gregory, "does that mean that how we respond to one another is important? You say something and I can either say, 'Man . . . that won't work' and shut you down, or I can say, 'Tell me more, that sounds interesting.' I just realized that the A, B, C triad fosters the former response. If B always feels that C is trying to find the weaknesses in her activities, this certainly does not foster quality conversation or dialogue. If our customers don't feel that we're listening to their aspirations, it's unlikely that they are going to say much of significance to us. Wait a minute . . . does this mean, well . . . does it mean that the way we respond to one another creates or destroys us? The way we respond to our team-mates creates or destroys us? The way our team responds to the other team creates or destroys us? The way we respond to our customers creates or destroys our business success? And . . . the way engineering responds to manufacturing creates or destroys our focus and attention to detail?"

Work Is Not Neutral

Marjorie smiles. "Yes, Gregory, work is not neutral. When I work, I express myself. Your response is important to me. You can either affirm or help improve what I am doing, or you can douse me with cold water, denigrating my efforts. When I work I am testing out ideas, possibilities, and aspirations. Your response as a co-worker, customer, or supplier is important. I'm creating myself with what I do. You're creating me in your response . . . or you're destroying me with your cynicism, off-handed remarks, or inattention. I'm beginning to see the wisdom in what Carol was saying, 'Work is conversation,' and 'Work is dialogue.' Vincent, you focus on trans-forming raw materials into finished products, but you take the ideas, the drawings, the process specifications given by engineer-ing and your manufacturing engineers. These are nothing more than ideas. So, do we not transform both raw materials and raw ideas in our company?"

"Never thought of it that way, Marjorie," comments Vincent, "but, yes, we do work more with raw ideas than with raw materi-als. It's easier to see a chunk of raw material, but without well-worked-out ideas, there is little in value we can add. Earlier we talked about the process of 'adding value' to raw materials and the process of 'generating value' through quality interaction

... quality interaction between one another, quality interaction between functions, quality interaction on teams, quality interaction between teams, and quality interaction with our customers' customers, customers, and our suppliers. It's becoming clear to me that without quality conversations, without quality dialogue and quality listening, many seeds of ideas never make it through the crust of disregard so typical of this place."

"Wow ... now I understand why we in HR have had to put so many rungs on the hierarchy ladder," exclaims Alan. "We might be good at adding value to matter, but we are typically not very adroit in valuing one another, individually or on teams. It's no wonder people want to climb the ladder so their subordinates will have to take them seriously. Power by position! It's of limited value in a fast-moving and fluid environment.... Do I have my work cut out for me! Our existing reward and review system is a major hindrance. We need a system that recognizes people's efforts and abilities at growing one another's ideas, insights, learnings, and visions. No, we don't need a system, we need people here who are exceptional in recognizing one another's abilities. I've got a lot to ponder this evening, but I want to continue to count on your help, it's been exciting."

Welcome Aboard

Wesley reaches out his hand to Alan and says, "Welcome aboard. The line is a rough and tumble place, but given our new approaches, you'd better become a key member of the team. And also we'll need the other staff folk to rethink their roles and join our efforts. In fact, let's take a minute to figure out how we can together reintegrate the staff into the line."

"Alan, you're not alone," comments Marjorie. "Our accounting system is excellent at identifying and tracking the costs and values of raw materials as they're transformed into finished products. We put asset numbers on all capital equipment. But alas, we have no ways to put asset numbers onto ideas, except the few that become patents or are trademarked. We have a way to value capital assets, but not knowledge assets. I too am going to have to think hard this evening."

Frank, who has hardly been heard from, steps to the front of the room. "The time is getting on, and we have covered so very much. Let's call it a day today. I suggest we sleep on these ideas, if we can. Sleeplessness seems to be a real sickness with us, so we might as well use our tossing and turning productively."

More laughter.

"Isn't it nice to see how we are lightening up?" notes Vincent. "See you all tomorrow—I'm heading to the tennis courts."

CHAPTER

5

FRIDAY

Taking Stock

It is just before 8:00 in the morning and Frank notices that everyone is already in the room.

He asks, "I wonder if someone would like to summarize where
we've come since I announced my sleepless nights and took the
bizarre step of tearing the organizational chart in half."

"Frank, why don't you do it? You've been quiet for some time in
our meetings," notes Gregory.

"OK, it might be good if I sort out all the ideas we've been
through. As you'll remember, I was bothered by the requests
for additional information systems resources. I was even more
bothered by our organization's slowness to respond to new
opportunities. We've also had difficulties listening, learning,

communicating, and deciding. Throw in a good deal of distrust engendered both by the A, B, C triad and the 'either/or' mode of thinking, a contribution of the industrial era, and it's no wonder we seem to be set in concrete. We can hardly jump over the lowest of heights with our scissors kick.

"We've discovered the importance of listening for our customers' aspirations, finding the small opportunities that begin to grow between our customers and their customers, and the power of 'both/and' thinking. We not only 'add value' to matter, but 'generate value' in quality conversation with one another. We transform raw ideas as well as raw materials. We not only need to improve our products and processes, but master dynamic teaming, redefine our interrelationships with our customers' customers, and customers and suppliers, and redefine our culture. In this regard, we need to shift from a culture of devaluing to one of valuing. As we do this, we'll be able to build off one another's capabilities and aspirations, releasing creative energy and insight. These insights are leading us to appreciate ideas and knowledge more. But breaking free of the underlying assumptions, the all-pervasive mindset of the industrial era, isn't easy, as we've experienced. Now, how do we make it real? How do we integrate the staff back in with the line? How do we help our colleagues within the company understand? And how do we engage our customers and suppliers in new ways? We have come a long way, but now the hard work begins."

Frank turns to Marjorie. "Could you please turn the flip chart to where you moved us from the value chain to the four overlapping circles, the valuing cluster?"

Marjorie flips through the pages and finds the one Frank seeks.

"Marjorie, two things stand out with your four circles, the valuing cluster," continues Frank, "the intense dialogue, symbolized by the arrows, which is essential, and second, the 'field of opportunities' at the overlap between our customers and our customers' customers. This leads to two questions: what can we do as an organization to spot capabilities, listen for aspirations, and better recognize the embryonic business opportunities? And second, how can we quickly mobilize our resources, and those of our suppliers and customers, to seize and deliver on the profitable opportunities?

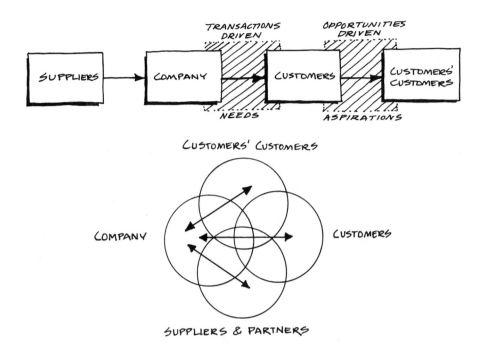

"In short, how do we actively listen and how do we quickly team the right resources?"

Virtual Enterprising

"It's an old and trite phrase, but let me use it anyway," says Wesley. "We'll need to move from a product push to a market pull position. I understand now that our work on the House of Quality isn't nearly adequate. In addition, I'm beginning to see that we can do twenty to thirty percent of our conceptual design with our customers, if we position ourselves that way through a quality dialogue. Moreover, if we choose carefully, we can get thirty to fifty percent of our detail engineering from our suppliers, but this requires a much closer working relationship with them.

"I also now better understand what people mean by 'virtual enterprising,'" he continues. "If we let the seeds of opportunities drive the process, and if we can effectively team among and between companies around specific opportunities, then the customer's customer sees us as if we were one company. Our 'virtual company' exists only as long as we're working the opportunity together. When another opportunity arises, we then create the appropriate coalition of companies to seize and deliver on it. In many ways this is nothing new. Aerospace companies have been teaming for years to deliver specific plane models. The computer industry is continually forming and reforming alliances around specific projects, such as the virtual team of IBM, Apple, and Motorola around the Power PC."

"I see other implications, Wesley, for this model," says Marjorie. "It forces us to think out of the box. Who's on the payroll of a virtual enterprise? What are the legal arrangements? How are the finances handled? What about the interweaving of information systems? As I think of it, virtual enterprising is forcing the staff functions to reexamine our models. I'm sure Alan and I would like your help in rethinking our roles in the virtual enterprising processes. I see Vincent wants to share something."

"Wesley, if I follow your logic about virtual enterprising," responds Vincent, "I could redefine our production model to also tap thirty to fifty percent of our resources from outside our company."

He continues, "Do you know what? As I look over the four overlapping circles, I see that we can let go of the model that we have to do everything ourselves . . . the so-called Henry Ford 'Rouge River Works' model. Strange, but it's a little relaxing. I've always felt that I needed to be ready to meet every contingency, whatever might happen, and this has caused me to build operational capacity we don't always need."

Marjorie is quick to pick up the implications. "Does that mean, Vincent, that our model has added expenses we may not have needed to incur?"

Vincent responds, "Now I see it much more clearly; yes, that's right. Also, instead of trying to just re-engineer our total production process, I need to also re-engineer the process of identifying and integrating external capabilities into specific projects. I'm going to need more staff support for these efforts, arranging the staffing levels, drawing up the legal agreements, running the numbers, and so forth. I see now that our skill in selecting good partners is a critical capability."

Carol sees some additional implications. "Does this mean, Wesley and Vincent, that if our marketing and sales folk better understand both our internal capabilities and those capabilities we can easily tap, then we can position ourselves better with our customers?"

Gregory is not going to be left out. "Carol, what you say is true if our sales people can also help us identify our customers' capabilities and aspirations. There's no reason why we shouldn't more actively tap these resources. But I realize that just saying this isn't enough. We'll need a level of discipline I haven't seen in this organization before. We're going to have to be much more rigorous in our approaches to our customers, customers' customers, and suppliers."

"Gregory, please say more," comments Frank.

Rhythm

"Frank, earlier you helped me shift from the 'break-fix' model to a much more proactive model where we look for patterns of service problems," responds Gregory. "Similarly, we need to be very systematic in the ways we approach our partners in the other three circles. We certainly can't reach out to everyone at once. Instead, what if we develop a rhythm of weekly meetings, say every Friday afternoon for four hours? Then . . ."

Vincent interrupts, "That's four hours out of forty, 10% of our time; that's way way way too much time for something like this. We've got to get product out the door and we don't have enough time as it is."

Marjorie looks at Vincent. "You're focused on adding value to the raw materials we purchase, aren't you? I suspect that Gregory's beginning to think about ways to generate value from the raw ideas we pick up from the market. Isn't that true, Gregory?"

"I didn't think of it quite that way, Marjorie, but yes," responds Gregory. "If we're spending 90% of our time transforming raw materials and only 10% transforming raw ideas, then we still haven't gotten it right. Given the nature of business today, we need to increase the time we spend on shaping raw ideas into timely products and services. Maybe we should spend 20 to 40% of our time on processing raw ideas instead."

"Put it that way, Gregory," adds Vincent, "and I find 10% looking better. Of course I'm not agreeing, but let's suppose we were to devote 10% of our time; how would we do it and who would be involved?"

"I haven't thought much about this before, but for the sake of argument, let me lay out a straw process," volunteers Wesley. "We need to spend time with our customers, customers' customers, and suppliers, getting to know their capabilities and aspirations. We can't pick them all. Perhaps we could begin with a small sampling of say 5% of our top customers, another 5% of our middle-range customers, and 5% of those who just buy on price. We also need internal time learning more about our own capabilities and aspirations."

"Keep going," encourages Frank.

Wesley looks around the room and continues, "Here, looking at the calendar, we have four Fridays in most months, but there are also four months with five Fridays. Let's say that we work internally during the first and third Friday afternoons, involve one or more customers on the second Friday of each month, and our suppliers on the fourth Friday. When the month has a fifth Friday, we will focus on our customers' customers."

But We Aren't Ready!

"Our people aren't ready to meet with our customers, Wesley," comments Vincent. "We have too much to sort out internally. If they join with us, they'll quickly discover we don't have our own act together. This is a very big risk you are suggesting."

"Vincent, I've heard this comment often. It's an easy way to put the brakes on," responds Marjorie. "I've worked in several different companies, and you know what? Most companies don't have their act together. I suspect that our suppliers and customers will feel very much at home with us, because they'll recognize themselves as well. Moreover, we're never going to get our act together if we don't learn how to master the process of dialogue and the process of dynamic teaming. Let's take a little more time to build on Wesley's suggestions. Wesley, who do you think should be involved in this process, just ourselves as senior staff?"

"No, not just ourselves; that would be too narrow," responds Wesley. "What if we made the meetings open to anyone who wants to come, especially the internal meetings?"

"I object—that could effectively shut down production," shouts Vincent. "We must keep this process under control."

Knowledge Assets

Marjorie says, "Earlier, I remember we talked about our knowledge assets, our experiences, our lessons learned, our training, and our capabilities; or to put it another way, our know-hows, know-whos, know-whens, know-wheres, and know-whys. Please excuse the grammar of putting these phrases in the plural, but we certainly have more than one of each of these embodied in our different professionals and in our different functions."

She continues, "The other day we started to compare the value of our capital assets and our knowledge assets. Wesley, Carol, and I have done some back-of-the-envelope calculations. We've estimated how long it takes to get an employee up to speed, how long it takes to cultivate and win a customer, the value of our various processes and information systems, the skills of our technical folk, and so forth. Our books show capital assets of just over $200 million. We estimate our knowledge assets to be equal to five to ten times this, from $1 to 2 billion. Everyone knows how carefully we monitor our capital asset return, but who among us carefully works our knowledge assets?"

No hands shoot up.

Wesley adds, "Remember on Tuesday we noted the distinction between 'either/or' and 'both/and' thinking? Clearly we need to manage both our capital *and* our knowledge assets. I'm convinced that the better we manage our knowledge, the higher the return on our capital!"

Frank nods his head slightly in agreement as he lets Marjorie and Wesley's words sink in. "How do we mobilize this knowledge base?"

"Frank, what if it mobilizes itself?" responds Carol. "Think about it—we always think we have to entice people to do something with some outside reward or compulsion. What if we give them room to define themselves, define their interests, define their capabilities, and define their aspirations? I like Wesley's suggestion that we open our meetings to any and everyone who would like to come. I know it seems risky, and we probably don't have the meeting space or know-how to create a productive meeting with a large group. Perhaps Alan knows of ways to handle such a meeting?"

Alan smiles. "I'd be delighted to help. We have talents in HR that are just what we need in this process. Incidentally, I'm amazed at the way we're discovering talents in one another here in this room that go way beyond our functional roles. And I know we'll find talents within our functions that will make a significant difference to our company. Back to your question . . ."

Knowledge Networking

Alan continues, "Over the last year we've been developing a knowledge networking process that divides any-size group into teams of four. It has proven to be a wonderful way of engendering quality dialogue, involving everyone, and developing meeting-wide consensus quicker than most other approaches. It also incorporates teamwork of teams, so participants can enrich and be enriched by the dialogues of other teams. For example, suppose we have a meeting of twenty people. Typically these twenty sit around a horseshoe table. Due to the pressures of time, when people have the floor, they want to say what's on their minds, and often fail to build on the last statements of their colleagues. In essence, they talk past one another.

"Now suppose that instead of one horseshoe table with twenty, they're divided into five tables of four. After a topic is introduced, each table can explore it. This gives everyone an opportunity to test out ideas, listen, and build upon one another. After a while, two move from each table to the next two tables, where they continue their dialogue. Results can be reported out and a general dialogue of the whole group can bring the meeting to a conclusion.

Typically the group is amazed at the commonality in their conclusions. The mathematics of this process are also impressive. In an hour, the twenty around the horseshoe table will have less than 60 minutes of quality conversations. With the teams of four, this same group will pack close to five hours of conversation into the hour, because they're working in parallel."

The Rhythm of Meetings

"We're also impressed with Harrison Owen's 'Open Space Technology,' which allows a group to set its own agenda at the beginning of the meeting and allows people to pick and choose those topics they want to delve into in greater depth. I'm sure my colleagues in HR can develop a process for your Friday meetings that will give everyone a significant level of involvement. Suppose we pick up on Wesley's suggestion of a rhythm of Friday meetings; they would be as follows: (As Alan summarizes Wesley's suggestions, Marjorie is writing them on the flip chart.)

- First Friday: Internal teamwork between project teams to discover capabilities and aspirations, and to share lessons learned, discover interrelationships, find leverages, open new business possibilities
- Second Friday: Meeting with selected customers from three strata: cutting-edge, middle, and price-pressurers
- Third Friday: Internal identification of patterns of opportunities and the forming of appropriate teams to seize and deliver on the opportunity
- Fourth Friday: Meeting with selected suppliers to discover capabilities and aspirations and to identify where they can support ongoing projects or develop new ones
- Fifth Friday: Focus on our customers' customers, exploring their aspirations, which will shape their relationships with our customers (four months a year have a fifth Friday)"

Alan continues, "Again this is off the top of my head, but we could develop a general rhythm for the actual meetings: (Marjorie continues to write)

- Agenda: The assembled group identifies the issues, themes, and opportunities they would like to work on (15 minutes)
- Context: In the next 15 minutes, the senior leadership team sets the business context
- Teams of Four: Participants cluster around the themes, working in teams of four (45 minutes)
- Teamwork of Teams: Two from each table move to the next two tables within the cluster or between clusters and continue working on the theme at this new table. This brings outside perspective and tends to weave together the dialogues of the other tables. (30 minutes)
- Home Teams: Participants return to their home teams and debrief, further weaving together ideas, insights, experience, and aspirations (15 minutes)
- Brief Break
- General Dialogue: The group as a whole or in multiple clusters of teams, depending on the number of participants, will briefly highlight findings, themes, issues, and especially business opportunities. These will become the focus of the next round of small-team work. (30 minutes)
- Opportunity Teams: Small teams of four will build upon the previous dialogues and focus on concrete opportunities, identifying the business context, the capabilities available, and the driving aspirations, and listing the available resources that can be committed to seize and deliver on this opportunity (30 minutes)
- Teamwork of Teams: Again two from each table will move to the next two tables to discover common areas to leverage, common capabilities, and ways to better leverage aspirations (30 minutes)
- General Dialogue: The key projects, themes, issues and opportunities are summarized and mapped for common reference (30 minutes)"

"Alan, if that has all come off the top of your head, I'd like to see how you are when you really get serious about something," remarks Gregory.

Hearty laughter.

"Wesley and Alan, I was afraid these Friday meetings might end up as time fillers, but I begin to see how we can both discover and work some very substantive issues," comments Carol. "I also begin to see a lot of other benefits. If our customers feel that we take their aspirations seriously, they'll probably be much more open with us. When they sense the range of capabilities available, it's likely their thinking will become bolder. This can, in fact, lead to even more business with us. And after we've gotten into the rhythm, we should be able to see the key patterns and excel at teaming capabilities. But one question: would we have the same meeting format for each of the Fridays?"

"It's likely we would find variations on it that work better for customers, for suppliers, and for customers' customers. I'm sure Wesley would join me in saying that ours are only suggestions," adds Alan. "We want to show that virtual enterprising, dynamic teaming, and knowledge networking are not vague abstract concepts, but are flesh and bone possibilities for us. They are do-able."

"Alan, you don't sound like the traditional HR person," congratulates Gregory. "Welcome to the line."

Alan chuckles; it's a laugh of relief.

Marjorie speaks. "Wesley and Alan, as you've been developing your thoughts, I've been thinking about the dynamics of the processes involved. When people are free to participate, we'll quickly discover the kind of talent we have in-house and the talent that's available in our customer and supplier communities. We'll also increase the level of trust, both internally and externally. By working in small teams, people will feel their contributions are valued. This helps to move us in a concrete way towards a culture of valuing. This is a powerful motivator. In addition, people will quickly discover how their own work fits into the larger business context. It will be easier for them to go into depth, knowing how it fits the larger whole. They can be more focused and effective. Why didn't we think of this approach before?"

Redefining the Staff

"Could it have been that we were too caught up in our boxes and lines organization?" asks Gregory. "But wait, we know that meetings, by themselves, will not change that much. We still have some pretty encrusted ways of doing finance, no offense meant, Marjorie, and our HR procedures, legal approaches, training classes, office arrangements, and information systems are all optimized for the industrial era. You know how skeptical I can be, but you've also found out that I'm open to change. Let me pose the toughest test I can think of. Can we suggest concrete ways our staff functions can redefine their approaches, individually and together, to support our new direction?"

Marjorie is again up at the flip chart and writes the names of the major staff functions. As people make suggestions, she lists them next to the function.

Finance:
- Develop an informal accounting of knowledge assets and intellectual capital
- Develop a "knowledge turns" measure, like inventory turns
- Develop a budgeting process where no more than 40% of the funds are allocated to functions; the remainder is available for opportunity teams, once they craft their plans against agreed criteria
- Develop a cost structure that acknowledges the cost of not using people's capabilities and aspirations
- Enhance the scrap tracking system to include good ideas that get prematurely scrapped from indifference

Human Resources:
- Develop a yellow pages-like listing of individual, functional, and company capabilities and aspirations every four months
- Develop a new approach to rewards, where everyone in the company has ten credit chits to give to others who've been effective in leveraging one another's capabilities for the benefit of our customers on a 360° basis. They must identify the contributions on the backs of the chits, and these notes are shared with their colleagues. The chits may or may not be signed.

- Reward flexibility, cross-teaming, openness and the ability to support growth
- Call employees "associates," "members," or "co-workers" rather than using the word "employee"
- Help middle managers discover new roles as project and program managers
- Develop dynamic teaming processes so each small, core opportunity team is supported by extended resources on an as-needed basis

Legal:

- Develop model teaming contracts for customers and suppliers to better support virtual enterprising
- Develop with finance a way of evaluating the business viability of these virtual enterprise undertakings

Training:

- Build learning into natural business processes, like the Friday meetings
- Develop ways to make the experience, skills, and learnings of team members more accessible to one another
- Develop ways to make tacit knowledge explicit and vice versa

IS:

- Develop a robust information systems infrastructure for dynamic teaming, using groupware such as Lotus Notes or a corporate-wide web approach
- Design a World Wide Web Home Page where it is easy to coordinate the company's various projects behind a membership firewall

Facilities:

- Create flexible office and meeting space

"As I look at these items," remarks Frank, "I can see how the various functions can collaborate with one another to make the practical changes necessary. Finance and HR need to team around the reward systems. Finance and legal can work on the pre-qualification of legal and financial models for virtual enterprising. HR and training can work to make us a true learning organization. HR, facilities, and IS can help us create an environment similar to Oticon's. These are starters. If we can involve others, I know we can extend the list significantly."

The Line Changes Also

"I can see that it isn't just the staff, but the line that also needs to change its thinking to make our new reality possible," remarks Wesley. "I see that our engineers will need to be much more open to collaborating with engineers in our supplier and customer companies. Moreover, I see that as we get better and better at listening for the aspirations of our customers, we'll have the seeds for new products and complementary services. We can also use complementary engineering capabilities elsewhere in the world. I was recently reading about how a Japanese engineering and construction company is using engineers in India, tied in over the latest in satellite communications and advanced CAD systems, to do its detail engineering."

Vincent looks around the room, "Wesley's right. If our integrated product development teams can leverage one another's capabilities, then we can bring in more variable resources from our supplier communities, so that we can cut time-to-market by having the production capabilities designed in at the conceptual design stage."

"I realize that changes in marketing and sales are perhaps even more profound," notes Carol. "We have a lot to actively unlearn, about telling and listening. I can see us teaming up with HR to design and conduct these Friday afternoon sessions. It would be a wonderful way to help our sales people learn to pick up on the subtle themes that excite our customers and suppliers. As they can experience the range of capabilities we have access to, internally and externally, I can envision a much more effective, motivated and focused sales force. We'll still sell the routine products from our catalog; now we'll train our customers to use our CD-ROM sales catalogs to place their own orders at a discount. This will free up our sales force to tackle the higher-margin custom work."

"It's remarkable," remarks Frank, "that our week together has gone in this direction. When I tore up the organizational chart, I expected you all to stake out your positions and fight for redefined turf. You haven't done it. Instead, you've been building upon one another's thinking in a remarkable way. How does it feel?"

"Frank, you know how hard-nosed I am," responds Vincent. "Well, I too have been struck by our process. I feel we're so much more open with one another. It feels so different. It's energizing."

Others smile and nod their heads in agreement with Vincent.

"It's nice to see some laughter coming back," notes Marjorie.

Overlapping Circles

"Marjorie, could you draw the four overlapping circles again on the flip chart? This time draw two sets of circles. On the one on the top, could you include reference to capabilities and aspirations? And on the bottom, could you simply number the various segments?" asks Frank.

Marjorie draws the figures.

"Frank, it's interesting that you've asked Marjorie to draw these figures," comments Wesley. "I was also thinking of them. What if we were to use the one on the top to work out a model of the capabilities and aspirations of each major customer or customer group? We could even use this in our Friday sessions, as it would help us discover the dynamics and the energy in the relationships. Where are you going with the figure on the bottom, Frank?"

"Once we identify capabilities and aspirations, we also need to look for the patterns at the overlaps," answers Frank. "Let's walk through it the way I've been thinking through it. We agree that we need to get good at identifying the opportunities at the overlap between our customers and their customers (1). We then identify the capabilities of our customers (2) that we can enhance, so they become even more responsive to their customers. This may involve bringing our suppliers and customers together (3) in a virtual

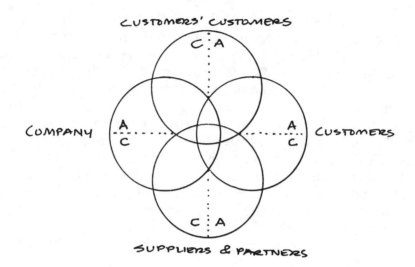

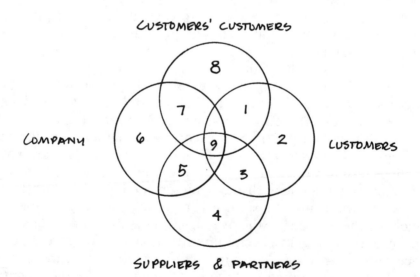

enterprise. We need to know as well the capabilities and aspirations of our suppliers and other partners (4). Therefore, our selection process (5) is critical. We ourselves need to excel in the teaming process (6). We also need a clear and crisp business idea, a way of leveraging our multiple capabilities. Perhaps the key to our success will be our ability to pick up the significant patterns of the aspirations of our customers' customers (7). Therefore, we have to be very smart in the ways we identify our customers' customers (8)."

"Frank, how many sleepless nights has it taken to master these models?" asks Gregory. "Oh, by the way, there is one number you didn't mention, number 9. What does it mean?"

"Vincent, any idea?" asks Frank.

Vincent looks puzzled.

"Vincent, you like tennis, don't you?" notes Frank.

"Yes."

"Well, when things really go smoothly, what are you doing?" asks Frank.

"My timing is on, my feet are right and my racket, well, it just does its thing . . . sweet spot, sweet spot, . . . is this what you're getting at? It's in the center of the racket. It's in the center of the overlapping circles (9). It's when all four circles are pulling together. Nice—it makes sense, but just like in tennis, it's very elusive and difficult to achieve."

Frank smiles.

"Fascinating . . . what makes it possible for us to master the sweet spot?" wonders Gregory. "Does it just happen, or is it a function of how we shape our relationships with our suppliers, customers, and customers' customers? I'm beginning to see that all these elements must be working together. This is why we need to reintegrate our staff into the line, this is why we need to excel at listening and picking up the patterns, this is why we need to think in terms of 'both/and' and this is why we need to be genuinely excited about our customers' aspirations."

"I see why we couldn't even have seen these things from the perspective of our industrial-era model," notes Vincent. "Things are so fragmented into little parts, little boxes, and little fiefdoms, that the larger context isn't even seen. Ouch! The only way we've been able to be successful has been with brute force. Not very elegant. Perhaps we've learned the lessons of the industrial era too well. We can see, but not much. And we don't bother to listen because we were too busy telling. Frank, is this what you wanted us to discover when you tore the organizational chart in half?"

Taking Responsibility

Frank responds, "No, I acted on a gut feeling. I didn't really understand how it imprisoned us. My eyes and ears have been opened through our dialogue. You all have certainly exceeded my expectations. And I've discovered so very much. It's beginning to feel more comfortable. I want you all to continue in your respective areas, but instead of seeing yourselves as bosses, could you become genuine mentors, mentors to one another, and mentors to those in your disciplines? You notice I'm trying to avoid using the old words of power and control. I haven't said 'your people,' because we don't own them. I'm not calling them 'employees,' because they're something more."

He continues, "What if we each take responsibility for building the best capabilities within our own areas, but do it in such a way that collaboration both internally and externally becomes a way of life? If we focus on not only identifying seeds of opportunities, but also planting them, we will find an excitement that's a very powerful motivator. I'm hoping that we master the process of putting together teams to plant, grow, and harvest these seeds. This means that our role is to set the context, mentor our resources, enhance the linkages with our customers and suppliers, participate actively in our Friday sessions. Our ultimate reward comes both from our customers and from our investors. We need to show them that we not only have the best products and services, but we've mastered a way of continually defining the standards for our industries. It's in this way that we'll be able to perform the Fosbury Flop; we'll be able to reach higher and grasp the unexpected, the non-linear and the unknown opportunity."

"Frank, this is a wonderful vision, a wonderful challenge," comments Wesley. "As a practical engineer, I've been envisioning a new organizational model, one where we can view our capabilities as nodes aligned around the circle. Then what lifts our spirits is our

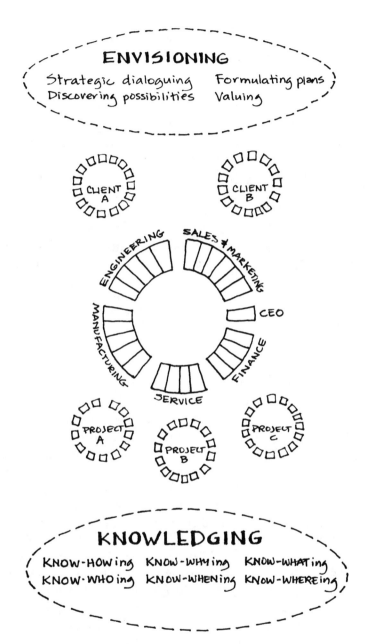

ability to tap into the visioning and aspirations of our customers and the market. This makes it possible for us to embolden our customers, because we value their visions. We can then deliver because we have mastered the 'knowledging' process, the process of continuously combining and recombining what we know, our know-how, know-when, know-where, know-why, and know-what. There's nothing static about this, just as there's nothing static about business. This is why I have put these 'know . . .' in the verb form by adding 'ing.' Yes, business is dynamic and ever changing. It is so exciting."

"You're right, Wesley," notes Alan. "The approach we've been developing makes so much more sense than the traditional change model. Instead of 'unfreezing, changing, and refreezing,' we're discovering a way to never refreeze, but instead agilely allocate and reallocate our resources given ever-changing business opportunities. Wesley, could you draw your model onto the four circles?"

The Four Circle Model

"Frank, you have a substitute for our former organizational chart," notes Alan. "We can identify and array the various resources we have within our company on this chart. There are no ups or downs in this model; instead everyone is around the circle. Each person is expected to do what he or she has agreed with the company, but also, and this is what is important, to be ready to take responsibility and to rise to the occasion. This way we can build a very porous model that still has focus and discipline. Our envisioning becomes our context generator and our knowledging provides the resources to deliver. Things are so much clearer. I can build on the previous suggestions and rebuild a reward system. The reason is that as people learn to discover and build off one another's capabilities, this is the best reward system any organization can have, because it brings whole people, people with ideas, thoughts, feelings, and passion, into a community of practice. It's exciting because we're going to be able to leverage our knowledge assets, our intellectual capital in new ways. Frank, sign me up!"

"We thought Gregory and Vincent were our skeptics, but frankly, I was very doubtful that we could ever get this far, as you will remember," comments Marjorie. "I see now that changing an organization isn't just a function of time, but rather is dependent upon people's willingness to take risks, be open, create an environment of trust, and then carefully listen to one another. We've really been transforming many raw ideas this week and it feels good. Look out GE! Look out Xerox! We're transforming ourselves, because we care, because we listen, because we ask the tough questions, because we are ready to model our ideas."

She continues, "Frank, something just struck me. We have such diversity on our staff, people with backgrounds from all parts of the world. More and more of our business is global. Have you been selecting people with this in mind?"

Frank smiles. "Yes, as a matter of fact. I've never really mentioned it to anyone, but I've sensed that it's important to be able to understand other cultures. Now it makes even more sense. If 'work is dialogue,' then we need people who have deeper levels of understanding of the cultures with which we'll be working. I've also noticed, and this week has really brought it out, that with diverse backgrounds we have to listen at a deeper level: we have to listen at a deeper level to one another, and we have to listen at a deeper level to the aspirations of our customers and our suppliers."

"Frank, you're ahead of us again," comments Carol. "But do you know what really got us started on Monday?"

"What are you getting at?" asks Frank.

"Frank, you're not the traditional 'boss,'" continues Carol. "On Monday I really believe you didn't know where we would go. You listened to your gut feelings in tearing up the organizational chart. You were open and trusted us to help find the solution. Most executives feel they have to always have the answers. You let your vulnerability show. How refreshing and challenging!"

"Thank you, Carol, and thank you all for being so open and honest with one another," Frank says with a smile. "Carol, when you drew the triad boxes, with A, B, and C, I understood for the first time what I haven't liked about our traditional understanding of the hierarchy. If you think of me as A, then my role has been to play one off against the other. I won't do that any longer. Instead, this week has helped me understand that we can still have a hierarchy, but that it can function in a profoundly different way. I've trusted you and I've been rewarded by a quality of interaction I've never seen before. Imagine if we create this kind of dialogue with our suppliers, partners, and customers? Our risks will go down significantly and our rewards will go up, and why? Because we'll be able to allocate our resources, our capital and knowledge assets, against substantive projects. It is indeed exciting. We're likely to have more sleepless nights, but not from the old reasons."

"Frank, as you were speaking," reflects Wesley, "I was hit by an 'aha' thought. Typically we want to satisfy our customers, but this is shortsighted. Our customers want to be listened to and to be taken seriously. They want a meaningful relationship that can last over time. A quality dialogue will give us this. Work as conversations. Work as dialogue. Work as meaning discovery. These are real, even to an engineer. I'm really excited about launching into our series of Friday afternoon meetings. I suspect that as we learn to listen to our customers, we will more quickly learn to listen to one another. Change will come from the outside more easily than from the inside. Frank began this week by revealing his uncertainty, his vulnerability, and his openness to us. We've decided to do the same with our customers. I know it will take a while to bring people along, but if we can build off the richness of the diversity within our company, and the diversity of the market, we have a very exciting time ahead."

"Wesley, you have just captured so nicely so much of what we have been through," responds Gregory. "I know you all have seen a marked change in my thinking this week, and frankly it is so energizing. If I may add my summary to the week, I now see our circle as only one-fourth of our world, the other three fourths involve our suppliers, customers, and customers' customers. What really holds us together is our ability to build upon one another's aspirations and visions, our ability to envision collaboratively. Moreover, we each have capabilities which we can combine and recombine given ever-changing business opportunities. We have learned to refer to this as the knowledging process where we can use one another's know-how or capabilities. Marjorie, if you are still up for it could you draw four overlapping circles with an oval for envisioning above and an oval for knowledging at the bottom. . . . Yes, that's it, elegantly simple, yet so dynamic."

Turning to Frank, Gregory says, "Frank, suggest we substitute this model for the organizational chart you tore in two on Monday." With a big grin, he continues, "I do not see any boxes or lines in this new organizational model . . . and now I do not miss them because I feel we have been able to connect at a much deeper level. Valuing and dialoguing have opened up a whole new horizon for me, and I know you held little hope for me as we began our process."

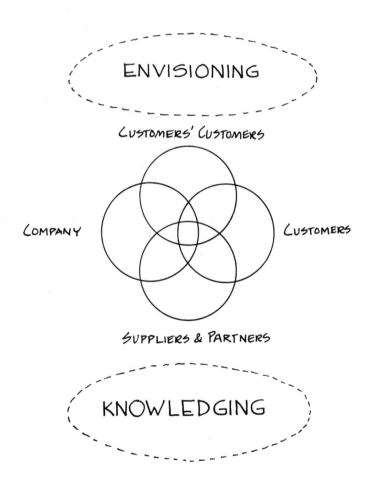

The others nod and smile in active support for these honest remarks.

Discoveryshops

Frank, looking highly relieved, turns to the group. "What are we waiting for? Let's start next week with our Friday afternoon series of meetings. They're not meetings, they're not workshops, they're something more. Let's call them 'Discoveryshops.' Alan, could you work with Wesley and Carol in designing the process? And by the way, welcome aboard, Alan and Marjorie; it's nice to be beyond the old staff/line split. We have a lot of work ahead.

"Oh, one last thing," adds Frank. "I wasn't quite as bold as you might have thought. After our meeting on Monday I retrieved the organizational chart from the basket and have kept it in reserve, just in case things got so confused that we would have to return to it. Well, we'll still have a hierarchy, but it will function very differently. We've gotten ourselves through this knothole this week. Life will go on, but we'll be living much more closely with the capabilities and aspirations of our customers, customers' customers, and suppliers. In fact, I realize that the word 'customers' may no longer be appropriate; perhaps we could use the word 'co-creators,' because we will indeed be creating our futures together."

Frank pulls out the torn organizational chart, and taking a lighter to it, lets it gently burn away. In its place he suggests everyone use the four overlapping circles which Marjorie just sketched. What's important is not who is reporting to whom, but how people are teaming to help our customers realize their dreams and aspirations. The process is as important as the form.

Smiles and laughter. New heights, new visions, and new capabilities!

The high of Friday afternoon was challenged by the reality of the next Monday, and many Mondays after that. The team persisted, and through sustained hard work, began to create a culture of valuing. They were helped because people throughout the organization already had things figured out. For example, Vincent helped his colleagues come to appreciate the tremendous wisdom on the shop floor among the supervisors and workers. The union stewards played a big role in mobilizing resources. Middle managers got a new lease on life. Project and program managers took it upon themselves to meet and exchange lessons learned.

Suppliers and customers became more open, slowly at first, but then with a force and energy that challenged Custom Products and Services at its core. The Friday afternoon meetings became a very significant competitive advantage because they fostered such a collaborative spirit.

Soon the company was involved in six major virtual enterprising efforts. It mastered the processes of dynamic teaming, so it could use not only its own knowledge assets, but those of others in the market in exciting ways. Profitability climbed steadily over the next two years and after.

There were setbacks and failures. Some mouthed the new terms, but walked in old ways; but even they found room to grow. In fact, people found they were growing in many different ways, especially because they were participating in one another's growth. The genetic code of the old hierarchy was broken, and they moved beyond the confinement of the A, B, C triad. The ultimate reward, being taken seriously on a daily basis by one's colleagues, became commonplace. The company reached a fluidity and agility it had not expected, because it realized that its strength was in weaving together and linking opportunities. The Internet Web became only one of many avenues, but it turned out to be a powerful metaphor for their new way of working, knowledge era enterprising.

PART TWO

Co-creating Through Virtual Enterprising, Dynamic Teaming, and Knowledge Networking

CHAPTER

6

INTRODUCTION: THE PAST AND FUTURE

The case study of Custom Products and Services in Part 1 shows some of the challenges before us. Frank Giardelli realizes he cannot continue to stuff computers into his existing organization and expect to leverage value out of these investments. As he looks at the last five years, he knows that he cannot get ahead without redefining the organizational context and without increasing his organization's market agility.

Giardelli and the vice presidents understand that their biggest challenge is to manage complexity rather than just cost and time. The swirling multiple interrelationships—both internal and external—with their suppliers, customers, and customers' customers, are often more chaotic than orderly. Only if the creative abilities of the people—employees, professionals, and managers—in the firm and between firms are unleashed can they expect to respond effectively to the multiple challenges of the market. Finely tuned bureaucracies with carefully defined policies, procedures, and job descriptions will be no match for the marketplace in the next millennium. They are too confining and rigid, and are always out of alignment with the market. They cannot maintain a creative dialogue with their suppliers, customers, and customers' customers. In their place, Giardelli and the others realize that they must master the processes of virtual enterprising, dynamic teaming, and knowledge networking that come through a vibrant dialogue with their suppliers, customers, and customers' customers. They also need a culture of valuing so that they can readily team their capable professionals with their suppliers and customers to quickly seize profitable market opportunities.

Giardelli knows it is not enough to just look up and envision the "dream organization" of the future, because the legacy of their past assumptions, attitudes, and decisions will turn their dreams into nightmares. To get ahead, they must look at the future and the past at the same time, and they must leverage their knowledge and aspirations, as well as those of their suppliers, customers, and customers' customers.

In Part 2 we explore the management and leadership challenges of the next millennium while also taking a long hard look at the past, the ideas and assumptions of the early and late industrial era. This past is still very much a part of our thinking, conditioning our technical and business reflexes. We can only bring about our desired future if we can sort out our past. The ideas and assumptions of this past, which flows with us, are largely bankrupt.

Bankruptcy of the Industrial Era

The currency of traditional assumptions, principles, and values of the industrial era is bankrupt. This bankruptcy will not be overcome simply by an infusion of new computer-based technology.

Agricultural-era principles could not cope with the onset of machinery-based technology. New forms of management and work were developed to utilize the power of the steam engine and all its derivatives. The industrial era used new principles to divide work, reward people, and control activities.

Steep hierarchies, the creation of the late industrial era, are under extreme pressure. They cannot provide the flexibility and responsiveness needed in our increasingly competitive and collaborative global markets. Instead, there is a need for more effective integration and teaming within companies and between them and their suppliers, partners, and customers.

Flatter network enterprises are beginning to emerge in place of hierarchies. This networking has two dimensions: (1) the technical infrastructure that links computer systems and people, and (2) the human process, networking with other people, linking knowledge and aspirations.

We are fascinated by the wonders of local- and wide-area networking technology, including the Internet and World Wide Web. These technologies are allowing us to bring together application processes, databases, and people in new ways. Networking technology is absolutely essential if we hope to build agile enterprises, but by itself it is not enough.

Human or knowledge networking is at the core of the integrative process. It is an ongoing process of reaching out to one another to form multiple cross-functional work teams within and between organizations. We need not only teams, but "teamwork of teams" and "networks of teams." These are new challenges, full of hidden surprises. But the early industrial era also had more than its share of "gotchas" encountered while people were figuring out how to harness the new technologies.

In steep hierarchies, work is broken down into smaller steps and different people are assigned to carry out these activities. They are structured according to "superior-subordinate" relationships. Everyone has a boss who determines what activities are to be carried out and how.

In a networking environment, people reach out to one another to work on whole sets of challenges in teams, and clusters of teams, in distributed environments across functional and organizational boundaries. Network enterprises build upon "peer-to-peer" relationships. People are expected to take initiatives, based upon their understanding of an agreed-upon context.

It has often been assumed that it is only a matter of time before networks of computers replace most people in our companies, as though people are the expendable item. Although fewer people will be needed to run our companies, as we have experienced through downsizing, this assumption of total expendability of people is misguided.

A sober realism is overtaking our naive fascination with computers. As we understand their limitations, we are beginning to appreciate human capabilities even more. For example, artificial intelligence and expert systems have not delivered what some had promised, primarily because rule-based systems have difficulty in capturing the larger *context* in which activities must be understood.

The re-emergence of interest in neural networking is indicative of a deeper appreciation of our human capability to see and respond to *multiple patterns* in real time. Instead of modeling the mind as a machine or even as a computer, neural networking starts with a more humble appreciation of the wonder of the networking capability of the billions of neurons in the human brain. Our human minds are able to see, interpret, reinterpret, and act on multiple patterns of impressions.[1] As we realize that the best databases are in people's heads, our challenge is to learn to network our visions and knowledge in new and creative ways.

How ironic that our quest for new forms of computer technology has increased our appreciation of human and team capabilities. Although people are able to communicate across the hall or around the world at the speed of light, thanks to computer networks, human distrust slows real communication to a snail's pace. Computer applications are accessible anywhere on the network, but not all departments have a common bill of materials. How are we to respond to the growing chasm between our technological capabilities and organizational lethargy?

Just as the dropping apple jolted Newton into a realization of gravity, a force that has been with us from the beginning of time, our technological advances are shaking the foundations of our assumptions about work and work organization. In the turmoil, we are discovering a whole new set of management and leadership challenges.

Management and Leadership Challenges of the Next Decade

As Giardelli and the vice presidents realized, their traditional bag of tricks, developed and honed during the industrial era, is inadequate for the knowledge era. They are not alone, for executives in Europe, Asia, Africa, Australia, and the Americas are facing a whole new set of management challenges:

1. How do we move beyond the extreme *fragmentation* of industrial-era companies?

2. How do we maintain *accountability* in flat, dynamic network organizations?

3. How do we support the *focusing and coordination* of multiple cross-functional task teams?

4. How do we build into the very structure of the organization the capacity for *continual learning* and *quick market responsiveness?*

We have all experienced organizational fragmentation, in which various functional departments focus only on their own tasks and ignore the concerns of others. It is clear that this fragmentation has to be repaired, because fragmented companies cannot deal with the rich complexity of global economies.

As we flatten the organization, the span of control increases. It is no longer as easy to look after all subordinates. Therefore, a new accountability strategy is needed, especially in a technically networked enterprise. Without a strong accountability strategy, it is easy for individuals and groups to go off in many different directions or get bogged down in swamp-like "group gropes."

The engineering, manufacturing, finance, marketing, sales, and service functions are being asked to work in parallel. In manufacturing, concurrent engineering is challenging design engineers and manufacturing engineers to develop products and processes together within their company and with other companies. Similar trends are emerging in the service sectors, such as the changes being made in investment banking.[2] As people work more in multiple cross-functional teams, they will need to be more self-directed and self-taught.[3] Moreover, they will need to coordinate their activities with other task teams, while also sharing their insights and experiences.

When these various task team efforts are under way, there will be a great deal of learning.[4] Too often this learning disappears into the ether with no net to catch it. Yet it is an invaluable corporate asset. One of the challenges of the knowledge era is to capture individual and team learning on a continuing basis, making it available to others in the enterprise. Much learning remains at the tacit level, and it often takes concerted effort to make this knowledge explicit and accessible to others.[5] "Time-to-learn" is as critical as "time-to-market."

Key Concepts

Several years ago the press feasted on the Japanese fifth-generation computer initiative.[6] It was feared that they would wrest the lead in high technology away from the rest of the world by unleashing the power of the microchip through parallel processing. This discussion diverted our attention from the real challenge: to unleash the power in human minds so that, working together, we can recognize and respond to the ever-changing opportunities of the market.

Fifth-generation management is not concerned with new ways of manipulating subordinates to one's advantage. Instead, it challenges us to rethink the basics: our values, attitudes, and assumptions about leadership, work, and time. It points to an elegantly simple understanding: We need to be in touch with ourselves—our visions, knowledge, thoughts, and feelings—and with one another in new and creative ways.[7] And it assumes that the various functions and companies are capable of working in parallel through virtual task-focusing teams. In short, fifth-generation management is a question of leadership. It is not being preoccupied with one's own power, but with how we *empower, energize,* and *enable* one another. It presupposes an integrative environment that puts people and companies in touch with one another's best capabilities.

The word *integration* has taken on a special mystique, especially thanks to our previous fascination with computer-integrated manufacturing (CIM) and computer-integrated enterprise (CIE). CIM and CIE have indicated, in some people's minds, that we are headed toward the "paperless and peopleless factory."[8] Some argue that automation, combined with computers, will make it possible for a few top executives to sit in their "command and control centers" and, with the aid of a few professionals, direct the day-to-day operations of the firm. After all, the hardware and software will have been connected together in one *automated* and *integrated* whole, from boardroom to shop floor. Strategic planning will be aided by executive decision support systems connected to operations planning, with orders being passed through computer-aided design systems to scheduling and numeric-control programming on the shop floor.

This vision of CIM and CIE is a dead end because it leaves people out of the equation, and people are what give an organization its flexibility, agility, and creativity.

Let us take another look at the meaning of *integration*. It seems to mean everything to everyone. It is often used as a synonym for connectivity (including interoperability) and interfacing. When the terms are blurred together, confusion follows. There are clear distinctions between the three terms, as shown in Figure 6.1.

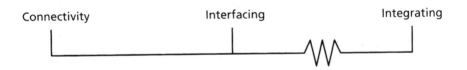

Figure 6.1 **Distinguishing the discontinuity between connectivity, interfacing, and integrating.**

It is one thing to connect offices or locations through telephone computer networks and to interface applications; it is something else entirely to integrate organizations. Connectivity and interfacing leave the organization pretty much as is, while integration changes the way organizations work.

Integration comes from the root *integer*. An integer is a whole number. It is not a fraction. The word *integer* comes from the Latin roots *in* = in and *tangere* = to touch. An integer is that which is in touch with itself. Many think of integration just in terms of physical connectivity. This is only a portion of the challenge.

The problem in many companies is that they function as a "collection of fractions." Engineering sees only a fraction of the constraints under which manufacturing operates. Manufacturing does not appreciate the serviceability constraints the field is under. Finance does not quite realize the artificiality of its desire to continue to burden direct labor. And too often top management has only a fractional understanding of what really goes on down on the shop floor. The real task of integration is to bring together, to put in touch, the creative thinking within and between enterprises in order to deal with whole challenges and opportunities. Integration builds on the synergy among and between professionals and companies. Connectivity and interfacing will not solve this problem.

Many companies have very fragmented views of their futures. There is little alignment across functions or with their key suppliers and customers. Many managers are not in touch with the talent in their own departments.[9] Too many are asked to fight fires, perform busywork, and do as they are told—not as they think. There are fractions, fractions, and more fractions.

Although *hierarchies* have been around for ages, steep hierarchies arose in the business world in the 1880s as a creation of the late industrial era. These structures embody fractional thinking, whereby everyone has narrowly defined and mutually exclusive areas of responsibility, much as the gears of a machine each have their assigned roles.

Networking is used in two different ways: (1) as a noun referring to a physical system of interconnecting elements, such as computer nodes and people, through electronic means, and (2) as an active verb, *to network*, to get in touch with ourselves, our visions and knowledge, and one another to deal with whole issues.

As used in this book, *integration* and *networking* complement each other. They refer to ongoing processes rather than a static state of affairs. I avoid the term "networked" because it assumes that it is possible to establish a networked environment once and for all. Instead, I prefer the terms *networking, integrating,* and *integrative* because they underscore the continuous nature of integration, which configures and reconfigures people and resources.

The *integrative process* puts us in touch with the whole, with one another, with customers, customers' customers, and with suppliers in ever-changing patterns of relationships. It also puts us in touch with our own wills, emotions, and knowledge. The integrative process is a process of human networking: networking our visions and knowledge so that we can take decisive action in response to concrete opportunities. Virtual enterprising, dynamic teaming, and knowledge networking are specific ways of networking. They all build upon the synergy created when people and companies are "in touch" with one another's capabilities and aspirations.

A good technically networked infrastructure is fast becoming a precondition for marketplace success, including a corporate-wide web and access to the World Wide Web. Even more important, however, is our human ability to network with one another on real business and technical opportunities. As we get better at this kind of networking, the need for the rigid command superstructure of steep hierarchies fades. Moreover, as more and more people experience the World Wide Web, they will understand the power of linkings, and the ability to follow threads of interest anywhere on the Web. Web weaving will quickly become a recognized form of networking interrelated interests and ideas. Companies will realize that they can more expertly weave together their interests with those of their suppliers and customers.

From Steep Hierarchies to Knowledge Networking

We have been plagued by those who take the official organizational chart, with its boxes and lines, too seriously. These traditional managers feel they must protect their *turf* (empire, territory, stovepipe, area of responsibility, or assignment). Their parochial interests often lead to debilitating political battles. This is why Giardelli realizes that he needs to tear his organizational chart in half.

A management strategy based on "command and control" is giving way to one centered on "focusing and coordinating" multiple teams within and between companies. As people come to understand themselves as resources capable of reaching out and participating on "multiple task-focused teams," to use Peter Drucker's term, we will be able to focus and coordinate enterprise resources more effectively.[10]

Ken Olsen, founder and former CEO of Digital Equipment Corporation, envisioned these changes in the following manner:

> But above all, we believe that we're taking part in changing the way organizations work. From our point of view, the companies that will survive are going to move from an environment of management control to one that allows a large number of people, all using their creative ability, their education, and their motivation, to take part.
>
> Now, this change won't be easy. But it has to come. And we're convinced that computer networking will be at the heart of these changes . . . the vehicle through which these changes are carried out.[11]

Olsen understood the need to nurture and grow the creative abilities, talents, and motivation of those in the enterprise, freeing them from the constraining control systems of the past. He knew computer networking would make it possible to integrate whole organizations around the world, allowing them to deliver quality goods and services in a more timely and targeted manner. This becomes especially critical as the combination of time-to-market and time-to-learn becomes a key differentiating factor in the competitive environment. A sense of *timing*, not just time, is also becoming essential for market success. Bringing products or services to market quickly does not help if they are the wrong ones.

A recognition of the increasing importance of the human element in the enterprise seems to be erupting spontaneously in many different areas. A number of Europeans, such as Professor Paul Kidd, are writing about "human-centered CIM systems (HCIM)."[12] In Japan, Kazuto Togino, former president of Komatsu Electronic Metals, has introduced the concept of "human integrated manufacturing" for many of the same reasons that Europeans are talking about HCIM.[13]

As Olsen has stressed, networking is making it possible to develop new forms of organization and new management approaches to put us in touch with one another and with ourselves in new and significant ways. The task of the 1990s and the early part of the next millennium is to build networked infrastructures and adjust our mindsets so that, working together, we will be adroit in our thinking and agile in our actions. Olsen's vision is of an "elegantly simple" enterprise.

In contrast, the automationist approach presupposes the computerization of steep hierarchies. Communication within these steep hierarchies is, by definition, "confusingly complex" because of all the little kingdoms through which one must go to resolve an issue. Automating and computerizing existing organizations, with all their distrust, petty politics, and disjointedness, only makes the mess faster, not better.

Network organizations operate by a different set of dynamics. They may become elegantly simple organizations. At first blush, elegant simplicity sounds like a contradiction. "Elegance" implies a good deal of sophistication, while "simplicity" seems to be its opposite. Yet when automobiles changed from manual to automatic transmissions, they went to an elegantly simple driver interface. The automatic transmission is elegant and complex, but the interface with the driver is simple.

An elegantly simple organization is one that is easy for customers, suppliers, and distributors to interact with because of its sophistication. Rarely do things fall through the cracks. People do not trip over one another. Action is crisp and decisive. There is responsiveness to the market. And there is integrity, because people have to be able to count on each other's word.

The Broadening Scope of Management

Traditionally, management theory has focused on relationships internal to the firm. Everyone's place can be clearly defined, and reporting relationships are clear. The shift to a broader enterprise perspective introduces a whole new set of dynamics.

The relationships between companies and their partners, suppliers, customers, and customers' customers is one of peer-to-peer relationships (Figure 6.2). These relationships are different from the superior-subordinate relationships in steep hierarchies.

Instead, the external relationships are based on trust and mutual benefit. There has to be careful listening, respect, and integrity among the parties involved. Figure 6.2 can also be stated in four overlapping circles, the concept developed in Part 1, Chapter 2:

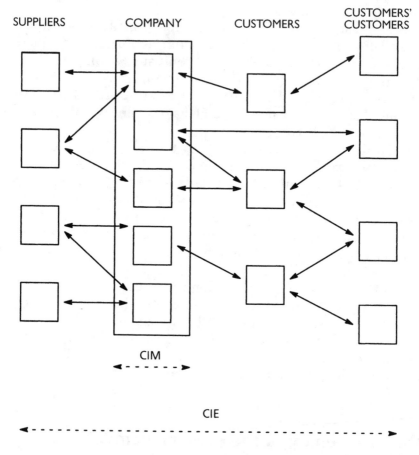

Figure 6.2 **Scope of CIM and CIE**

Certainly, Just-in-Time (JIT) and Total Quality relationships are not possible between cooperating partners without a good deal of openness and respect. As companies link themselves through electronic data interchange (EDI), technical data exchange, and the

Internet, they are starting to share long-range plans and purchasing intent, something that was unheard of just a few years ago.

This shift in perspectives is forcing a re-evaluation of traditional command and control theory. It is not possible to command external resources in the same way in which internal resources can be dominated. Instead, the fine art of alliance building between peers becomes critical.

CIM focuses primarily on the interaction of functions within a firm. CIE puts this interaction within the larger context of the firm's set of relationships; it represents the extended enterprise. Computer networking both enables and demands the exchange of information within the firm and among firms. For example, aerospace firms are linking themselves in multiple networks with other prime contractors and their subcontractors, as well as with the government.

In the CIE environment, business success will increasingly depend on the knowledge resources of the firms rather than on their fixed capital. We are witnessing a shift in the sources of wealth between two eras, the industrial era and the knowledge era.

Chapter Focuses

In order to understand this shift, we must place the discussion within a larger historical context and include the sources of wealth, types of organization, and conceptual principles that underlie the industrial and knowledge eras. These elements will be discussed in greater detail in subsequent chapters; the focus of each chapter is indicated by the chapter number in Figure 6.3.

Chapter 7 discusses the five generations of computers and managements and relates them to the historical eras. It also describes several visions of the type of organization that lies beyond the organizational bottleneck. Chapter 8 explores the attempts to computerize existing steep hierarchies. Chapter 9 looks at the conceptual principles of the early and late industrial eras, while Chapter 10 discusses those of the early knowledge era. The transition between the industrial and knowledge eras is the focus of Chapter 11; Chapter 12 discusses ten practical considerations in managing knowledge-era enterprises.

Historical Eras

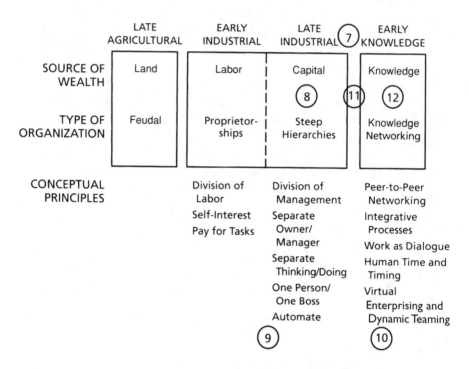

	LATE AGRICULTURAL	EARLY INDUSTRIAL	LATE INDUSTRIAL ⑦	EARLY KNOWLEDGE
SOURCE OF WEALTH	Land	Labor	Capital ⑧ ⑪	Knowledge ⑫
TYPE OF ORGANIZATION	Feudal	Proprietor-ships	Steep Hierarchies	Knowledge Networking
CONCEPTUAL PRINCIPLES		Division of Labor / Self-Interest / Pay for Tasks	Division of Management / Separate Owner/Manager / Separate Thinking/Doing / One Person/One Boss / Automate ⑨	Peer-to-Peer Networking / Integrative Processes / Work as Dialogue / Human Time and Timing / Virtual Enterprising and Dynamic Teaming ⑩

Figure 6.3 **The focus of each chapter**

This discussion picks up many of the themes introduced in the dialogue in Part l. The repetition of themes, or iteration of ideas, is part of the process of unlearning, learning, and re-learning basic relationships. The shift from the industrial to the knowledge era is primarily one of attitudes, values, and norms. It can only come through a struggle of thought, because most of the changes are counterintuitive. We are so conditioned by the vocabulary of the industrial era that it is often difficult to think in new terms. We continually need to look at the past and future, re-sorting our knowledge and expanding our visions.

CHAPTER

7

FIVE GENERATIONS OF COMPUTERS AND MANAGEMENT

The evolution of computers offers an interesting parallel to what we are being challenged to do organizationally.[1] Computers are breaking out of a bottleneck created by the architectural assumptions of the initial computer era. Business organizations are also up against a bottleneck created, in part, by the success of the industrial era. Can we break out?

Generations of Computers

In the early 1980s, the Japanese, under MITI (Ministry for International Trade and Industry) initiated their fifth-generation computer project. It created quite a stir and sparked similar initiatives in the United States and Europe: MCC (Microelectronic Computer Center) and ESPRIT (European Strategic Program for Research and Development in Information Technology). The five generations of computer technology are defined in Figure 7.1.[2]

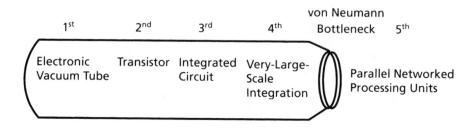

Figure 7.1 **Generations of computer technology**

Computers of the first four generations pass all information through a single central processing unit (CPU). This single CPU has been described as the "von Neumann bottleneck," after John von Neumann, mathematician and computer pioneer.

According to von Neumann's 1945 paper, "First Draft of a Report on EDVAC (Electronic Discrete Variable Computer)," the computer needs five key components: a central arithmetic logic unit, a central control unit to orchestrate operations, a memory unit, an input unit, and an output unit.[3] It should use binary numbers, operate electronically, and perform its operations one at a time, or sequentially. COBOL, FORTRAN, BASIC, C, and other computer languages have followed this strategy of stepping through their programs in a sequential manner, although some languages are now being adapted for parallel work.

The key to the fifth-generation computer, parallel processing, is in the networking of multiple processing units. In parallel processing, two or more interconnected processors simultaneously process different portions of the same application. This linking provides a new challenge: to divide the problem so that the multiple processors can work on portions of the same problem concurrently, then piece together the solution. Parallel processing is opening up a whole new frontier of exploration because of its speed.

In addition to parallel processing, networking is making it possible to run multiple applications in parallel on different computer processors by linking distributed databases on a network. Not only the computer but also people and applications can begin to work in parallel, especially as we develop more effective user interfaces.

The computer industry is developing common windowing interfaces that allow users to open multiple windows and interact with several different applications concurrently, wherever the applications may be on the computer network. This makes it possible for departments to work in parallel: design engineers, manufacturing engineers, and marketing specialists can look at the same drawings, process plans, and market projects at the same time, even if they are widely separated by distance. It also makes it possible for companies to work together effectively. Ingersol Milling Machine works concurrently with its customers to design new automobile transfer lines. A Japanese engineering and construction company used Indian engineers in India for detail design. Through voice, electronic mail, and the Internet they can discuss alternatives to the design, process plans, and marketing strategy in an iterative and interactive manner.

Generations of Management

Fifth-generation computing and networking make possible new ways of working together, but organizational assumptions too often block effective use of this technology. We are still wedded to the organizational forms that evolved to meet the needs of the industrial revolution.

As the industrial era began, proprietorships emerged as a convenient way to organize people, resources, and technology. After about a hundred years, steep hierarchies developed. We have attempted to apply the principles of the matrix organization to these hierarchies to increase cross-functional communication and most recently we have been re-engineering our business processes. We are also still interfacing people and applications with the use of computer-based networking.

Just as computers have outgrown their initial single-CPU architecture, so too management is facing its own bottleneck. If we can break through, then we can enable, empower, and energize the creative abilities of not only our people but those in our supplier and customer organizations.

Figure 7.2 shows the five generations of management[4] and illustrates the dilemma that we face.

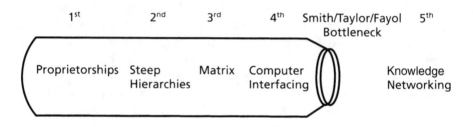

1st	2nd	3rd	4th	Smith/Taylor/Fayol	5th
				Bottleneck	
Proprietorships	Steep	Matrix	Computer		Knowledge
	Hierarchies		Interfacing		Networking

Figure 7.2 **Generations of management**

In the first four generations of enterprise management, raw materials and information were passed *serially* from one department or function to the next. Fifth-generation management makes it possible for the functional departments to work in *parallel* through the use of multiple task-focusing teams within and between companies. But in order to achieve this parallel capability, we must break through a bottleneck created by our acceptance of the assumptions implicit in Adam Smith's pin-making factory with its division and subdivision of labor,[5] reinforced by Frederick Winslow Taylor's theories of scientific management,[6] and Henri Fayol's fourteen principles,[7] which set the rationale for the unity of command, span of control, and scalar principles used in today's industrial-era organizations.

Fayol's fourth principle, unity of command, suggests that people cannot bear dual command; it is a key underpinning of the sequential operation of steep hierarchies. Fayol also emphasized division of work, authority and responsibility, unity of direction, centralization, the scalar chain, and order (a place for everyone and everyone in his place]—all of which reinforce the rigidity and bureaucracy of our steep hierarchies.[8] The assumptions behind these principles led to a simple calculus of importance: the higher up a person is, the more important that person appears to be, as illustrated in Figure 7.3.

Figure 7.3 **Hierarchy and calculus of importance**

This model of the calculus of importance assumes that "thinking" goes on at the top of the corporation and "doing" at the bottom; information is sucked up and summarized through executive support systems, so top management can make the right decisions. The irony of this model is that those who add value to the product are usually the least valued in the organization.

The model also supports the idea that power is concentrated at the top of the hierarchy, and it assumes the traditional series of sequential handoffs from one function to another. Research has shown that this visualization of the hierarchical model is, in most companies, a fantasy.[9] Many products and services, especially in the aerospace, automobile, and financial service industries, require a high degree of coordination among functions (or competent centers of excellence). Real business problems are not easily fragmented into the cubbyholes of functional hierarchies.

This realization was one of the forces leading to the initial widespread acceptance of the matrix model. Third-generation management, the matrix organization, attempts to overcome some of the problems inherent in second-generation management by breaking away from Fayol's unity of command and the notion of "one person/one boss." In a matrix organization, two or more managers share power over a single subordinate. This allows the organization to encompass multiple dimensions at the same time, whether they are functions, products, geographic areas, markets, or any combination of these factors. Although matrix organizations have been widely used by some companies, they have not come to terms with the underlying model of the steep hierarchy articulated by Fayol.

Stanley Davis, who in 1977 co-authored with Paul Lawrence one of the basic texts on matrix organizations,[10] now recognizes the inadequacy of this approach. Davis says that the matrix organization has "never truly lived up to its promise."[11] Although it continues in limited form, it has never adequately addressed the issue of the distribution of power. More often than not, the matrix is simply grafted onto the hierarchical structure without changing the existing system's rewards, accounting approach, or power distribution.

Davis realizes that no management approach has evolved to replace the "singular industrial hierarchy," the steep hierarchy, because we have not figured out a way to resolve conflicts among two or more bosses. Here Davis has put his finger on the dilemma we face. The one person/one boss approach is inadequate, but if this is given up, how do we manage accountability? What holds the organization together? How is responsibility assigned?

Davis suggests that the best management structure to replace the hierarchy is networking, because it relies "not on an informal web of personal contacts, but on a technological web of information handling systems."[12] Is Davis giving us a glimpse of the fourth- or fifth-generation organization? Is it really information handling systems that are needed, or do we not need to give visibility to the multiple cross-functional task teams that really get the work done, both within and between companies?

Fourth-generation management uses computers and networking to interface the various functions, both horizontally and vertically. This is often incorrectly called "integration" because the disparate parts of the company are connected with one another. Most of what is going on now leaves the formal organizational structure unchanged and simply adds connectivity and interfacing between the boxes (functions and departments), using translators (software) to facilitate communication and interoperability among application programs where necessary.

Ironically, as we stated earlier, we are busy stuffing third-, fourth-, and fifth-generation computer technology into second-generation organizations, steep hierarchies (Figure 7.4). To be sure, some of this technology is being introduced in matrixed and interfaced organizations, but unfortunately, these organizational modes are still hierarchical at their core. Simple re-engineering of key processes does not, by itself, bring the dynamic teaming and virtual enterprising necessary for ongoing success.

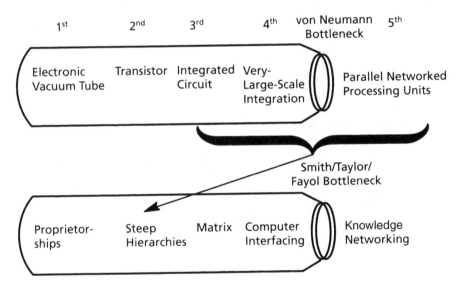

Figure 7.4 **Third-, fourth-, and fifth-generation computer technology being grafted onto second-generation management**

If we hope to put advanced computer-based technology into fifth-generation management organizations, we must pay more attention to the unique characteristics of integrative enterprises based on knowledge networking. We need to find a way to break through the Smith/Taylor/Fayol bottleneck. We must develop fifth-generation management capabilities in our enterprises through virtual enterprising, dynamic teaming, and capability networking so that we will be able to leverage our knowledge much more effectively than we do now.[13]

Part of the problem in breaking out of second-generation management organizations is an attitudinal one. We put too much faith in the computer and not enough in ourselves. Real integration is people dependent. It is not possible to put "integrative enterprises" on automatic pilot and expect them to run themselves.

True integration is an ongoing process; it is fragile and requires continual nurturing. It is more dependent on the values of the enterprise and the integrity of those employed than on the quality of the computer systems chosen. As cross-functional teams are configured and reconfigured, respect, trust, and honesty between people are essential. Game-playing stymies effective teamwork.

We have not taken our own history seriously enough, nor have we understood the major shifts between historical eras ideally suited to the late industrial era, while fifth-generation management and leadership will help us leverage our individual and corporate knowledge for the new knowledge era.

The first four generations of management are a creation of the industrial era. Only as we get beyond them can we expect to tap the fuller potential of both our people- and our computer-based systems. It is likely that as companies introduce corporate-wide webs (CWWs), they will begin to experience first-hand the power of dynamically linking interests, themes, and capabilities. These CWWs will help us recapture the art of conversation and dialogue, and they will make knowledge much more accessible.

Historical Eras

Each historical era has had its dominant form of wealth and its unique form of organization. In the West, the wealth of the late agricultural era rested in the land. People and resources were organized under the feudal system. As the early industrial era began, about 1780, with the invention of the steam engine, the source of wealth shifted to labor, and proprietorships became a key form of organization. In the 1880s, with the advent of the railroads, telephone, and telegraph companies, wealth relied more and more upon capital. Moreover, as large national corporations emerged, steep hierarchies began to displace proprietorships.

There was a major discontinuity between the agricultural and industrial eras, as people unlearned the old and learned to interact in new ways. New ideas of roles and responsibilities displaced the old feudal models. Now in the 1990s, we are witnessing the beginning of another era, the early knowledge era. It is again a time of discontinuity, although we do not readily recognize the need to unlearn industrial-era values and assumptions. We are still very much under the spell of the late industrial era, and it is hard to break through the bottleneck (Figure 7.4).

Historical Eras

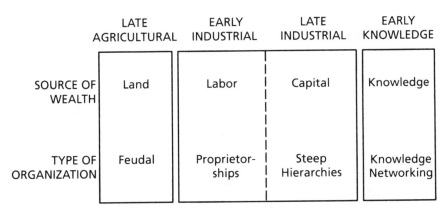

	LATE AGRICULTURAL	EARLY INDUSTRIAL	LATE INDUSTRIAL	EARLY KNOWLEDGE
SOURCE OF WEALTH	Land	Labor	Capital	Knowledge
TYPE OF ORGANIZATION	Feudal	Proprietor-ships	Steep Hierarchies	Knowledge Networking

Figure 7.5 **Sources of wealth and types of organizations**

The transition into the early knowledge era is not necessarily a simple or cumulative process. There are many new principles to be learned, while some of the older principles must be unlearned.[14] The gap between the eras suggests that we will have to work as hard as Frank Giardelli and the vice presidents to rethink our basic attitudes. Attitudes are often tougher barriers than the tightest bottleneck, because they are so much a part of everyday life.

During the whaling era, sailors often passed the time by rigging elaborately designed sailing ships in tiny glass bottles. In many ways, the industrial era has encased us in a glass bottle. The bottle is barely perceptible because it is the only home we know. We have always expected work life and jobs to be confined and confining.[15] We readily accept being stuffed into narrowly defined jobs, as though there were no alternative. The first four generations of management are an artifact of the industrial era. Figure 7.6 shows the interrelationship between the generations of management and the historical eras.

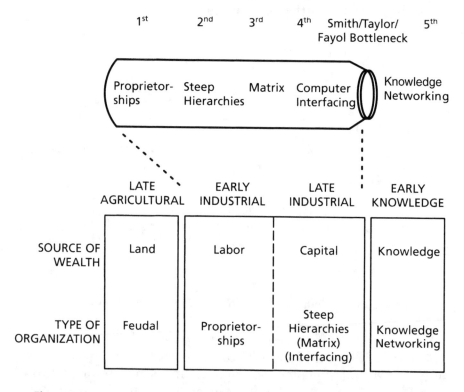

Figure 7.6 **Interrelating generations of management and historical eras**

The knowledge era's source of wealth is not just accumulated knowledge but also our human ability to recognize new patterns and interrelate them with the old patterns that flow with us. Like detectives, we are constantly sorting out ideas, impressions, hunches, intuitions, and understanding. We are learning, unlearning, and relearning. We possess the ability to sort out significant patterns in new events. Knowledge is not something that is possessed like a commodity. Instead, it represents a capability to see broad new patterns among fuzzy old ideas and new impressions and relate them in a larger context. This is why I have used the word "knowledging" in this revised edition.

What does it mean when we say that the basis of wealth is shifting from that which is "possessed as a commodity" to a "human capability"? Known facts can be possessed, but the human process of "knowledging" is a much richer and more dynamic phenomenon. This suggests that an organization that helps facilitate the knowledging process will be able to see the significant patterns in the market and respond more effectively than companies that are bogged down in routine bureaucracy. Some companies, such as Skandia and the Canadian Imperial Bank of Commerce, are working hard to help their employees understand the value of "intellectual capital."[16]

"Knowledging" is more than just "knowing," because it suggests an active and continual process of interrelating patterns. It is more than the accumulation of and access to information, because it looks at both the known (information) and the visionary (what could be). Our quest to better understand the knowledging process will lead us to explore a whole new set of concepts, including "intellectual capital," "organizational intelligence," and "collaborative intelligence." We will soon realize that we process not only raw materials, but also raw ideas. In fact, "idea transformation" processes are as critical as "material transformation" processes, if not more so. In this regard, the Fraunhofer Institute in Germany is sponsoring a process called AIM for "active idea management."[17]

It is fascinating to see that there is a growing awareness that people seek "meaning" in what they do. Long gone are the days when we focused just on satisfaction, one of the most ethereal of phenomena. People want to understand the whats and the whys of what they are doing, not just the hows. We want to understand the larger whole, the context within which we are doing a particular task. Some even want to feel that there is a larger purpose connected to our efforts. Gradually we will hear more about "significance" than we do about "satisfaction." We will also go beyond "needs" and "wants" to an era in which people's and companies' aspirations are taken more seriously. Indeed knowledging is a process of refining meaning and significance in concrete situations. It helps bring out the robust and spirited nature of those involved.

Knowledging wants to see the particular within the context of the whole. It is small wonder that we find people studying chaos theory, complexity, fractals, holonics, general systems theory, and the like. What is the learning organization but a community that wants to discover the meaning of what it is doing within the larger context of business and life?

Knowledging is full of subtlety. There is much that we know, but that we do not know how to describe or put into words. Much of this knowledge remains below the threshold of our ability to talk about it. Ikujiro Nonaka and Hirotaka Takeuchi, professors at Hitotsubashi University in Japan, have written an exciting study of the *Knowledge-Creating Company*.[18] They explore the process of making tacit knowledge explicit and vice versa.

Shoshana Zuboff, a professor at Harvard Business School, has used the word "informate" to describe the human challenge of moving from primary experiences to working on multiple levels of abstraction while using the computer.[19] For example, as boiler-room operators shift from manually turning off steam valves to monitoring and regulating pressure at their computer terminals, they must operate through the mediation of the computer. Computer-mediated work, as Zuboff explains, challenges us to work on higher planes of abstraction, the process she defines as "informating."

The creation of a software package, next-generation micropro-cessor, new financial service, or multi-axis lathe involves both knowledge and vision. Knowledging, the basis of wealth in the knowledge era, is a dynamic and ongoing process that involves our human capabilities to see existing patterns and at the same time envision new patterns.

In the industrial era, we have assumed that it is possible to figure out everything ahead of time, divide the work up among various functions, then monitor and control what is done so that it meets the expected outcome. As with an ocean liner, the challenge has been to hold the effort on course, making only minor corrections for changes in winds and currents. In applying automation and computer-based solutions to the steep hierarchy, we have assumed that the task is to use these resources to phase out manual operations. Often these efforts have simply automated existing messes, making them faster, not better.

This model is out of synchronization with the changing expectations of the market. Instead of large ocean liners, we need swift runabouts that can customize solutions to particular needs. Our knowledge and ability to see patterns and nuances in patterns becomes the key asset of the enterprise.

The industrial era defined fixed resources. The knowledge era needs to draw upon variable or virtual resources to meet unique market and customer demands in a timely manner by configuring and reconfiguring the appropriate capabilities and competencies within and between companies to seize concrete and profitable market opportunities.

How much of the knowledge needed to run an enterprise can be captured in a firm's automated systems, applications, databases, and manual procedures? I have asked this question of many different groups. They almost always agree that we cannot capture much more than 30 percent. Some think it is no more than 10 percent. In either case, it is clear that the real knowledge needed to run an enterprise resides in the heads of those working there. The task then becomes one of networking the right people to handle task-focused assignments. In addition, multiple teams must be networked in order to achieve teamwork of teams. This suggests a whole new vision of what might be possible outside the industrial-era bottle.

Looking Beyond the Bottleneck

It has been twenty-three years since Joseph Harrington, Jr., published *Computer Integrated Manufacturing* and Daniel Bell wrote *The Coming Post-Industrial Society*, and seventeen years since Jay Galbraith brought out *Designing Complex Organizations*.[20] Each, in his own way, saw the industrial era being superseded by something new: Harrington envisioned computers linking engineering and manufacturing, Galbraith suggested that matrix organizations would bring more effective integration in complex hierarchies, and

Bell predicted that post-industrial society would be organized around knowledge. Each, in his own way, was looking beyond the bottleneck.

Even though Harrington's concept of computer-integrated manufacturing (CIM) has become a rallying cry for all sorts of "integration" activities, the concept will hardly sit still long enough for an agreed-upon definition to emerge. Galbraith's concept of the matrix organization has not proven to be the cure-all that was once expected because most power has remained within discrete functions. We are still struggling to understand what an organization based on knowledge instead of land, labor, or capital might be like.

Three recent publications by Peter Drucker, Stanley Davis, and Richard Nolan give some informed insights into the evolving post-industrial organization envisioned by Bell.[21]

Drucker: Vision of the "New Organization"

Drucker expects businesses of the future to have half as many levels of management as are typical today. They will be knowledge-based and essentially self-directing. The traditional command and control model will have little meaning. In short, these businesses will have little resemblance to the businesses of today.[22]

Today work is done in departments or functions. Tomorrow, Drucker suggests, the activities of the business will be carried out by many ad hoc "task-focused teams." The departments will serve as bases of resources, technical and human, and as providers of standards. Instead of working sequentially, the various functions will work together in synchrony, with teams taking projects from inception to market. The emerging organization will go beyond a matrix, thus requiring greater self-discipline and individual responsibility. It will be held together by clear, simple, common objectives and coordinated like a symphony orchestra, but without a score. It will have to write its own music as it goes.

Drucker lists four challenges of these emerging information-based organizations:

1. Developing rewards, recognition, and career opportunities for specialists.

2. Creating a unified vision in an organization of specialists.

3. Devising the management structure for an organization of task forces.

4. Ensuring the supply, preparation, and testing of top management people.[23]

Drucker finds examples of his vision in large symphony orchestras, hospitals, and even the British civil administration in India. He says we can only see dimly the outlines of this new form of organization. Some of its characteristics are known, but "the job of actually building the information-based organization is still ahead of us—it is the managerial challenge of the future."[24] It is likely that we will need to learn how to structure organizations around multiple overlapping networks of teams, instead of simply spinning off ad hoc teams as needed.

Davis: Networking Will Encompass Hierarchies

Stanley Davis expects a shift in focus from hierarchical organizations to networked ones, although "networks will not replace or supplement hierarchies; rather, the two will be encompassed within a broader conception that embraces both."[25]

What is this broader conception? Davis is not specific and adds that we are still struggling to figure out just what this means. He introduces into the discussion new considerations of *time* and *space*. By bringing a vision of the future into the present, present activities take on more directionality. A firm's space does not need to be physically defined by the four walls of its factory or office building, since it can extend through computer terminals right onto the customer's site. Like Drucker, Davis sees a shift from working sequentially to using multiple functions simultaneously.

What do these visions have to do with fifth-generation management? First, Drucker's vision places significant new demands on the human component of the organization. Second, the efforts of multiple task-focused teams will need to be continually integrated into the total effort of the enterprise. And Davis suggests that the emerging knowledge-based organization will be built around the *network*.

Fifth-generation management embodies values and attitudes that make it possible to leverage networking technology so people can remain in touch with one another in ever-changing constellations of work teams. Richard Nolan, Alex Pollock, and James Ware describe much of this shift.

Nolan: The Twenty-First-Century Organization

Richard Nolan suggests that the bureaucratic hierarchical form of organization used by most companies today is obsolete.[26] He suggests that the organizational structure of the twenty-first century will have to take the form of a network in order to compete.

Companies that try simply to modify their existing bureaucratic hierarchies will "fall short of becoming globally cost-competitive, market-driven, or achieving a lasting competitive advantage."[27] These companies will not have the flexibility or adaptability to meet market demands primarily because of the shift from relatively stable to dynamic markets. Moreover, there is also a shift in knowledge requirements from relatively simple needs to complex interdependencies.

Nolan and his colleagues picture this shift as shown in Figure 7.7. The entrepreneurial form represents first-generation management. Bureaucracy, or steep hierarchy, is second-generation management. The networked organization requires fifth-generation management. The circles indicate multiple task-focusing teams. One of the teams involves participants from either a supplier or a customer organization or both. Third-generation matrix organizations and fourth-generation interfaced hierarchies are simply superimposed on the steep hierarchy.

A New Intellectual Foundation for Manufacturing

The first part of the 1990s has brought with it significant developments in manufacturing thought. Once people realized CIM had been over-hyped and that business process re-engineering is limited in scope, efforts began in various parts of the world to lay a new foundation for understanding manufacturing (and by implication, the service and government sectors as well). The Japanese are

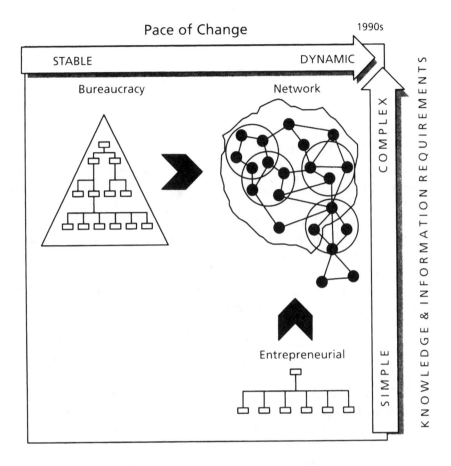

Figure 7.7 **Organizational forms and environmental demands**[28]

working on the concepts of holonic management, the Germans are exploring fractal enterprises, the Americans seek to probe the breadth of agility in manufacturing. In parallel, efforts are underway to tap more explicitly the knowledge, learning, innovation, creativity, and intellectual capital in our companies.

These efforts represent a tremendous intellectual ferment. The above-mentioned initiatives are often developed in isolation from one another, and yet their occurrence is similar to the way in which the forsythias bloom on the same day in the spring all over town. There are common themes and threads that run through these efforts. All are rediscovering the importance of people in the workplace. They recognize the need to use not just hands but heads. And they envision organizations that are open to quality dialogue, internally and with other organizations.

Holonic Management

Japan has conceived and inspired an international collaborative research program in manufacturing, the Intelligent Manufacturing Systems (IMS) program. A multi-year program begun in the early 1990s, it will carry out joint international research, pre-competitive development, systematic organization, and standardization for the next generation of manufacturing technologies. Manufacturing companies and universities in Australia, Canada, the European Community (EC), European Free Trade Association (EFTA), Japan, and the United States are involved.

The IMS program sponsors six projects in (1) clean manufacturing in the process industry, (2) global concurrent engineering, (3) global enterprise integration in the 21st century, (4) rapid product development, (5) holonic manufacturing systems (HMS), and (6) knowledge systematization and configuration systems for design and manufacturing (Gnosis).[29]

The fifth project, on holonic manufacturing systems, is of particular interest for our discussion. Hitachi, the project coordinator, has been joined by thirty-two other companies and universities in Australia, Belgium, Canada, Finland, Germany, Italy, Spain, Switzerland, the United Kingdom, and the United States. Maekawa in Japan is often referred to as an excellent example of a holonic enterprise.

Arthur Koestler, a Hungarian author and philosopher, coined the concept "holon" in his 1967 book, *The Ghost in the Machine*.[30] He used the word holon to describe a basic unit of organization in biological and social systems. *Holos* in Greek refers to the whole, and *on* is a part, such as in "prot*on*" or "electr*on*." Holon refers to the interplay between the parts and the whole.

Koestler observed that in living organisms and in social organizations, entirely self-supporting, non-interacting entities do not exist. Every identifiable unit of an organization, such as a single cell in an animal or a family unit in a society, comprises more basic units (plasma and nucleus, parents and siblings) while at the same time forming a part of a larger unit of organization (a muscle tissue or a community). A holon, as Koestler uses the term, is an identifiable part of a system that has a unique identity, yet is made up of subordinate parts and is in turn part of a larger whole.

Although there has been some excellent academic work on holonics in the United States,[31] the bulk of the interest, until recently, has been in Japan. I first heard the term in 1989 from Kazuto Togino, then President of Komatsu Metals.

The strength of a holonic organization, or holarchy, is that it enables the construction of very complex systems that are nonetheless efficient in the use of resources, highly resilient to disturbances (both internal and external), and adaptable to changes in the environment in which they exist.

The stability of holons and holarchies stems from holons being self-reliant units, which have a degree of independence and handle circumstances and problems on their particular level of existence without asking higher-level holons for assistance. Holons can also receive instruction from and, to a certain extent, be controlled by higher-level holons. The self-reliant characteristic ensures that holons are stable, able to survive disturbances. The subordination to higher-level holons ensures the effective operation of the larger whole.

Potential applications of holonic management systems include the computer simulation of steel rolling mill cooling controls, the fixturing of workpieces, robot motion control, flexible manufacturing cells, assembly stations, flexible assembly, and machining inspection. Besides these specific applications, there are general applications in continuous processing industries, machining, assembly, transportation, and systems optimization.

Holonic management is conceived as a way to manage very complex systems with efficient use of resources. It seeks resiliency to disturbances, both internal and external. It recognizes the importance of being adaptive to changes. The operating units, the parts, need to be self-configurable, synergistic, and self-responsible. Wherever possible these units should re-use existing knowledge and capabilities. These characteristics are possible when the whole, the larger context, is understood. We might say that the units have a great deal of freedom for independent action, but within the larger business context. The two words that occur continually in the literature on holonics are "autonomy" and "coordination."

Although the HMS and the German focus on fractal enterprises have developed independently, there is much in common, both conceptually and practically.

Warnecke: *Fractal Enterprises*

Professor Hans-Juergen Warnecke, president of the Fraunhofer Institute in Germany, brought out, together with Manfred Hueser, *The Fractal Company: A Revolution in Corporate Culture* in 1992.[32] The Fraunhofer Institute is extremely well positioned in Germany. Its role is to be a bridge between the universities and industry, the services, and government. Whereas the Max Planck Institute focuses on basic research in Germany, the Fraunhofer Institute is dedicated to applied research. Its nearly 7,000 employees are deployed in forty-seven locations throughout the country.

Even though Warnecke has been a strong proponent of CIM, he has also recognized its limits. In typical factories, as in most businesses, there are too many interrelated variables that typically have non-linear relationships. It is not possible to plan for and control all activities in a company. Therefore he recognizes the need to rethink the way that we organize, staff, and manage our companies.

Instead of vertical communication, he argues for more horizontal dialogue. Inspired by developments in chaos theory, he envisions the enterprise as dynamic fractals. Each component is independent, so that it can make its own decisions, and yet lives within the context of the larger whole, which it must understand. This is similar to the holonic idea of "autonomy" and "coordination."

Perhaps we can better understand a fractal by thinking of a head of broccoli. If we were to break off an individual branch, we would quickly discover that this branch is both unique and yet the same as the whole. There is no other branch exactly like it, but at the same time it echoes the shape and form of the whole head. It is "self-similar," but not exactly alike.

Each part of an enterprise (including each person) has its unique characteristics, yet each element understands itself within the context of the larger whole. Each element is free to self-optimize, self-design, self-create, and self-organize, but always within the context of the larger business mission. Instead of always waiting to be told what to do, each of the elements of the enterprises is expected to continually size up the larger whole, communicate with the other elements (fractals) and act in such a way that it optimizes both its operation and the organization as a whole. Each element is expected to be self-responsible for interrelating its own efforts with the total organization.

Since first publishing *The Fractal Company* book in 1992, the Fraunhofer Institute has been working with over forty companies to help them more effectively use their business and technical resources through a fractal approach. They recently published the interim results of eighteen projects that involve work on six levels.[33]

- Cultural
- Strategic
- Social-Informational
- Economic and Financial
- Information
- Process and Material Flow

Much of the concrete consulting work is led by Dr. Wilfried Sihn and his colleagues at the Fraunhofer Institute for Production Engineering and Automation (IPA) in Stuttgart. He is forceful in his determination to bring about cultural change in our manufacturing companies. He is well aware of the need for increased trust in our companies as a precondition of quick and flexible response to changing market conditions. Even though the roots of IPA are in industrial production and automation, Sihn and his colleagues have been working not just in manufacturing, but also with services, including hospitals. One project of interest focuses on "active idea management (AIM)" in a hospital setting.

The co-worker in a fractal enterprise is not only a co-worker, but he or she is also a co-knower, co-thinker, co-envisioner, co-decider, and co-responsible. . . . Much of the inner creativity of each person is unused. Yet creativity brings new and better ways of achieving our goals and determines more effective ways of working ("doing the right thing").[34]

Much of the cultural and transformation work ahead involves our evolving use of language. The concept "active idea management" is an important one, because many are now realizing that we transform raw ideas as much as we transform raw matter. We have developed physical logistical systems to a high art, but are still rather primitive in our idea logistical systems. We can process raw materials swiftly and in high volume, but our idea-processing systems leave good ideas strewn all over the place.

Language evolution will come through simple, yet powerful changes. For example, we all remember how boring grammar lessons were in high school, especially those prepositions. Yet, in the shift from the industrial era to the knowledge era, we will find that we shift from the preposition "for" to the preposition "with." In the industrial era we work "for" someone. In the knowledge era we work "with" our colleagues. The above quotation from the AIM project illustrates this change. The use of "co-" is another way to say "with." Working "with" requires a cultural change, a change in which trust and openness are essential and we discover and build upon one another's capabilities. No longer are we just "doing tasks" or "tending machines"; on the contrary, we are being asked to continually envision and co-create possibilities. These are the directions of the fractal projects of the Fraunhofer Institute.

Change comes not just through language and culture, but through the interrelationship of all six of the themes listed above. An excellent example of a fractal organization is Mettler-Toledo in Albstadt, Germany.[35] The company has been producing industrial scales for over 140 years. In the mid 1980s it was facing an economic crisis that threatened its future. Radical steps were needed and the manager Johann Tikart, together with his colleagues, introduced a series of significant reforms, with major success.

In spite of reducing their headcount from 300 to 200 in the last ten years, their sales have increased from 40 million deutsche marks to over 100 million DMs. While reducing headcount, they have redesigned their processes around head content. They have evolved a set of operating norms that are oriented towards delivery, the market, and co-workers. They realize that they cannot be successful without delivery at the promised time. They have redesigned their processes so that they only produce against customer orders. This has led them to be much more in dialogue with their market, developing new products through cross-functional teams together with their customers. They also realized that it is not individual success, but success in the market that counts. Through openness and trust they are able to create an environment that continually improves, developing creative product and process solutions that better meet the expectations of their customers.

There are about 80 co-workers involved in new product development, 90 in production, and only 25 in support. They have a simple flat hierarchy in which people are free to talk with and work with one another without asking permission of the higher-ups. New products are developed in six months now, instead of eighteen. They use world-class techniques to improve their development processes, including concurrent engineering, Quality Function Deployment, Design for Assembly, Failure Mode and Effect Analysis, and the Taguchi Method. Once a product is put into production, the production co-workers take responsibility individually for an entire order, including assembly, documentation, and shipping. Because they produce only against orders, the production co-workers understand that they must be ready to work from 50% to 200% capacity. There are three pay levels: part-qualified assembler, fully qualified assembler, and specialist. The supervisors function as mentors.

Many of Mettler-Toledo's changes began even before they knew about fractal concepts. They have done things that have been repeated in many other companies, both in Germany and in other parts of the world. However, they have been successful because they implemented changes in culture, business strategy, social and informal relationships, economic models, information processing, and process flow. They have created an open and fast-moving environment in which individuals and teams take responsibility for their own areas of responsibility. They are truly self-organizing, self-optimizing, and self-similar in their approaches. Everyone understands the operating principles and norms, and so can adjust to both opportunities and disturbances in the market. Success has come with the changes over the last ten years. In 1994 Mettler-Toledo won a German national prize in innovation, a so-called "industrial Oscar." If we weigh their results, then their continued success is an inspiration to other companies that it pays to transform the old industrial-era model into a more knowledge-intense approach.

The fast-moving and adaptive model of Mettler-Toledo is what the Agility Forum in the United States is also pursuing.

Goldman, Nagel, and Preiss: *Agile Competitors and Virtual Organizations*

In 1991 a small group of manufacturing executives spent six months thinking through the characteristics of the next-generation manufacturing model.[36] They realized that it was not going to be enough to just be flexible. Instead, companies needed to be "agile." They needed to be able to quickly team their resources and capabilities internally and externally with other companies.

Rick Dove has put these developments into a historical perspective.[37] In the feudal age, a craftsperson would do an entire job from start to finish, like a cobbler making shoes. Then Henry Ford divided work into minute steps. This mass production produced a lot of "Tin Lizzies," the Model T, but its legacy has been to confine workers in little job boxes. Then along came the MIT study of the Toyota production system, and manufacturing had a new concept, "lean."[38] Lean is synonymous, in many ways, with flexibility. The agility study has found that companies need to be more than just flexible; they need to be agile. They need to be able to spring, like a gymnast, after ever-changing opportunities.

Out of this intense study has grown the Agile Manufacturing Enterprise Forum (now called the Agility Forum) headed by Rusty Patterson, on loan from Texas Instruments. The Agility Forum is a volunteer association of companies that are working to discover how they can implement, throughout their companies, agile capabilities. Steve Goldman, Roger Nagel, and Kenneth Preiss have captured the spirit and direction of the efforts in their recent book, *Agile Competitors and Virtual Organizations: Strategies for Enriching the Customer*.[39] Agile companies can develop market-segmenting, knowledge-based, and service-oriented products that can easily be customized to the requirements of individual customers. They find an excellent example in a company like Asea Brown Boveri (ABB), which has created a web of smaller, independent units that can act on their own authority, yet can pull together on the larger projects.

The agility concept is spreading to the European community. Paul Kidd, in England, has written an excellent study of agility that is different and yet complements nicely the work of Goldman, Nagel, and Preiss.[40] Kidd adds a more technical understanding of agility in the manufacturing process.

Why agility? To enrich customers. In other words, agility is not an end in itself, but a way to help make our customers more successful. This is certainly a different approach from the "customer beware" days. How do we enrich our customers? We enrich them by teaming capabilities internally and with our suppliers and customers. This is a different approach from building walls around jobs and between companies.

Agile companies are self-organizing. They are not rigid and bureaucratic. People who need to work together, be it through concurrent engineering or product support, simply team up. Through this fluid and adaptive approach, companies can ride the waves of market changes, even getting out ahead of the wave and directing its course. This takes excellence in leveraging the capabilities of people and information systems.

The Agility Forum understands that successful implementation is in the details. It has commissioned several cross-company working teams to explore ways to enhance product development processes, human resources, marketing, and logistics. There is an annual conference at which there are reports on the progress of these working teams. At the last conference, Ted Goranson presented a fascinating description of the whaling industry as a model of agility.[41] Many in the audience wondered what an industry that has been dead for over a hundred years had to teach us today.

According to Goranson, the United States dominated the whaling industry for over a hundred years. Even though they tried hard, the English and the Dutch could not break in. They had equally good ships and sailing captains. Why were they not successful?

The Americans benefited from three things. First, when the captains returned to New Bedford and Nantucket, they would share their logs, in detail, with the other captains in port. Second, they believed it bad luck for a ship to set out twice with the same crew. Therefore, they continually changed the members of their crews. Third, everyone was in agreement at the beginning of a journey as to the percentage of the profits they would get at the end of the journey. Therefore, everyone had a stake in the trip's success.

As the captains openly shared their logs, they were really processing their knowledge. They may have done this because many were Quakers, and it was a Quaker tradition to be open and honest. Nevertheless, the results helped the captains understand wind, current, weather and the probable location of the whales.

Even though it may have been a superstition, the continual redistribution of crews meant that the learnings of previous journeys were spread throughout the fleet. These two processes, the sharing of logs and the redistribution of crews, were, in hindsight, wise norms. This leads us to pose the question, what wise norms lead our companies? Certainly Mettler-Toledo has been developing its own set of norms that drive its successful business. The Goldman, Nagel, and Preiss book is full of other examples of companies that are smartly moving towards success in agilely deploying and redeploying their resources.

Many of us will soon be experiencing Boeing's new 777. Several years ago some wise executives from Boeing and United Airlines, excluding the lawyers from the room, wrote up a simple collaborative agreement:[42]

> *In order to launch on-time a truly great airplane, we have a responsibility to work together to design, produce and introduce an airplane that exceeds the expectations of flight crews, cabin crews, and maintenance and support teams and ultimately our passengers and shippers.*
>
> *From day one:*
>
> * *Best dispatch reliability in the industry*
> * *Great customer appeal in the industry*
> * *User friendly and everything works*

This simple agreement created a spirit of openness and trust between Boeing, United, and Boeing's other customers. For the first time ever, United Airlines personnel were invited to share space with the Boeing design engineers as they were designing the plane. In this way, United and the other airline representatives that were also present were able to bring their knowledge and experience right into the design phase. This is an excellent example of what Goldman, Nagel, and Preiss refer to as "enriching the customer" and what the whaling captains did in Nantucket. Let us step back at this point and ask, what are these changes and what do they mean?

Holonics, fractals, and agility . . . different approaches from different parts of the world. Are there common messages?

Although the words and language may be different, the direction is the same. We need people's heads and not just their hands. Instead of being told what to do, co-workers will take responsibility for both their own processes and for the larger whole. The parts may be autonomous, but they also need to collaborate with other parts to optimize the whole. Each element of the fractal may be different, but they all participate in a similar undertaking that provides the context and direction for their efforts. And as agile resources are teamed and re-teamed within and between companies into virtual enterprises, it is necessary to see how everyone is helping to enrich the customers. These three initiatives are helping to evolve the international language of manufacturing so that Hitachi in Japan, Broken Hill Properties in Australia, Mettler-Toledo in Germany, and Texas Instruments and Allan-Bradley in the United States are all evolving in similar ways. As the lessons of holonics, fractals, and agility are better learned, these companies and others will not only be able to respond to opportunities, but they will be able to create new opportunities and trends. They will be able to rewrite the rules of their industries, as C. K. Prahalad and Gary Hamel suggest.[43] They will be able to recognize the ways in which developments in technology are continually rewriting the rules of business, whether we are aware of it or not, as Dan Burrus explains in *Technotrends*.[44]

Are these three initiatives the final words on the future of manufacturing? Probably not. It took the industrial era from fifty to one hundred and fifty years to replace agriculture as the dominant economic activity. We are probably in another twenty- to fifty-year period of transition. There are others who are bringing equally rich insights.

Nonaka and Takeuchi:
The Knowledge-Creating Company

Inspired by Michael Polanyi's distinction between tacit and explicit knowledge, Nonaka and Takeuchi provide us with a carefully thought-through and well-documented approach to knowledge creation.[45] Their work is extremely timely as more and more people are focusing on knowledge, creativity, and innovation.

Nonaka and Takeuchi realize that much of a company's knowledge is located in highly subjective insights, intuitions, hunches, ideals, values, images, symbols, metaphors, and analogies. If properly understood and developed, these resources can add tremendous value to the daily operation of the company. It is necessary for a company to consciously develop processes to mine these ideas and insights. They provide a number of excellent examples of how companies such as Honda, Canon, Kraft General Foods, NEC, and 3M process their knowledge.

They find that middle managers make ideal project and program leaders because they are able to both understand the aspirations and metaphors of top management and communicate with and inspire professionals in the organization. Their concept is of "middle-up-down" management. It is refreshing to see someone who sees middle management in a positive light, because for too long middle managers have been the neglected and abused element in many companies, especially as we have gone through the recent period of downsizing.

Nonaka and Takeuchi present some tough challenges to Western managers and organizational theoreticians. They question whether Peter Senge's work on the learning organization does not continue the Cartesian split between mind and body, something that they feel has plagued Western thought for several centuries. They also question the West's notions of "best practices" and "benchmarking" because they believe it is not enough to just learn about other ways of doing something. Instead, companies need to actively process what they are learning to make it their own. And they question our approach to the virtual corporation that easily combines the knowledge of the company, supplier, and customer.[46] These challenges are on target and timely and if we can take them seriously we can get beyond our "management theory of the month" syndrome. We need to pause and come to terms with the quality thought of these two men if we hope to move our companies to another level of understanding. They are no strangers to the West, as both did their doctoral studies at the University of California at Berkeley.

If we follow their thought, we will need to do a better job of combining both action and reflection. We need to process both matter and ideas more effectively. If Nonaka and Takeuchi slow us down a bit, we will only be richer in our efforts. They are not alone. S. K. Chakraborty of the Indian Institute of Management in Calcutta suggests that instead of just brainstorming, we need to learn the art of "brain stilling."[47] We need to learn to quiet down so that we can hear one another more effectively, and so that we can also hear our suppliers and customers in new ways.

Nonaka and Takeuchi recognize that the creation of new knowledge has as much to do with ideals as it does with ideas. This certainly suggests that culture and values are as critical as quality and process re-engineering, if not more so. Certainly their work will deepen the efforts in holonics, fractals, and agility in substantive ways.

In fact, their metaphor for the emerging organization is the "hypertext organization." As more and more business people experience the World Wide Web, they will better understand the hypertext metaphor that makes dynamic linking and web weaving a way of life. The hypertext organization has three elements: the business-system layer (the hierarchy), the project-team layer, and the knowledge-base layer.[48] A hypertext organization is really a layered web of relationships capable of processing a wide variety of ideas very effectively. There are other voices helping us understand this emerging model.

Helgesen: *The Web of Inclusion*

In 1990 Sally Helgesen studied ways in which women led a construction firm, a group of radio stations, the Girl Scouts, and the management training institute for Ford. She found upon further reflection that these lessons apply to business in general.[49] In 1995 she applied these insights to Intel, the Miami Herald, Boston's Beth Israel Hospital, Anixter Inc., and Nickelodeon. Her book, *The*

Web of Inclusion, explores the web metaphor for organizing highly adaptive companies.[50]

Helgesen makes use of the discovery of quantum physicists that matter is both particle and wave. She finds the web to be both pattern and process. As a pattern, she found that the organizations run by women in her first study were much like a spider's web. "The structures were circular in shape, with the leader at the central point, and lines radiating outward to various points."[51] This is somewhat like the model of the pizza organizational structure developed by Eastman Chemical discussed earlier. Helgesen found that the structures were "continually being built up, stretched, altered, modified, and transformed."[52]

She also found that the leaders were continually bringing everyone into the circle, increasing communication with everyone and encouraging participation among and between people. These web-like structures were more circular than hierarchical. The leaders felt comfortable being in the midst of the action, rather than on top of the organization, and they liked to build consensus rather than just issue orders. By creating a collegial atmosphere, people could focus on what needed to be done, rather than who had the authority to command that it be done. With the flexibility of a web, it was easy for people to move around and connect and reconnect with one another as needed. This structure is what Helgesen calls the *web of inclusion*. It works because people feel valued, and in feeling valued, they more easily value one another. This, in turn, increases trust and openness.

As a process, Helgesen finds the web to be characterized by open conversation throughout the entire organization. Distinctions between positions and roles and between thinking and doing are blurred. In the web, power is more easily redistributed and it is easier to continually redefine the organization. The web is inclusive of resources outside the organization, and as it easily interacts both internally and externally, it is a continual-learning model. Helgesen illustrates these insights not just with women leaders, but with examples involving both men and women.

The literature on holonics, fractals, and agility hardly, if at all, mentions the web metaphor. There is also relatively little consideration of human emotions. Roxanne Emmerich is developing the notion of "emotional literacy" in business, a way to tap important energy in oneself and one another.

As I reflect on Helgesen's work I find that much of the discussion of employee empowerment misses the mark. We do not get empowered by our bosses. Instead we discover within ourselves and one another talents, capabilities, knowledge, and aspirations. We become one another's palette of capabilities with which we team to seize concrete opportunities. The web metaphor has so much more to do with energy as inspiration, innovation, and creativity than it does with power. Already we can see on the Internet communities forming around different themes and moving through different stages of community. In these communities, it does not matter what size office, fancy title, or type of car one has. Instead, it is the ability to listen, share, and contribute that counts. It is the quality of what is said and how it is said that captures attention, not one's rank in the world. Interestingly enough, in the anonymity of cyberspace, people can sometimes be much more open with their thoughts and feelings.

At a recent meeting of those involved in a community exploring the nature of intellectual capital,[53] we discovered a spectrum of involvement in organic communities on the Internet. These communities range from communities of interest to those of commitment as people become involved in the life of the on-line dialogue. They sometimes become communities of practice, in which people are working together on a joint undertaking. Finally a few reach the community of co-creation. In actuality, different people in the community are at different points in the same interaction, so perhaps we should not think of this in strictly linear terms. The communities of disinterest are probably typical of most of us in our work-a-day world. We are in situations that are less than inspiring.

Leaders in our organizations have the challenge to mentor vibrant communities of commitment, practice, and co-creation, which are able to see the big picture while focusing on the specifics, to seize and deliver on the opportunity. So much of business is dependent upon our ability to weave webs of inclusive relationships in which people feel valued and inspired to give more of themselves.

Helgesen has provided vivid ways of thinking about our evolving organizations. She has captured many of the characteristics of the self-organizing companies that Margaret Wheatley explores in her excellent book, *Leadership and the New Science.*[54]

Self-Organizing and Intelligent Enterprises

The concept of self-organizing appears in discussions of holonics, fractals, and agility. It is a term that seems easy to understand, but in reality is a major challenge. What are the norms and principles of self-organization? What prevents a self-organized team from organizing itself in a mini-hierarchy? What are the values, norms, and principles that give the self-organizing process vitality and endurance? Certainly, Helgesen's book contributes significantly to our exploration of this area, but it is clear that we are just at the beginning. There are already some examples of networking and webbing organizations.

For example, each of us who uses a VISA card participates in a world-wide organization that has neither centralized hierarchy nor a command-and-control structure—although its products are created by over 23,000 financial institutions and accepted in more than 200 countries around the world, and it provides 355 million people with 7.2 billion transactions exceeding $650 billion annually.

Conceived in the late 1960s by Dee Hock and a few others, it is owned by all member companies, its power and functions are distributed to the maximum degree possible, its governance is distributed, it is infinitely malleable and yet extremely durable, and it can easily embrace diversity and change. It finds its own order in the chaotic world of financial transaction. In fact, Hock has coined the word "chaord" (spoken "kay-ord"), a composite of chaos and order, to characterize VISA. He calls it a chaordic organization.[55]

What is clear is that we are not simply re-engineering the old to up its efficiency, we are reconceiving the way we organize and work together. We see this in Boeing, VISA, and Oticon. We see it in the "lifelong learning" project of ABB Network Controls in Sweden, which has been building a culture and community in which the co-workers and management take responsibility for their own and one another's competency development.[56]

Since *Fifth Generation Management* was first published in 1990, there have been a goodly number of excellent books dealing with the same and closely related topics. Tom Peter's *Liberation Management* and his more recent book, *The Tom Peters Seminar*, show his passion to help us break loose from our old moorings.[57] He is our "change coach" and he does not just call the plays from the sidelines, but jumps into the fray. Other significant authors who come to mind are James Quinn Brian, Charles Handy, James O'Toole, and Gifford and Elizabeth Pinchot.[58] The deans of the science of networking are Jessica Lipnack and Jeff Stamps. Their books, new and old, are always rich and insightful.[59]

There is a growing literature on intelligent organizations, collaborative intelligence, intellectual capital, and knowledge assets. Michael McMaster, who brings a deep understanding of complexity to organizations, has just published *The Intelligence Advantage: Organising for Complexity*.[60] Organizations have intelligence of their own, distinct from the individuals within them, emerging from the interplay of founders, members, society, technology, and competition. This intelligence can be understood and increased by design, a position also taken by Nonaka and Takeuchi. Dialogue, language, and conversation are the necessary elements for developing a corporate intelligence that allows creation beyond individual intelligence.

In a similar vein, George Por is focusing on collaborative intelligence.[61] It is one thing to have intelligent individuals in an organization, but something quite different to have intelligent organizations. This reminds us of Peter Senge's question as to why the work of a committee represents an IQ of 65 when those sitting around the table average from 120 to 140 in IQ?

Several colleagues are doing excellent work on intellectual capital, although relatively little has been published.[62] Leif Edvinsson is leading an effort at Skandia in Sweden to identify the company's intellectual capital. They are now publishing an Intellectual Capital supplement to their balance sheet. Rather than looking back at past results, they hope their work will provide a set of navigational tools to look effectively at the future. Hubert St. Onge, who leads the Leadership Center at the Canadian Imperial Bank of

Commerce in Toronto, has helped his bank set up a "knowledge lending practice." Banks traditionally loan against the capital assets of a company, but when the company is knowledge intensive another approach is needed. Gordon Petrash has helped Dow Chemical put in place an intellectual asset management program. Working on the premise that intellectual properties will be more valuable than a company's physical assets in the 21st century, Petrash has developed a way of working out, classifying, and better leveraging their knowledge assets. Dave Marsing at Intel has worked hard to create a vibrant culture, capable of valuing and building upon difference, at their plant in Albuquerque. These examples show that these changes are occurring not just in the manufacturing world, but also in the services.

When I first wrote this book in the late 1980s, Drucker, Davis, and Nolan were pointing the way. Since then we have seen the development of holonics, fractals, and agility. Nonaka and Takeuchi have highlighted the knowledge-creating capabilities of companies and more intense work is going on around intelligent organizations and intellectual capital.

Still, many companies are not looking beyond fourth-generation management. Instead, they are busy trying to overcome their fragmentation by computerizing their existing steep hierarchies. What results can we expect?

CHAPTER

8

COMPUTERIZING STEEP HIERARCHIES: WILL IT WORK?

After two hundred years of working to divide and subdivide enterprises, we find ourselves today trying to integrate these same processes with computers and networks. In spite of the enthusiasm for computer-integrated manufacturing, computer-integrated enterprise, and the Internet, it isn't easy. Why?

George Hess, vice president of Ingersoll Milling Machine, caricatures our present industrial-era organizations as "human disintegrated manufacturing."[1] He dislikes the "fragmentation virus" affecting our organizations. Certainly the endless turf battles, the need for middle managers as expediters, and the seas of irrelevant data all give testimony to Hess's observation. But these are merely symptoms of deeper problems.

How do we begin to address the extreme fragmentation that is so common in our manufacturing and service organizations? Is the problem really in the way that we organize ourselves? After all, structure is supposed to follow strategy. Yet structure too often develops a life of its own. Even a structure that has outlived its usefulness will resist the pressure to change or get out of the way. The traditional steep hierarchical corporate structure, that familiar pyramidal mobile with the boss at the top and department heads and middle managers dangling beneath, cannot cope with the rapidly changing customer demands and technological pressures of today's marketplace, as we have been discussing.

Can the imposition of computer-based technology, by itself, transform the corporate structure into one that allows the vast potential of CIM and CIE to be realized? Or must the old corporate species die to make room for the new? Figure 8.1 shows the focus of this chapter.

Historical Perspective

In *The Wealth of Nations*, Adam Smith theorizes about the division and subdivision of labor, one of the key concepts of the industrial revolution.[2] He uses as his model a pin-making factory in which the manufacturing process is broken into a sequence of simple steps, each of which is performed by a specialist who does nothing else (Figure 8.2).

It is perfectly natural to organize the work of a small-scale proprietorship such as a small shipyard, a group making shoes, or a textile import concern according to this idea of the division of labor. The owner coordinates the various activities necessary to acquire the raw materials, divide up the work, and sell the products. Market forces determine the interplay between these and other enterprises, as suggested by Adam Smith's concept of the "invisible hand": as the proprietorships look after their own self-interest, the general economy prospers. Government's role is to establish the ground rules for this competition.

Smith's idea of the role of self-interest is a macroeconomic concept: as proprietorships try to maximize their own positions,

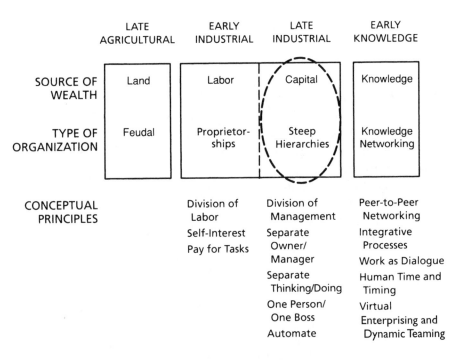

Historical Eras

	LATE AGRICULTURAL	EARLY INDUSTRIAL	LATE INDUSTRIAL	EARLY KNOWLEDGE
SOURCE OF WEALTH	Land	Labor	Capital	Knowledge
TYPE OF ORGANIZATION	Feudal	Proprietor-ships	Steep Hierarchies	Knowledge Networking
CONCEPTUAL PRINCIPLES		Division of Labor Self-Interest Pay for Tasks	Division of Management Separate Owner/Manager Separate Thinking/Doing One Person/One Boss Automate	Peer-to-Peer Networking Integrative Processes Work as Dialogue Human Time and Timing Virtual Enterprising and Dynamic Teaming

Figure 8.1 **The focus of the chapter: steep hierarchies**

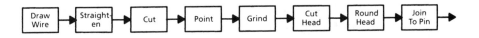

Draw Wire → Straighten → Cut → Point → Grind → Cut Head → Round Head → Join To Pin →

Figure 8.2 **Division and subdivision of labor in pin-making factory**

society benefits from optimum employment and the creation of wealth. Within an enterprise, however, self-interest often works to the detriment of the company. As each function competes to maximize its own position, it diverts resources from other vital functions, and the corporation as a whole suffers. If engineering does not devote time and expense to understanding how its designs create problems in manufacturing, resources are wasted on engineering change orders (ECOs).

Steep hierarchies are a creation of the last hundred years. They evolved out of the early industrial-era proprietorship, according to Alfred Chandler in *Managerial Hierarchies*.[3]

The Emergence of Steep Hierarchies

In the 1880s and 1890s, steep managerial hierarchies began to appear in the United States, Europe, Asia, and elsewhere. In the United States, the railroad and telegraph companies needed extended management structures to span the large geographic areas covered by their companies.[4]

Chandler notes that in these companies, "The visible hand of managerial direction has replaced the invisible hand of market mechanisms . . . in coordinating flows and allocating resources in major modern industries."[5] Chandler's work focuses on this shift from the market-driven proprietorships, guided by Smith's "invisible hand," to the "visible hand" of managers who were no longer the owners of evolving firms, such as Pillsbury, Procter & Gamble, Eastman Kodak, Sony, Nokia, Alcan, Siemens, and Volvo.

These firms were faced with the task of organizing their managerial ranks to coordinate high-volume production with national and international distribution. Careful planning and scheduling, as well as standardization, were critical to achieving economies of scale. Through mergers, consolidations, and other strategies, many of these companies expanded forward into distribution and back into raw materials. This "vertical integration" helped them reduce costs, increase profits, and build barriers against other potential competitors.

In other words, integration is not a new concept.

As they evolved, these firms employed middle- and top-level salaried managers to monitor and control the work of their operating units. Gradually, multi-unit enterprises emerged, with work divided among the functions.

This form of organization brought many advantages. Unit costs could be kept lower through coordinated buying and distribution. The internal flow of goods between operational units could be coordinated through effective planning and scheduling. Facilities, personnel, and cash flow could be managed more effectively.

Managers within steep hierarchies had to develop whole new sets of procedures, policies, and standards to coordinate their activities. New managers had to be recruited and trained. Many activities had to be differentiated.

These needs brought about a division and subdivision of management that paralleled Adam Smith's earlier concept of the division and subdivision of labor, especially with respect to two key features: sequential work and narrowly defined tasks (Figure 8.3).

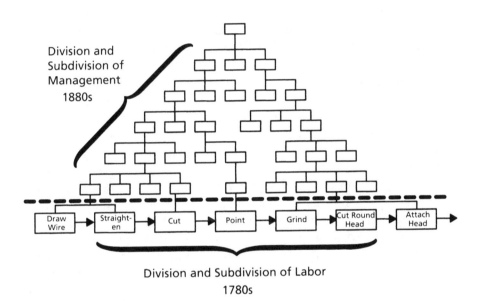

Figure 8.3 Division and subdivision of management and labor with sequential work and narrowly defined tasks

This division and subdivision of management made it easier to manage the growing capital resources of the firm. As a result, new accounting procedures were devised to assign costs, budget for capital investments, and allocate expenses.

New strategies were needed to support both the differentiation of the functions and the integration necessary to coordinate diverse but interconnected activities. Lawrence and Lorsch's classic study, *Organization and Its Environment*, traces the way the organizational structure became the key integrating influence within the enterprise.[6] Clearly articulated departmental charters and job definitions helped define who was responsible for each task. This challenge represented an attempt to establish clearly defined spheres of *authority* and *responsibility* in order to maintain *accountability*. Reward strategies and accounting procedures became key to keeping the companies focused and coordinated.

There are many examples of this process. As companies such as Pennsylvania Railroad, Western Union, Eastman Kodak, John Deere, General Electric, and General Motors grew, their managerial hierarchies increased in size and complexity. In the 1920s, General Motors (GM) and Du Pont pioneered the multidivisional structure with autonomous product divisions. At GM, the divisions ranged from Cadillac, at the top of the line, to Chevrolet at the bottom. At Du Pont, the divisions specialized in explosives, films, fibers, and chemicals. Executives of both companies added centralized staff at headquarters to coordinate the long-range financial development of these divisions. As more and more layers were added, the steep hierarchies of today took shape.

Many of the problems that we face today are the result of using the division of labor as a model for the division and subdivision of management. Even the multidivisional approaches, such as those of General Motors and Du Pont, rely on distinct functions within each division. The sequential model of functional handoffs has not changed, even within divisions, although both companies are working to change this today. Many companies are plagued by their managers' preoccupation with their turf. As information is passed sequentially from one function to another, it is lost or misinterpreted in the handoff. Decisions are made from the narrow confines of one function, without an understanding of the larger context. These problems are endemic in steep hierarchies.

The Structure of Steep Hierarchies

Steep hierarchies may have ten to fifteen layers of management, with a complex set of operating procedures to determine reporting channels, authority levels, departmental charters, job definitions, and operating policies (Figure 8.4). Their structure is based on the assumption that *thinking* will be done at the top of the organization, *doing* at the bottom. Middle management's role is to summarize information for top management and to instruct, monitor, and control subordinates. To ensure responsibility and accountability, each person has only one boss.

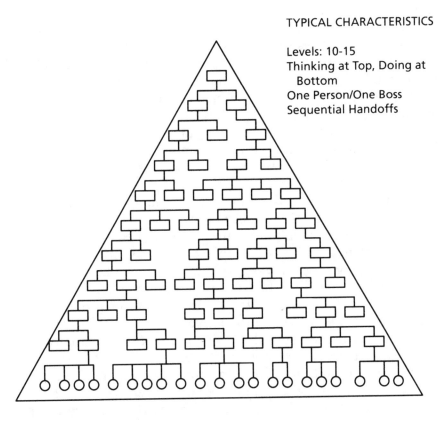

TYPICAL CHARACTERISTICS

Levels: 10-15
Thinking at Top, Doing at
    Bottom
One Person/One Boss
Sequential Handoffs

Figure 8.4 **Steep hierarchy**

Steep hierarchies work by a sequence of handoffs: each department completes its work, then passes the results on to the next department. It is easy to see why all-encompassing bureaucratic procedures are necessary in this environment to integrate the various functions. When established procedures and policies fail to cope with specific situations, the problems are tossed upstairs to the next managerial level—a natural safety valve for the lower levels.

Steep hierarchies in their different forms have worked well over the last hundred years. Despite their recognized shortcomings and growing obsolescence, they have proved quite useful in solving a broad range of managerial problems as they have evolved over the years.

The industrial revolution was fueled not only by an entrepreneurial spirit, but also by a steady flow of technological innovations. The steam engine, the spinning jenny, and metallurgical techniques helped fuel the visions of the industrialists.

The early industrial era combined the division and subdivision of labor with a system that sent work to craftspersons in their homes.[7] As concentrations of equipment began to grow in the 1880s, a shift to professional management necessitated the building of an organizational hierarchy. Functions took over responsibility for the various aspects of the firm. Each function, such as engineering, finance, marketing, or manufacturing, was responsible for building up its own capabilities.

Once these functional hierarchies were defined, they could more easily absorb new technology. When a new lathe, milling machine, or steel-making process was introduced into the hierarchy, there was usually no need to change the way the organization worked. The function that acquired the improved tool or process simply became more efficient and productive.

In spite of the success of these hierarchies, there are many issues that steep hierarchies cannot handle. In their success are the seeds of their failure, and these are being noted not only by Drucker and Davis but by many other contemporary writers.[8] Part of the problem has been that while we have had many theories about hierarchical organizations, we know little about how they actually operate. For example, Teicholz and Orr see the factory as "a seething caldron of emotion, perspiration, nobility, foolishness, greed, sincerity, selfishness, idealism, vanity, and generosity." They go on to note that its "actual operation is almost impossible to diagram because it is shrouded in a fog raised by the heat of human activity."[9] This quotation may be overly dramatic, but it does point to many of the human elements overlooked in most studies of the manufacturing environment.

Robert Reich, Secretary of Labor, notes that America's successes have occurred principally in large, mass-production markets that require what he calls "superstructures of management," his term for what we are calling steep hierarchies.[10] The nation's basic industries—steel, automobiles, petrochemicals, and machinery—mastered the art of high-volume, standardized production. Now, faced with the competitive demands of a world economy that requires flexible systems in products and processes, American companies are playing a catch-up game.

Many manufacturing organizations have simply grown in an unplanned manner, like the Winchester House in San Jose, California. This Victorian mansion, built by the Winchester rifle heiress over thirty years, has staircases leading to nowhere, a chimney that rises four floors to stop just short of the ceiling, and doors that open to blank walls—all because of the owner's obsession that if the builders stopped working, the spirits of those who had been killed by her husband's rifle would come back to haunt her.

Although few if any manufacturing firms are driven by such obsessiveness, most have their share of projects that go nowhere, reports that are necessitated because one department does not trust another, and endless meetings that are held because departments do not understand or appreciate the constraints under which other departments are working. So much information is fragmented within these jumbled hierarchical environments. How can it be sorted out and made available to those who really need it? This deficiency has created a vacuum that is drawing computer-based systems into the hierarchies in an attempt to reverse the fragmentation. The explosive interest in CIM and integration exemplifies this way of thinking.

Computerizing Steep Hierarchies

In the early days of the computer, it seemed only natural to budget computer equipment in the same way as other projected equipment purchases. Individual functional departments had large volumes of repetitious information to process. Computers nicely streamlined and shortened these operations. Each department wanted a computer to support its activities. Finance had accounting to worry about, manufacturing was concerned about tracking inventory, and engineering desired tools to support design and drafting. These functions pulled in both hardware and software to do work that had always been done manually. In fact, most computerization initiatives have been focused on replacing manual operations with the supposed efficiency of the computer. Few efforts have been designed to use computers in qualitatively new ways.

Another dynamic has also been at work: the politics of information management. In steep hierarchies, the information a person controls is directly correlated with that person's power base. In many organizations, information has become currency, doled out to friends and withheld from others.

Figure 8.5 shows a steep hierarchy with computer systems

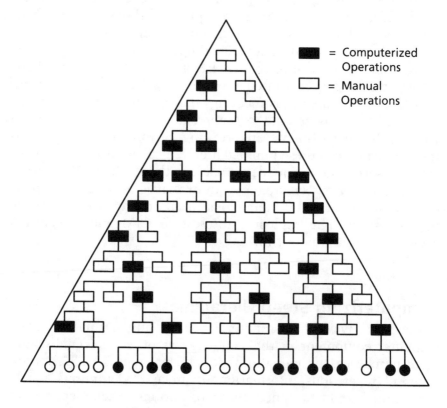

Figure 8.5 **Steep hierarchy with computer systems**

within various departments. Not every department has a computer; they are distributed unevenly within the hierarchy. Different functions have different styles of computing: some are very hierarchical, others distributed.

Each company configures computer systems differently. Some have these resources widely distributed; others have resources concentrated in limited areas. Still other companies have introduced different levels of computing, from large applications packages to word processing and electronic mail systems. Some have more inclusive networks than others. And, of course, the situation is changing all the time as companies add and upgrade systems and tie them together with networks, both internally and with their suppliers and customers.

However, there are some important trends that cut across most companies and industries. Initially, computers thrived in the "glass houses" of the computer centers doing batch operations. Frustrations with centralized and bureaucratic management information systems (MIS) often led to departmental computing. Time-share computing added flexibility to these systems, as professionals used dumb terminals to access their applications and mail. We have just been through the PC wave, where everyone has wanted his or her own terminal.

Gradually, companies are moving from large, centralized, hierarchical computing to peer-to-peer computing, using local and wide-area networking to link terminals, PCs, and workstations. Windowing and client/server technology are making it easier to access files and applications anywhere on the network. Cooperative work-group computing (teamware) is spreading, as is interest in relational and object-oriented programming and databases. The Internet is perhaps the hottest topic today. The World Wide Web is linking all who care to be linked. Companies are also setting up their own corporate-wide webs for internal usage, protecting proprietary discussions from the outside by so-called "firewalls." There is also tremendous pressure from users to establish open systems, including industry-approved user interfaces.

These technological developments will make it much easier for enterprises to work in parallel, by creating multiple task-focusing teams from the different functions and companies to deal with market and customer complexity. Unfortunately, our attitudes and understanding are not maturing as fast as the technology. It is easy to become dazzled by technology and overlook the human and organizational changes necessary to leverage this technology.

Some Unexpected Consequences

When John Deere and Company tried to computerize and integrate its Waterloo, Iowa, tractor works in the early 1980s, it encountered a few surprises. It developed a computer-based system that allowed it to track work-in-process, download programs, schedule operations, and track maintenance. It built high-bay storage capacity so it could easily store and retrieve parts. When the systems were all put into operation, they did not work as they were supposed to. Why not?

Deere discovered, after much reflection, that it had simply computerized and automated operations as they existed in a manual mode. After much soul-searching, Deere realized that it had computerized the contradictions, confusion, and inconsistencies of its existing operations. Reflecting upon this experience, Jim Lardner, a Deere vice president, recommends that companies simplify existing operations before introducing heavy computerization.[11]

Deere subsequently embarked on a "Total War on Waste," incorporating notions of Just-in-Time (JIT) and Total Quality. The interplay between CIM-related efforts, JIT, and Total Quality has enabled Deere to sort out and simplify many of its processes and, where appropriate, computerize and automate them. Deere may be further along on the learning curve than many other companies.

In the 1970s, many companies and government agencies believed it would be possible to develop what some affectionately called the "Great Database in the Sky." Surely the computer would be powerful enough to help run the entire operation. The U.S. Air Force spent millions of dollars on such an effort, only to find it an impossibility. They failed because of two unforeseen problems: first, the available hardware and software were not flexible enough; and second, they tripped over naming conventions. They found that traditional flat data files together with COBOL or FORTRAN did not provide the flexibility to interrelate multiple operations. Each functional group in the organization had its own naming conventions. They underestimated the difficulty of achieving agreement across the organization regarding the definition of key terms. They had assumed the problem was one of bits and bytes, but they learned that the challenge was to hammer out a consistent set of meanings and a definition of key terms between people in different functions.

Two lessons stand out in these examples. First, simplify operations before automating or computerizing them. Those who naively chant "Automate or evaporate!" need to understand that an automated mess is not a better mess—just a faster one. Second, standardize terms across the organization. Without cross-functional understanding, cross-functional computerization will flounder in a sea of turf battles and unresolved definitions.

We often underestimate the complexity of our organizations. Although the organizational chart of steep hierarchies makes us think we understand the organization, the hidden networks of interrelationships, the informal organizations, the old-boy networks, and the political chit systems are major factors in running the operation.

Since George Homans's classic study *The Human Group* in 1950, there has been a growing interest in how organizations actually constitute themselves in spite of their formal organizational models.[12] In order to get the work out the door, people form alliances and coalitions that cut across traditional boundaries. These invisible networks are often the real strength of the company, yet traditional computerization approaches are blind to their existence.

Until recently, the main thrust in industry was to attempt to automate and computerize existing organizations, with all their idiosyncrasies and contradictions. We should certainly try to make manual operations more efficient with the aid of the computer. But what happens when we do this?

Critical Computerization Issues

As our enterprises are connected and interfaced, we face a new range of issues related to computerization and the networking of business and government organizations. Who will own the information? To what extent will this information be managed, that is manipulated, to make some look good? What are the hidden assumptions in embedded software applications? And how do the values and politics of the organization influence the management of information?

Many companies have not come near answering all of these questions. Certainly many have tried, through their business process re-engineering efforts, and some good progress has been made. As companies move more towards client/server technology and groupware, a whole new set of challenges is arising. Moreover, as more business is done through the Internet, additional problems and opportunities are ahead.

The use we make of existing technology often reflects our self- and organizational self-understanding. As we suggested in the previous chapter, rather than using computer-based technology to support the steep hierarchy, we are finding ways to use it in web-like arrangements. Hypertext and hyperlinking are making possible an open and free-form mode of connections. This will lead to our working in parallel both within and between companies. We will, in effect, be breaking out of the von Neumann bottleneck.

Key Interrelationships of Computerization Issues

One of the fundamental tenets of steep hierarchies is the notion of ownership of one's turf, be it individual or functional. This is implicitly the message of the proverbial organization chart. It *is* small wonder that information should be managed and that political fighting should be a way of life. What value do trust and integrity have in such an environment?

As computer and networking systems are introduced, how will the enterprise begin to deal with the new dynamic of communication? How will it deal with meanings that are hidden in applications? When will it begin to get consistency of definitions between functions? Will horizontal communication be encouraged? Will trust and openness be developed? These assets are not easily bought: they must be homegrown and carefully nurtured. A computer vendor cannot install trust in a user environment.

In the process of defining an organization, implicit values are also defined. An organization is not a neutral body. Its structure shapes the attitudes and values of those involved in it. These values also shape policy, reward systems, and accounting procedures. Computer systems and networking are not neutral in their impact on the organization. They are not just more capital equipment, justified by return-on-investment formulas or hurdle rates. Their value is in the way in which they help all elements of the enterprise to work together. In many instances, this has still to be realized.

David Stroll of Digital Equipment Corporation suggests that computers and networking are beginning to dissolve the traditional structure of organizations, the high walls that have separated functions. This creates anxiety and uncertainty as people lose the protection of these traditional boundaries. At the same time, Stroll adds, the clock of organizational interaction is speeded up as companies are required to respond more quickly to market changes.[13] This increasing complexity adds further stress. Enterprises are being forced to interrelate multiple factors—marketing, design, manufacturing, cost, and service—in new ways. These changes are forcing functions to work iteratively, rather than just sequentially.

We are putting powerful new technology in traditional, industrial-era steep hierarchies. Either we learn to adapt to this new technology and leverage its capabilities, or we may find our companies imploding as they choke on complexity and their inability to sort out multiple interrelated variables.

The chapter began by asking whether computerization of steep hierarchies will work. The answer is clear: no.

One of the biggest problems is not in the technology but in our attitudes. As long as we persist in thinking in terms of "boxes and lines," in terms of the "ownership" of these boxes, and in terms of the "ownership" of data, collaboration between multiple functions will continue to be politicized and a climate of distrust and fragmentation will persist.

We are just beginning to recognize the right questions to ask about a fifth-generation management approach that can lead to the effective leadership of flatter network enterprises. For example, how will accountability be maintained? How will knowledge be shared? How will the various functions work together and yet not trip over one another? How do we reverse the trend toward fragmentation that is so common today?

If computerizing the steep hierarchy is not the answer, what is? The answer lies in an attitudinal shift. If we can come to terms with some of the assumptions we have been making about organizations and power, we will be able to use the resources of the computer and networking in exciting new ways. Our challenge is to rethink the conceptual principles that underlie the steep hierarchy. The breakthrough to fifth-generation management will be made, not by money, but by will. The next chapter looks back at the conceptual principles of the industrial era that still confine us in the bottle.

CHAPTER

9

STEEP HIERARCHIES: BREAKING FREE

Like the smile of the Cheshire Cat in *Alice in Wonderland,* integration seems elusive. When the smiling promises on the slick brochures fail to materialize in the plant, serious second thoughts set in. We are confined and uncomfortable, but we do not know how to break free.

Chapter 8 suggested that the problem is putting advanced computer technology in second-generation organizations' steep hierarchies. But won't these organizations evolve as this new technology is introduced? No, because steep hierarchies have a life of their own. Like persistent dandelions that continue to spring up, no matter what we do, the conceptual principles of the steep hierarchies seem to permeate all our thoughts and actions. They continue to hold us captive.

The division and subdivision of labor, self-interest in one's own turf, and simpleminded tasks were convenient principles to support the transition from the agricultural period to the industrial era, yet they still shape our thinking today. The division and subdivision of management, creation of a management group separate from the owners, separation of thinking and doing, a command structure in which each person has only one boss, the desire to automate—all these conceptual principles keep us in a full nelson.

In this chapter we will discuss these conceptual principles and the attempts to break out of them through various attempts at integration. It may well be that the technology cannot overpower these principles. If so, we must find a new set of basic ideas around which to organize both the manufacturing and service sectors. Figure 9.1 highlights the areas of consideration in this chapter. We will first review the conceptual principles, then move into a discussion of the forces leading toward technical integration.

Conceptual Principles of the Early Industrial Era

The transition from the late agricultural era to the early industrial era was accompanied by a profound conceptual shift. This shift between eras was an exciting period, shaped by the rise in scientific thought, political shifts, technological innovations, and many other factors. This section focuses on three conceptual principles that helped shape the fabric of the early industrial era: (1) the division and subdivision of labor, (2) self-interest, and (3) pay for narrowly defined tasks.

The Division and Subdivision of Labor and Self-Interest

Two simple interrelated principles put forth by Adam Smith became the foundation upon which the industrial era was built.[1] These two key ideas, the division and subdivision of labor and self-interest, are easy to grasp.

Smith believed that there had been four stages of society: hunting, pasturing, farming, and the one he was ushering in, commerce.

Historical Eras

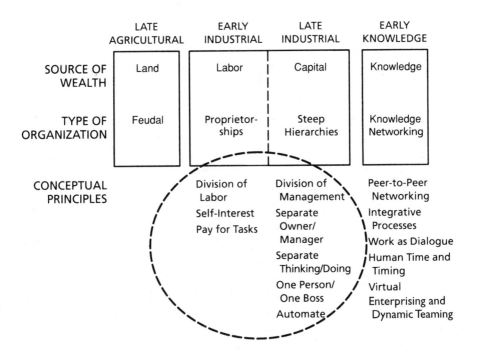

Figure 9.1 **Chapter focus: eight conceptual principles of the industrial eras**

He saw his task as one of redefining economic life to help people understand that their own efforts could become the basis for the wealth of nations. He felt a need to go beyond the mercantilism of the sixteenth and seventeenth centuries, which argued that gains through international trade were the principal factor in promoting national power. He was also influenced by and wanted to push beyond the French Physiocrats, who sought to establish a science of economics based on the laws of nature rather than on the concept of divine law that had supported the feudal era.

The Physiocrats saw agricultural labor and land as the sources of a nation's wealth: land combined with human labor produced bounty from the fields, creating a surplus that nourished all classes. Smith felt that this was too limited a concept. He was sure that more wealth could be generated through the proper application of labor in manufacturing, using the principle of the division of labor. At the same time, he was influenced by the Physiocrats' discussion of self-interest. They believed that individuals know their own interests best, and that as they act to fulfill their interests, society is benefited. The Physiocrats expounded the maxim *laissez faire, laissez passer*—that is, let things alone, let them take their course. Smith's acceptance of this concept of self-interest was reinforced by his reading of Bernard Mandeville's *The Fable of the Bees*, subtitled *Private Greed, Public Benefit.*[2] In order to defuse the storm created by Mandeville's writing, Smith wrote that as each person "intends only his gain, he is . . . led by an invisible hand to promote an end which is not his intention. . . . By pursuing his own interest he frequently promotes that of society more effectively than when he really intends to promote it."[3]

Whereas Mandeville put envy and vanity on a metaphorical pedestal as ministers of commerce and industry, Smith chose a much more innocuous and acceptable metaphor, that of the invisible hand, to represent self-interest. Who could be against a seemingly benevolent "helping hand" that looked after things much as parents looked after their children?

This principle of self-interest, teamed with the division of labor, would give birth to the industrial era. Labor, based on skill, dexterity, and judgment (according to Smith) could best be used under two conditions: (1) if people were allowed to follow their natural interests, specializing in those professions of greatest interest and selling their surplus in the market; and (2) if work were divided into fairly simple steps so that individual workers could specialize in just one step in a larger process.

This second point was illustrated by Smith's discussion of the pin-making factory (Figure 8.2) that divided the process into eighteen steps (although only eight are shown). This division and subdivision of labor was to make it possible to easily employ the unskilled, train them in the individual steps, and thereby greatly increase the quantity of work produced. Smith saw three factors bringing this about. First, as each worker specialized, he or she would gain greater dexterity in that particular function; second, time would not be lost going from one step to the next; and third, as the worker concentrated on a particular function, he or she would "invent a great number of machines" that would facilitate these efforts and "abridge" the labor content.[4]

Smith believed that division of labor would increase the workers' skill and dexterity as they repeated the same function daily. But he was also aware that there would be a consequence: the workers would be "stupefied" by the repetition of the task, losing contact with the overall process. This would cut down on the workers' judgment, one of the key aspects of his definition of the nature of work. Smith never really reconciled this conflicting consequence of his division and subdivision of labor. History has shown that in some instances the division of labor has enhanced a worker's skills and dexterity, but in many others it has stupefied the worker.

Smith had a broad view of the interaction of the various components of the economy. He understood that capital formation was essential for the investments necessary to develop manufacturing concerns and to pay wages. He also figured in the rent that could be generated by the use of land. These two elements, land and capital, when combined with productive labor, would provide the basis of an expanding economy. Capital formation became essential to the development of the later industrial period.

In a historical context, Smith's principles made sense. Since Smith's time, though, their importance has become so exaggerated that it is hard for us to see their growing obsolescence.

Although Smith also dealt at length with the role wages were to play in his economic model, it was Charles Babbage who developed a more precise approach for relating wages and tasks. Babbage, best known for his development of the digital computer, had a profound impact on thought regarding the ways in which work should be organized and rewarded.

Pay for Narrowly Defined Tasks

Babbage's *On the Economy of Machinery and Manufacturers*, published in 1832, helped establish a scientific approach to the study of management.[5] Concerned with the design and manufacture of machinery, its use, and the organization of labor, Babbage reinforced the work of Smith and anticipated themes that would later be articulated by Frederick Taylor.

Babbage clearly believed that a worker should be paid only for the task performed:

The master manufacturer, by dividing the work to be executed into different processes, each requiring different degrees of skill and force, can purchase exactly the precise quantity of both which is necessary for each process; whereas, if the whole work were executed by one workman, that person must possess sufficient skill to perform the most difficult, and sufficient strength to execute the most laborious of the operations into which the art is divided.[6]

Like Smith's division of labor and self-interest, Babbage's payment for narrowly defined tasks made sense in the context of the times. Processes were generally well known and easily divided into simple steps. It made sense to pay only for what a person did, not for what he or she knew. This approach was also easier to administer because it could be related to clock time: the worker would agree to give up a specified amount of time for an agreed wage. As the division of labor was extended to the division of management, the same pay strategy was extended to staff professionals and to the middle levels of the steep hierarchy.

For hourly workers through middle management, we still largely operate on Babbage's principle of payment for narrowly defined tasks. This approach makes less sense today, however, because now we rely more on people's knowledge and awareness of how operations are interrelated.

The gap is growing between Babbage's pay-for-tasks approach and the approach that is needed in the knowledge era. We need a compensation system that recognizes not only knowledge but vision and skill in focusing on and responding to the themes of the market, whether from a marketing, engineering, manufacturing, finance, or service perspective. The Japanese recognize and reward people for three qualities: will, emotion, and knowledge. *Will* is a measure of engagement; *emotion* or *heart* determines, among other things, the quality of interaction with others; and *knowledge* involves memory and vision.

In summary, the three conceptual principles that made the early industrial era possible—division of labor, self-interest, and payment for tasks—must be redefined to fit the knowledge era. These principles are preventing us from being able to leverage the full potential of the technology and human capabilities of the knowledge era. We cannot overcome them by simply ignoring or forgetting them, because they will not easily let us go. They are so much a part of the intellectual woodwork of our thinking that, without a conscious rethinking of their role, we cannot get free. At the same time, we also have to come to terms with the conceptual principles of the late industrial era.

Conceptual Principles of the Late Industrial Era

Around the 1880s, the growing size, complexity, and geographic extent of corporations ushered in the late industrial era and its characteristic organizational structure, the steep hierarchy. In addition to those of the early industrial era, five new conceptual principles characterized the late industrial era: (1) the division and subdivision of management, (2) the separation of ownership and management, (3) the separation of thinking and doing, (4) the notion that each person should have just one boss, and (5) the drive to automate.

Division and Subdivision of Management

Some argue that managerial hierarchies are as old as human history, having arisen in military, political, and religious forms; however, this overlooks the difference between steep and flat hierarchies. Anthropologists point out that most tribes, clans, and family farms have had surprisingly flat hierarchies: the Roman Catholic Church, for example, has only four levels. Nevertheless, many accept the idea that steep hierarchies are a natural part of life.

The impetus toward steep hierarchies began in industries that spanned the continent. As railroads, telegraphs, and telephones spread, companies discovered a need to develop duplicate structures in diverse geographic locations. Each unit needed a general manager, functional managers, and direct reports to summarize information, pass on orders, and monitor activities.

Figure 8.3 illustrates the development of the management infrastructure as it was built above the division of labor. It shows how we became wedded to the box-and-line model. Each box is seen as being owned by its incumbent; the lines show the accepted channels of communication. No wonder many corporations have spent millions to carefully define management jobs and departmental charters. If the company is to be competitive, the organization must run like a clock; every function is expected to mesh with the others, like so many cogs in a series of gears. This is possible only when everyone knows his or her place.

This organizational system, which our business grandfathers and grandmothers thought of as integration, is at the heart of many of our problems in today's large enterprises. When each of the functions is preoccupied with hanging on to its narrowly defined charter and looking out for its own self-interest, it is not surprising that ideas fall through the cracks or drown in a sea of politics. Managers retreat into their foxholes, protected by barbed wire (Figure 9.2).

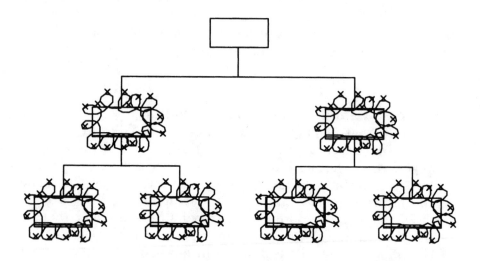

Figure 9.2 **Foxhole management**

Large organizations need some division of responsibility, of course, but the lines between functions should not represent unscalable walls. We will need to think of the areas as much more blurred and fuzzy, and indeed overlapping. Instead of treating marketing, research and development, finance, engineering, manufacturing, process control, service, human resources, and MIS as little empires unto themselves, we must realize that there is substantial overlap in their concerns. Each of the functions is really a resource center for the entire enterprise.

Separation of Ownership and Management

The industrial era is characterized by advances not only in technology but also in legal doctrine. The interplay of the two is critical. The corporation has evolved over the last few centuries. It was established in English law at least as early as the fourteenth century, when it applied primarily to religious bodies, towns, and guilds, both craft and mercantile.

Gradually the legal principles of the corporation were defined: it could hold property, sue and be sued, and endure beyond the lives of its members. The first corporations were established by grant from the king. In many ways, they served as a device by which royal power was both administered and expanded. These early corporations were often granted monopoly rights to a particular area or economic field of activity.

In the sixteenth and seventeenth centuries, the corporate concept was expanded to allow for joint stock trading. This made it possible to concentrate capital for the economic expansion of the corporation and added a new dimension to the purpose and role of the corporation.

Whereas the charters of the early corporations allowed private persons to serve public purposes, nineteenth-century charters became instruments by which private groups used the corporation for their own interests. When some of these interests became excessive, legislation such as the Sherman Antitrust Law of 1890 began to set limits on them.

With the growth of the modern corporation, especially in the latter part of the last century, there arose the industrial bureaucracy, characterized by its hierarchy of functions and authority. Management was professionalized and there was a proliferation of written rules, orders, and record keeping.[7] Some corporations, striving to integrate mass production with mass distribution systems, found that they needed well-defined areas of responsibility and well-defined procedures to coordinate their diverse activities.

The bureaucracy, the organizational chart, the departmental charters, and the job descriptions were the integrating structures of these large corporations.[8]

Thus proprietorships of the early industrial revolution gave way to the steep hierarchies of the late industrial era. Capital could now be concentrated and expended to extend the power of the enterprise. Accountability could be maintained through the structure of the hierarchy.

Direct involvement of the owners lessened. As professional managers took responsibility for the daily affairs of the corporation and ownership was diffused, the influence of the stockholders receded. The board of directors, representing the owners, was not involved in the daily activities of the corporation in the same way in which the proprietor had been.

The modern corporation does not have the same types of checks and balances built into its structure that the U.S. Constitution has built into the structure of government. Some scholars have bemoaned the fact that the corporation does not maintain the democratic traditions that we expect in the political arena. But many others admire the corporation because it can quickly take decisive action. This has been important in developing the goods and services that have contributed to our rising standard of living.

Even so, many now worry that the corporation is not responsive enough to rapid changes in the marketplace. To compete in a global economy, companies need shorter product life cycles, concurrent engineering, greater cross-functional coordination, and external coordination with suppliers and distribution channels.

The bureaucracy, essential in the era of mass production, is now getting in the way in the era of "mass customization," to use Stanley Davis's term.[9] Mass customization requires that functions work together closely so that 20 percent of a core product can be redesigned to meet different customer expectations.

The classic integration of the vertically defined corporation is not the integration that we are seeking today, which involves putting the diverse parts of the corporation in touch with one another so that products and processes can be developed in parallel rather than in sequence. Boards of directors should understand that their responsibility is more than fiduciary, and should challenge top management to break down the artificial boundaries between functions. Some chief executives, like Jack Welch of General Electric, have already taken steps to remove bureaucratic cholesterol by "delayering" their corporations and moving toward flatter network organizations.[10]

In short, as proprietorships shifted to corporations and bureaucratic management began to dominate the steep hierarchy, the seeds of inflexibility were sown. This inflexibility has been amplified by separating thinking and doing.

Separation of Thinking and Doing

Frederick Winslow Taylor, in recounting the origin of scientific management before a special congressional committee in 1903, told of having gone to work at Midvale Steel Works in 1878. As a lathe operator, he participated in limiting output to about one-third of what it might have been, which was the custom of the time. This "soldiering," under the piecework system, allowed operators to restrict the flow of work.[11]

Later, after his promotion to "gang boss" in this machine shop at Midvale, the workers asked him not to be a "piece-work hog." He explained that as an operator, he had not broken a single rate set by the group but that, as a supervisor, he intended to get more work out of them.

Taylor's firsthand experience in the machine shop convinced him that it was necessary to gain control of the production process. To this end, he believed that scientific data had to be used to separate planning and doing:

> Thus all of the planning which under the old system was done by the workman, as a result of his personal experience, must by necessity under the new system be done by the management in accordance with the laws of science. . . . It is also clear that in most cases one type of man is needed to plan ahead and an entirely different type to execute the work.[12]

Taylor considered the most prominent single element in modern scientific management to be the "task." He and his colleagues, Frank and Lillian Gilbreth, envisioned the tasks of every worker being fully planned out by management at least one day in advance. The planning office was to provide complete written instructions as to what was to be done, how it would be done, and exactly how much time was to be allowed for each task. If the worker fulfilled the instructions within the allotted time, he or she would receive a bonus of from 30 to 100 percent of the base pay.

Taylor believed that under this new system the workers would "grow happier and more prosperous, instead of being overworked." But to achieve the separation of thinking and doing, a "mental revolution" would be necessary. "Both sides [management and labor] must recognize as essential the substitution of exact scientific investigation and knowledge for the old individual judgment or opinion . . . in all matters relating to the work done in the establishment."[13]

Robert Reich sums up Taylor's contribution: "This separation of thinkers from doers was the apogee of specialization: Planning was to be distinct from execution, brain distinct from brawn, head from hand, white collar from blue collar."[14] The separation of thinking and doing was a natural outcome of Taylor's desire to increase specialization through simplification of individual tasks, to use predetermined rules to coordinate these tasks, and to monitor and control performance. Each level of the organization had its planning assignment.

Although they were resisted at first, Taylor's principles spread throughout American industry following World War I, then were accepted in Europe and even in the Soviet Union, where Lenin heartily embraced them. Rules and plans multiplied within every large organization. Top management was responsible for the strategic plans of the enterprise. Middle management formulated the operating rules, and standard operating procedures were established for the lower levels.

Taylor's approach was, in effect, an extension of the principles established by Smith and Babbage. Taylor believed he was establishing a scientific foundation for the industrial revolution. His approach made sense in the drive toward large-scale mass production, especially when companies were assumed to be structured like machines. Just as every part of the machine had its function, so each department was to follow the sequential steps specified by the overall plans.

Thus industry developed a system of rigid job classifications, work rules, and narrowly defined departmental charters. Monitoring and control systems set up to ensure conformity to these plans, such as cost accounting, inventory control, and financial reporting, were supposed to give top management overall control of the system. Each person was assigned his or her area of responsibility, and lines of authority were clearly specified on the organizational chart.

While Taylor reinforced the thought of Adam Smith on the shop floor, it was Henri Fayol and a few others who articulated this same type of thinking for management.

One Person/One Boss

Henri Fayol, a Frenchman, rose to the position of managing director of a large coal mine, Comambault, in 1888. At that time, the firm was on the verge of bankruptcy. When he retired in 1918, it was in an extremely strong financial position. Fayol attributed the success of the firm to his system of management, which he described in *General and Industrial Management*, published in 1916 and translated into English in 1929.[15]

Fayol identified five components of management: planning, organizing, commanding, coordinating, and controlling. Although he and Taylor developed their ideas independently, they reflect a remarkable similarity of spirit. In his work, Fayol emphasized division of responsibilities (leading to specialization of functions), authority of position (boxes), unity of command (one person/one boss, where each person reports to only one boss), and the scalar chain (the gangplank principle with the lines on an organizational chart indicating the chain of command).

Clearly, the underlying notion was that the chain of command would be the mechanism of integration within the enterprise. With highly specialized roles tied together by the chain of command, each role and function could be planned, organized, coordinated, and controlled. Communications would go through prescribed channels, people would perform and be evaluated on their narrowly defined tasks, and authoritative leadership would be the norm.

Other authors of the era reinforced these same ideas. In 1937 Lyndall Urwick wrote the following:

The considerations which appear of greatest importance were that there should be clear lines of authority running from the top into every corner of the undertaking and that the responsibility of subordinates exercising delegated authority should be precisely defined.[16]

Undoubtedly, Urwick was reflecting his experience in the British army during World War I as much as his experience as a manager in a chocolate candy company in the 1920s.

Two American counterparts of these two Europeans were James Mooney, a vice president and director of General Motors, and Allan Reiley. Reflecting the same general line of thinking as Fayol's and anticipating Urwick's approach, Mooney and Reiley wrote:

The subordinate is always responsible to his immediate superior for doing his job. The superior remains responsible for getting it done, and this same relationship, based on coordinated responsibility, is reported up to the top leader, whose authority makes him responsible for the whole.[17]

These three writers were in agreement that specialization and departmentalization were essential and that the chain of command was capable of integrating the various activities. As Paul Lawrence and Jay Lorsch point out, these ideas of authority were implicit in the legal definition of the corporation: "They were rooted in the traditional concept of the master-servant relationship, which had been carried over to the employer-employee relationship."[18]

The influence of Fayol, Urwick, and Mooney is evident in most enterprises. The concept of the chain of command and the idea that each person should have only one boss seem bred into us. Yet those who work within this model have an uncomfortable sense of a gap between theory and real life: the miscommunication, the politics, the "back-stabbing," and the cracks through which information falls attest to fundamental problems. Somehow, in spite of it all, human nature and ingenuity often rise above the conditions to get the job done. As Jay Galbraith has noted, "Informal organization processes arise spontaneously and are the processes through which the organization accomplishes most of its work, despite the formally designed structure."[19]

There is a growing awareness that division of labor, functionalization, and specialization often lead to extreme fragmentation. Chester Barnard, in his 1938 classic *Functions of the Executive,* was one of the first to question the notions that were leading to organizational fragmentation.[20] For example, he explored the five bases upon which an organization can be specialized: (1) the place work is done, (2) the time it is done, (3) the people by whom it is done, (4) the things upon which it is done, and (5) the method or processes employed. He noted that on the surface, specialization seems straightforward, but when these factors are introduced, it becomes more complex.[21] For example, many companies continue to struggle with the competing interests of product lines, geographic responsibility, and industry orientation. To which aspect of this equation should one be more loyal?

Functionalization and specialization also seem to be getting in the way as companies try to build more flexibility into their operations. As more and more companies realize that they must compete in a world market, customer responsiveness becomes critical, not only to survive but also to build market share and profitability. These companies suffer from rigid work rules on the shop floor as well as from narrow-minded functional managers who are more interested in their own success than that of the enterprise.

Industry observers have taken issue with the shallowness and rigidity of the Smith/Taylor/Fayol bottleneck. In his work *Administrative Behavior,* Herbert Simon points out the ambiguities of the seemingly straightforward notions of work specialization.[22] Robert Reich observes that a more flexible system of production "cannot be simply grafted onto business organizations that are highly specialized for producing long runs of standard goods."[23] Peter Drucker teaches that "top management is a function and a responsibility rather than a rank and a privilege," as would be suggested by the steep hierarchy model. Moreover, he points out that "people are a resource rather than a cost," and "the purpose of a business is to create a customer."[24] And George Hess, a practical, hands-on manager, speaks of the "human disintegrated manufacturing" characteristic of so many of our steep hierarchies.[25]

In spite of their shortcomings, the conceptual principles underlying the steep hierarchy seem to be anchored in concrete. They have withstood the assaults of Douglas McGregor's classic work on Theory X and Y, *The Human Side of Enterprise,* published almost thirty years ago,[26] as well as those of more recent authors such as Robert Hayes and Steven Wheelwright, Tom Peters, and Stanley Davis.

The irony is that technological developments may themselves force more profound organizational changes than all of the theorists combined. For example, the conventional wisdom has been that computers will enhance the overall efficiency of steep hierarchies. It should be clear by now that simply computerizing steep hierarchies leads to a spaghetti-like mess of interfaced systems: inflexible and incompatible.

As time and timing, particularly time-to-market and market timing, become the factors that distinguish the market leaders, the need to put people and processes in touch in dynamic ways is ever more pressing. Networking can help facilitate this process of communication, but unfortunately we are still seeking the magic solution or the major innovation that can do our work for us. We are still under the spell of the promise of automation.

Automation

The concept of automation has a long history. The early Greeks, seeking freedom from the routine toil and drudgery of labor, conceived of devices that might take over certain tasks. The word *automation* is derived from the Greek word *automatos*, meaning "self-acting." It refers to an apparatus, process, or system that is capable of operating by itself in an unassisted manner.

Aristotle, in *Politics*, foresaw an automated shuttle and harp capable of working or playing at a spoken command or even in anticipation:

> There is only one condition on which we can imagine managers not needing subordinates, and masters not needing slaves. This condition would be that each [inanimate] instrument could do its own work, at the word of command or by intelligent anticipation, like the statues of Daedalus or the tripods made by Hephaestus, of which Homer relates that, of their own motion, they entered the conclave of Gods on Olympus, as if a shuttle should weave of itself, and a plectrum should do its own harp-playing.[27]

Today, Aristotle's vision is being realized. Engineering drawings are transformed into post-processed tool paths and sent out over distributed numerical control (DNC) systems directly to the machining centers. Some flexible manufacturing systems (FMS) are close to being instruments that can do their own work, like the statues of Daedalus. They are backed up by other systems that can help schedule processes and products. Given these developments, can we expect the continuation of this process until all of manufacturing is totally automated? Doesn't this make it easy to equate automation and CIM, with CIM being the total connection of all automated activities?

Some authors, such as Teicholz and Orr, have chosen to define CIM as if it were a natural continuation of the automationist tradition:

> *Computer-integrated manufacturing (CIM) is the term used to describe the complete automation of the factory, with all processes functioning under computer control and only digital information tying them together. In CIM, the need for paper is eliminated, and so also are most human jobs. CIM is the ostensible evolutionary outcome of computer-aided design and drafting and computer-aided manufacturing (CADD/CAM).*

> *Why is CIM desirable? Because it reduces the human component of manufacturing and thereby relieves the process of its most expensive and error-prone ingredient...*[28]

This definition is an excellent example of the automationist point of view taken to its logical conclusion. It implies that the enemy is the human element, because it is "error-prone." Paper and people, the two variables that do not lend themselves to consistency and predictability, will be removed by CIM. But what is the underlying assumption of this definition? It is routine work. In the Teicholz and Orr conceptualization of CIM, routine processes are handled by hardware and software, not people.

Also implicit in this definition is a focus on the factory floor, where the most direct labor takes place. But what about the interaction between marketing and engineering? Is it outside the scope of CIM? It is probably excluded in Teicholz and Orr's definition. Certainly their choice of topics in the *Computer Integrated*

Manufacturing Handbook shows a clear focus on engineering and manufacturing.

Is there a place in CIM for the other functions, such as marketing, sales, finance, and service? Are the people there also to be replaced by automation because they are "error-prone"? It may seem so, but there is more to the story. It is one thing for Aristotle to envision the automated shuttle; it is another to bring it about throughout all functions in an organization. We are clearly not anywhere near there yet. Aristotle envisioned an automation in which managers will not need subordinates and masters will not need slaves.

Two of Aristotle's ideas have particularly influenced the way we interact with one another. The first is the *master-servant* relationship; the second deals with the ancients' disdain for labor or work. The master-servant principle is embodied in our organizations and in labor laws concerning agency and ownership. This idea is most clearly manifested in the notion of employer-employee, a modern term for the old master-servant idea. This notion assumes that the master or employer has the right to be arbitrary, to decide without consulting the servant or employee. There is a lot of precedent and legal doctrine surrounding management prerogatives that are embodied in labor-management contracts and laws.

A disdain for labor and work (these terms are being used synonymously) was built into the Greek language. To them, work was a curse and nothing else. Their name for work, *ponos*, has the same root as the Latin *poena*, meaning "sorrow." For the Greeks, *ponos* was colored with the same sense of a burdensome task that we feel in the words *fatigue* and *travail*. Hesiod defined happiness as a life free from work. According to Homer, the gods hated humankind and out of spite condemned men and women to a life of toil. The Greeks deplored the mechanical arts as brutalizing the mind and making it unfit to think about truth. Even free artisans and craftsmen were scorned as hardly better than slaves. Such intolerance was natural in a society where most heavy labor was done by slaves.[29]

The old Western prejudices remain in assumptions about job design, training, authority, and responsibility. People still believe that the higher a person is in the hierarchy, the more important he or she is. Often those professionals and workers who add the most value to the product are the least valued in the organization. Even though direct labor costs now constitute only 2 to 15 percent of total costs, the drive to automate persists.

Several tentative conclusions can be reached at this point. First, automation is one way to deal with the negative connotations of work and labor as toil. Laborers are not expected to be thinkers; they do not have the leisure. Therefore, they have to be trained and closely supervised, or so we are taught by the tradition carried on by Charles Babbage, Frederick Winslow Taylor, and others. When Teicholz and Orr speak of labor as "error-prone," are they not reinforcing this centuries-old prejudice?

Second, the thinking behind the master-servant model also assumes that the former does the thinking and the latter the doing. Why should we ask labor or even some professionals their opinion about what is going on? Are they not supposed to do only what they were trained to do? This might have made sense in Taylor's era, which was characterized by routine production processes. But it makes less sense when companies are faced with the need to continually change and upgrade their technologies, forge closer links with their suppliers and customers, manage for quality and excellence, and deal with shorter product cycles.

Two consequences result from this prejudice against labor and from the master-servant model: (1) middle-level professionals and labor are not taken seriously as thinkers, and (2) professionals and middle managers are to be replaced if possible with automation so their "error-proneness" does not muck up the works.

This line of reasoning, in turn, leads to two fundamental problems:

1. We fail to listen to and benefit from the insights, knowledge, and visions of those who are actually doing the work.

2. Automation often reduces the flexibility of the organization, especially at a time when flexibility is most needed.

Automation has an important role to play, especially in addressing routine tasks, but there is a growing shift toward nonroutine activities, where teams of professionals and managers must be supported, not eliminated.

Aristotle's concept of automation has continued to evolve into the industrial era's "machine model," in which all parts of the organization mesh like clockwork gears.

As our thinking evolved, we first spoke of hard automation, then soft automation, and now CIM, the supposed "paperless and peopleless factory." Figure 9.3 illustrates this evolution.

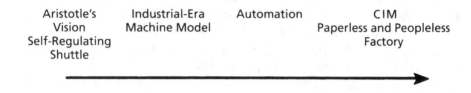

| Aristotle's Vision Self-Regulating Shuttle | Industrial-Era Machine Model | Automation | CIM Paperless and Peopleless Factory |

Figure 9.3 **Automationist's linear view of CIM**

The problem with this linear thinking is that it misses the critical dimension of integration. The automationists are doing us a disservice by equating total automation with CIM, because CIM is something qualitatively different from a paperless and peopleless factory. It makes more sense to think of CIM and CIE as a partnership between people and technology.

In the CIM literature there is tension and a great deal of uncertainty as to whether CIM is heading toward the paperless and peopleless enterprise, or whether integration, assisted by the computer and networking, will enable people to work together. In most manufacturing establishments, the direct labor base is shrinking, as are management ranks. Many companies that once maintained eight to fifteen levels of management now find that they can operate with four to six levels. Our enterprises of the future will produce more with fewer people, but each person will be more valuable. Since there is always room for new and dynamic companies, new employment opportunities will replace the jobs that fall to automation.

Automation and CIM

To be sure, a lot of money has been spent on industrial automation, often with success. Flexible manufacturing systems are proving their worth in a good many installations. The slash is coming out of CAD/CAM, as engineering departments send parts programs directly to numerical control (NC) equipment on the shop floor and as they learn the rules of design for assembly (DFA). Bar coding is spreading. Companies are finally obtaining the training required for successful MRP II efforts. In the service sector, airlines are making money from their computer-based reservation systems, banks are extending their automated teller machines, and distributors are putting terminals on their customers' premises.

The picture is anything but black and white. The landscape is a patchwork quilt of successes together with numerous unpublicized failures. With these general successes, is it not a matter of time before interfacing becomes integration? Yes and no. Third- and fourth-generation computers will be used long into the future, even as fifth-generation computers become more commercially viable. These successes represent isolated accomplishments within the hierarchy rather than true steps toward integration. We can expect the old ways of organization to persist well into the next century.

Given the hold that the conceptual principles of the early and late industrial era still have on our thinking, it is not surprising that we should want to computerize and network our steep hierarchies. However, although computers and networking may be flexible, there is an inherent inflexibility in the thinking underlying steep hierarchies, and this is a significant source of the problem.

Bill Lawrence, plant manager of the Texas Instruments facility in Sherman, Texas, remarked during an Automation Forum meeting that he regretted investing $3 million in a state-of-the-art computerized high-bay storage facility.[30] Even though it provided great flexibility to move work in process in and out, it was of less value as the company moved to a Just-in-Time approach. He now wishes that that money could be available to invest in the training and education of his plant personnel.

In 1987, Lawrence's facility received the prestigious LEAD Award (Leadership and Excellence in the Application and Development of CIM) from the Computer and Automated Systems Association of the Society of Manufacturing Engineers, in part because of the human climate of openness and trust that he created. Certainly he was trying to break out of the attitudes of the industrial era, although the web of capital investment decisions made over the years did not make it easy. In many ways, Lawrence's values and approach are unique. Most managers are still "CIMizing" their steep hierarchies.

This trend can be seen in the "reference model" being developed by a wide variety of groups in the United States, Europe, and Japan. The Factory Automation System of Computer Aided Manufacturing-International (CAM-I); the U.S. Air Force's Factory of the Future project; the Purdue Workshop's Reference Model for CIM; the International Standards Organization's Technical Committee 184, Working Group 5's model; the National Institute of Standards and Technology's Automated Manufacturing Research Facility; and even the European CIM/Open Systems Architecture model all, in their own ways, focus on interconnecting the technologies of various levels of the organization.

The working notion is that of hierarchical control. Even though the structures being modeled are not hierarchical, this approach tends to cast them in a hierarchical mindset (Figure 9.4).

The two key words related to this structure are *hierarchical* and *control*. The model presupposes the steep hierarchy and assumes that the key concept is control, with orders coming down from the top and information filtering up, much as they have done for the past hundred years in the manual mode.

Many people are working on standards so that there will be well-defined protocol between levels, and so that equipment from different vendors will fit into one structure. Industry's search for more open standards to allow for interoperability, has given a strong boost to UNIX, Manufacturing Automation Protocol (MAP), Technical and Office Protocol (TOP), Initial Graphics Exchange Specification (IGES), Product Data Exchange Specification (PDES), Electronic Design Interchange Format (EDIF), various graphic interchange standards, and X/Open. These efforts will continue to grow in importance as connectivity and interoperability become central issues.

Integration: An Evolving Concept

Computer-integrated manufacturing is a marvelously vague concept that defies easy definition. The father of CIM, Joe Harrington,

Levels:

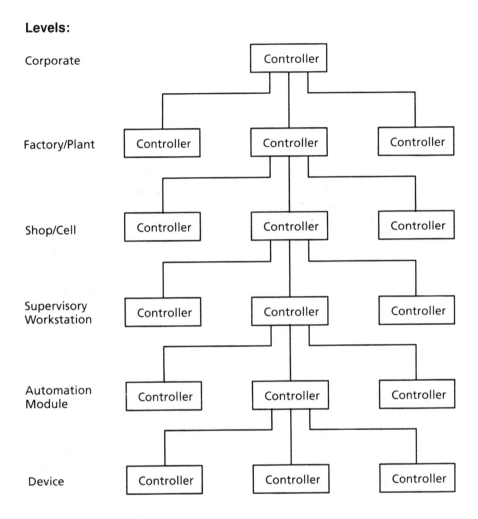

Figure 9.4 **Typical hierarchical control system**

Jr., who coined the term in 1973, studied the way in which computer applications were beginning to penetrate the engineering and operations functions of manufacturing organizations. He realized that a good number of the major manufacturing functions were "potentially susceptible to computer control."[31] He also recognized the human impact of CIM, stating that "the functions of management at all levels will undergo a major change."[32]

Ten years later, by the time Harrington wrote his second book, *Understanding the Manufacturing Process*,[33] he had broadened his concept of CIM to include the entire manufacturing company. He considered manufacturing a "monolithic function." This second book discussed how the functions could interact as a seamless whole.

Harrington was helpful to Dennis Wisnosky and Dan Shunk in designing the U.S. Air Force's Integrated Computer Aided Manufacturing (ICAM) program in the mid-1970s, and their work, in turn, influenced Harrington's second book. The ICAM program was visionary in showing that a new approach was necessary to achieve integration in manufacturing firms. Wisnosky and Shunk developed a "wheel" to illustrate the architecture of their ICAM project and to show the various elements that had to work together (Figure 9.5). They were among the first to understand the web of interdependencies needed for integration. Their work represents the first major step in shifting the focus of manufacturing from a series of sequential operations to parallel processing. The ICAM program has spent over $100 million to develop tools, techniques, and processes to support manufacturing integration and has influenced the CIM project efforts of many companies.

The growing use of the word "architecture" is itself a recognition that various activities are interrelated and should be coordinated. Companies are now developing material architectures, information systems architectures, data architectures, and distribution architectures.

The Air Force's ICAM program recognizes the role of data as central to any integration effort. Data is to be common and shareable across functions. This concept still remains ahead of its time, because most major companies will not seriously begin to attack the data architecture challenge until well into the 1990s.

The ICAM program recognizes the need for ways to analyze and document the major activities performed within the manufacturing establishment. The Structured Analysis and Design Technique methodology, developed by Douglas Ross of Softech, was adapted for the ICAM program with his help.[35] It is called ICAM DEFinition methodology 0, or $IDEF_0$. The ICAM program also

Figure 9.5 **U.S. Air Force's ICAM architecture**[34]

recognizes the importance of being able to identify the key information items (data entities) that should be captured, architected, and managed in an integrated manner. This has led to the creation of ICAM DEFinition methodology 1 for data architectures (IDEF$_1$), with the support of Dr. Robert R. Brown of Hughes, Stewart Coleman, and Dan Appleton of DACOM.

The need to simulate events in time led to the development of a simulation language, called ICAM DEFinition 2, or IDEF$_2$, from work primarily done by Pritsker & Associates. These IDEF methodologies have found widespread use, especially in the aerospace industry; they are now spreading to other industries as companies work to integrate diverse functions.

In response to this challenge, the ICAM program and the National Institute of Standards and Technology (NIST, formerly the National Bureau of Standards) also initiated the Initial Graphics Exchange Specification (IGES), which uses a neutral file format to enable CAD drawings to be translated from one vendor's system to another's. Roger Nagel, then of the NBS, Philip Kennicott of General Electric, and Walt Braithwaite of Boeing provided the first version of IGES. IGES has proved to be extremely important in integrating information from dissimilar CAD systems, and has undergone continual improvements under the leadership of Brad Smith of NIST.

NIST has taken responsibility for the continued evolution of IGES and has added a new initiative, also inspired by Air Force work, called Product Data Exchange Specification (PDES). PDES is intended to be a more intelligent and structured file format that transmits not only graphic representations, but bills of material, forms and features, tolerances, test specifications, and the like. PDES is expected to grow into an internationally recognized standard called Standard for the Transfer and Exchange of Product model data (STEP) as part of the Department of Defense's Computer-aided Acquisition and Logistics Support system (CALS). CALS is now understood as "Commerce at Lightening Speed" because firms can interconnect electronically.

It is likely that the IGES and PDES efforts will become more significant as the Electronic Data Interchange (EDI) movement picks up speed. EDI, at this point, is primarily concerned with the ordering and invoicing cycles between companies and their suppliers, although its horizon is broadening fast. As experience is gained with EDI, there is a growing desire to include technical data interchange (TDI), which consists of product and process specifications like PDES, so that work can be bid on and managed between prime contractors and second- and third-tier suppliers. EDI and TDI are harbingers of the kinds of interorganizational integration challenges that loom on the horizon. They also illustrate how companies will communicate with one another based on their strategic alliances.

At about the same time that Harrington and the Air Force's ICAM staff were rethinking the intraorganizational elements of integration, John Hall was independently sketching out the first wheel for the Computer and Automated Systems Association (CASA) of the Society of Manufacturing Engineers (SME). This wheel has evolved from an engineering and operations perspective to one that involves the entire enterprise. The latest iteration of the CASA wheel[36] includes not only the engineering and manufacturing functions, but also marketing, finance, strategic planning, human resource management, and general management (Figure 9.6). It also recognizes the role of information resource management and communications (networking) along with common data.[37]

The CASA/SME CIM wheel is built around a focus on customers. It involves people and teamwork within the larger manufacturing context.

The ICAM and CASA wheels are significant in that they represent initial attempts to focus on the interaction among and between functions. John Hall has told me that as he was developing the CASA/SME wheel he was aware of the inadequacy of the traditional hierarchical organization to foster effective collaboration between functions.[38]

There is, however, a growing awareness that CIM is too limited a concept, especially with its emphasis on computers and manufacturing. More and more, there is a desire to take an enterprise perspective that includes a recognition of the important role people play. This is why the CASA wheel is now called the *enterprise wheel*. For many of the same reasons, Computer Aided Manufacturing-International (CAM-I) in Austin, Texas is supporting a working group attempting to define the outlines of computer integrative enterprises.

CIM and People

Where do people really fit into these models? In most of the reference models, there is almost no discussion of the human element. In a few there is an awareness that people have to be accounted for, but it is unclear how to do this. For example, the European ESPRIT CIM/OSA (European Strategic Program for Research and Development in Information Technology, Computer Integrated Manufacturing/Open Systems Architecture) project description booklet includes the following paragraph:

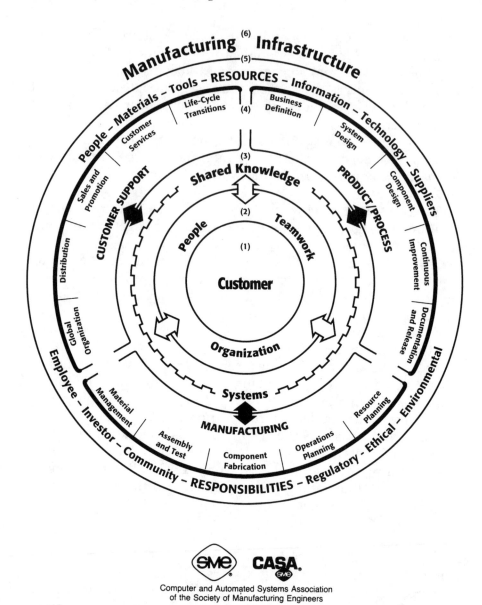

Figure 9.6 **CASA/SME CIM enterprise wheel (reprinted from the CASA/SME** *New Manufacturing Enterprise Wheel*, **with permission from the Society of Manufacturing Engineers, Dearborn, Michigan, copyright 1993, third edition.)**

From these short descriptions of the key points governing the CIM philosophy, it must be stressed that the human still plays a dominant role in its realization and execution. **The human operates and programs computers.**

S(He) is involved in the complicated information transfer structures (communication equipment, information definition, and data transfer software). It is unthinkable that the design, manufacturing and installation processes could be handled without human participation. The current state of the art is still such that people are the dominant factor in this total process. ***The point is that we had better make sure that in all our automation plans and strategies, the person is not forgotten.***[39] [Emphasis added.]

It is a step in the right direction when Kidd and others introduce the idea of human-centered CIM into the European CIM discussions. But is an admonition not to forget the human element adequate? Is technology destined to remove the human element? We may feel bad about this, so we remind ourselves that humans can at least operate and program computers. Luckily they will continue to have a role—at least for a while.

Joseph Harrington, Jr., saw CIM as a "control and communication structure." He felt that the competitive pressures of the marketplace would challenge companies to begin the process of reintegration:

The term computer-integrated manufacturing does not mean an automated factory. People are very much involved. New skills are required at the working level and, of course, in the supervision of the working level. New skills are certainly involved at the next higher level, the planning and control level. Additionally, the managerial function changes radically. At least half the present functions of top and middle managers are removed to the data processor and the true functions of managers—innovation; management of people, money, and legal affairs; the selection of objectives and policies—become full-time regimens for the manager. It appears, too, that the day of the specialist is passing. The managers of tomorrow must be multispecialists (not generalists). ***Thus, a new kind of manager at all levels is required.*** *The impact of computer-integrated* *manufacturing falls as heavily on the man as on the machine, a situation surely to be met with reluctance, if not outright opposition in many quarters.*[40] [Emphasis added.]

Harrington makes it clear that he does not see CIM as simply automating the factory, as proposed by Teicholz and Orr. He foresees more involvement of people in the process, with much of the machine-tending work done by the computer at the work cell, allowing professionals and managers to be more innovative and to concentrate on managing people, money, objectives, and policies. He advocates "multispecialists" in place of narrow specialists or even generalists. As CIM changes the way traditional functions work together, this recognition will play an even more important role. In the future, cross-functional team members will need to be multispecialists as they work in virtual teams in virtual organizations, in much the same spirit as that of the task-focused teams of Drucker.

Implicit in Harrington's concept of CIM is an awareness that the computer will assist with the routine, freeing laborers, professionals, and managers to focus on the nonroutine. In his own way Harrington agrees with Olsen and anticipates Tom Peters's idea of the need to thrive on chaos.[41]

Interestingly enough, a working group of the Czechoslovakian Academy of Sciences produced a study in 1968 stating that computers would help free people from their machine-tending chores, pushing them into more involvement with planning and innovation, functions that require a higher level of creativity.[42] One way to encourage this ability was to enhance the artistic, dramatic, and musical environment. The theater and concert house were seen as important sources of creative inspiration. If Harrington is right in stating that there is a qualitative shift in the roles of laborers, professionals, and managers, then the Czechoslovakian insight is right on target. In fact, if Harrington is right, we are going to have to rethink both our cultural and educational foundations. A stimulating and creative environment may well be a significant factor in encouraging innovation in the workplace.

Harrington's thesis concerning this shift in roles has been confirmed in studies done jointly by Nolan, Norton, and Company (NNC), an information systems consulting firm, and Digital Equipment Corporation. NNC reports that three-fourths of a typical company's resources are used to transform information about products and processes and one-fourth to transform raw materials into finished goods. Thus our approach to structure and organization has to be qualitatively different from that of the industrial era.[43]

Zuboff also understands the limits of the hierarchy in an "informated organization." She believes that if we cannot come to terms with the new conditions of work, we will find "knowledge and authority on a collision course."[44] Knowledge represents our ability to see information from different levels of abstraction, while authority represents the power of the position within the hierarchy.

This means that CIM is not a linear descendant of Aristotle's notion of automation. Instead, there is a discontinuity in the process. CIM and HCIM represent a new partnership between people and a computer-based, networked technology that enables professionals and managers to interact in new and more dynamic ways (see Figure 9.7).

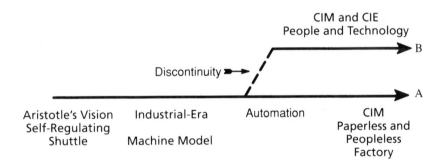

Figure 9.7 **Discontinuity in shift to CIM partnership**

In Figure 9.7, Teicholz and Orr represent track A, the automationist point of view. Harrington, on the other hand, recognized that CIM sets us on a new course, represented by track B. By implication, Harrington raises this question: how can we change the quality of interaction between functions so that there is more innovation and creativity? He highlights the idea of multispecialists—people with knowledge and skill in several areas—rather than specialists. He implies that there is a need for in-depth capabilities tempered with a broad understanding of the interplay of functions. In spite of Harrington's thoughts, the reminder in the ESPRIT CIM/OSA booklet, and Lawrence's remarks, the trend is to impose CIM on the steep hierarchy. It seems as though the automationist tradition has the upper hand—perhaps because of our preoccupation with technology. Thus the shift from CIM to CIE will require a fundamental rethinking of industrial-era conceptual principles. We need a new set of conceptual principles to support the emerging knowledge era, especially if we hope to achieve a break with the automationist mentality and free ourselves from the confinement of second-generation management. The next chapter explores the conceptual principles of the early knowledge era.

CHAPTER

10

KNOWLEDGE NETWORKING: ENHANCING ORGANIZATIONS

In spite of all the noble words in corporate annual reports about people being the corporation's most important asset, the industrial-era mentality tells us that it may be only a matter of time before our positions are automated out of existence. Moreover, many companies have used their business process re-engineering projects to thin out employees.

Reactions to this threat have taken many forms: participative management, job enlargement, job redesign, sociotechnical systems, employee involvement, and Quality of Work Life, and most recently a shift to the use of teams. These efforts have been an attempt to develop more meaningful task assignments. Their success has been limited, not because they are wrong in their vision and values, but because the task is so large and the vested interests are so well entrenched.

What is needed is a set of conceptual principles that redefines the central role of professionals—including managers and workers—as they work alone and on multiple teams within the company and between companies. These conceptual principles should help us use the 70 to 90 percent of the knowledge needed to run the enterprise, which is still in our heads. To leverage this valuable reservoir of knowledge, skill, and experience, we must create working conditions under which our learning, insights, vision, capabilities, and aspirations can be more effectively utilized. This chapter focuses on five principles, highlighted in Figure 10.1, from the perspective of the historical eras.

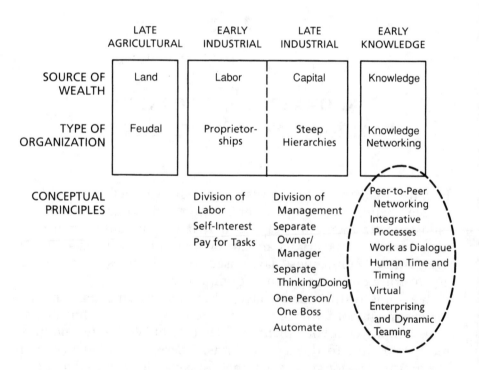

Historical Eras

	LATE AGRICULTURAL	EARLY INDUSTRIAL	LATE INDUSTRIAL	EARLY KNOWLEDGE
SOURCE OF WEALTH	Land	Labor	Capital	Knowledge
TYPE OF ORGANIZATION	Feudal	Proprietor-ships	Steep Hierarchies	Knowledge Networking
CONCEPTUAL PRINCIPLES		Division of Labor Self-Interest Pay for Tasks	Division of Management Separate Owner/Manager Separate Thinking/Doing One Person/One Boss Automate	Peer-to-Peer Networking Integrative Processes Work as Dialogue Human Time and Timing Virtual Enterprising and Dynamic Teaming

Figure 10.1 **Chapter focus: conceptual principles of the early knowledge era**

These conceptual principles are not new creations, but rather are reflections of an understanding of the fundamental nature of our humanness. In order to appreciate the significance of these principles, we must first look at the pressures being exerted on steep hierarchies from both business and technical sources.

Steep Hierarchies under Pressure

Recognizing the energy-sapping effects of top-heavy management, many corporations, such as General Electric, Eastman Chemical, and Ford, are "delayering" themselves and cutting management positions. Executives are learning to lead with fewer levels of management below them.

At the same time, companies are producing more with less direct labor because of better work methods, re-engineering, and automation. Depending on the industry, the typical cost of direct labor is now 2 to 15 percent of total costs. The trend toward a flatter hierarchy (Figure 10.2) is attributable not so much to automation as to business factors—the realization that our organizations are overstaffed and that layer upon layer of paper pushers and report expediters make the organization sluggish and unresponsive to the market.

What happens when we flatten the hierarchy? We get a little less of the same thing. Even though there are fewer levels of management, people still suppose that their box is sacred territory that must be defended at all costs. Organizational flattening treats only the symptoms; it does not fundamentally redefine relationships between people and functions in the organization. Functions still work sequentially, making decisions from fragmented perspectives.

Suppose, instead, we were to think of ourselves and our positions within the organization not as fixed little empires, but as resources available to others. If we were to see ourselves not as boxes but as nodes in a network, not as cogs in a gear but as knowledge contributors and decision points, our support of one another would increase dramatically.

To shift from rectangles to ovals in a drawing is one thing, but it is something quite different to emotionally and intellectually

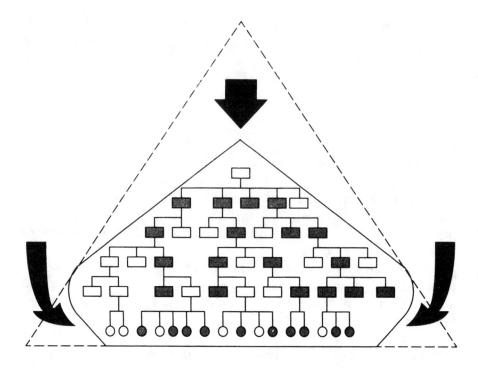

Figure 10.2 **Steep hierarchies under pressure**

accept the changes this implies. It is wrenching to give up the comfort of known job boundaries and established reporting relationships. When we first see ourselves as resources in a network of other people, we cannot help but feel vulnerable. Yet this vulnerability brings challenge and excitement to the work environment.

We are beginning to understand that it will take resources from many functions, working together, to distinguish and respond to opportunity patterns so that knowledge-era organizations will have the necessary market resiliency. Organizational learning and the ability to synthesize information are essential. Management must draw upon these multiple capabilities to perform tasks, much as a conductor draws on the instruments in an orchestra or a coach mentors a basketball team.

Figure 10.3 symbolizes this change by replacing the boxes with ovals. To be meaningful, a switch in attitudes and expectations is also needed. The boxes of the traditional hierarchy have come to represent the turf that is owned and controlled by the position. The ovals represent a capacity and knowledge resource that is available to join and team with others in order to deal with the multiple challenges of the enterprise. (I first wrote this before the article by C. K. Prahalad and Gary Hamel on core competencies came out.[1] They have contributed greatly to our understanding of the role of core capabilities and competencies.)

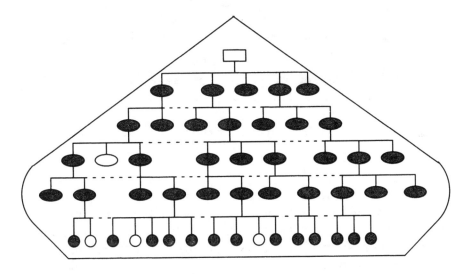

Figure 10.3 **Shift from boxes to people as resource centers in human networking enterprises**

In the network enterprise, each position, or oval, represents a person with capabilities, skills, and experience. Instead of mutually exclusive tasks (jobs) and departmental assignments (charters), enterprises blend the talents of different people around focused tasks to respond to real business opportunities (Figure 10.4). Thus individual talents, knowledge, experience, and aspirations become more important resources in network enterprises than they ever could be in steep hierarchies. (When I first wrote this I was thinking of teaming within companies. Now it is clear that much of our teaming of capabilities occurs among and between our suppliers, partners, and customers.)

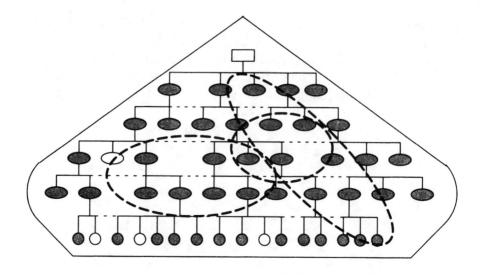

Figure 10.4 **Designating cross-functional virtual task teams**

Thanks, in part, to ready access to computer network infrastructures, companies are using more cross-functional task teams internally and externally. These teams may appear under many different names: project teams, concurrent engineering teams, competency teams, account teams, network teams, bid teams, task forces, and steering committees. The idea of using teams is not new. Alvin Toffler has been writing for years about "adhocracy," the use of short-term task forces,[2] but it has been hard for many executives to conceive of organizations with the randomness that an ad-hocracy suggests.

Instead of a random ad hoc approach, we need to structure an increasing amount of the enterprise's work around well-defined multiple cross-functional teams, even if executives may worry about maintaining focus and coordination within such a fluid organization. Nevertheless, we know we must experiment—because, as Leslie Berkes suggests, the pyramidal organizational structure is no longer working.[3]

How do we find cohesion and structure in a fluid and dynamic environment? One way is to understand the conceptual principles that can help us to lead and manage knowledge-era enterprises.

Conceptual Principles of the Early Knowledge Era

Although the exploration of knowledge-era principles will be new, what they recognize will not be. Was gravity created when Newton discovered it? Did the sun stop revolving around the earth when Copernicus proposed his heliocentric theory?

I suggest that there are five conceptual principles of the early knowledge era: (1) peer-to-peer knowledge networking, (2) the integrative process, (3) work as dialogue, (4) human time and timing, and (5) virtual enterprising and dynamic teaming. To understand these concepts, we will explore each theme individually, then look at their interrelationships. This is part of a reinterpretation process that we will need in order to work our way out of the constraining legacy of the industrial era.

Peer-to-Peer Knowledge Networking

Peer-to-peer knowledge networking has three aspects: technology, information, and people. The technology of peer-to-peer networking allows each node to communicate directly with every other node, without having to filter through a hierarchical arrangement. Peer-to-peer information assumes that people and applications have ready access wherever the information may be located. And peer-to-peer knowledge networking assumes that individuals have access to one another's knowledge wherever it may be in the enterprise. In all three instances, we have moved beyond the superior-subordinate attitude of industrial-era steep hierarchies.

In the early days of computing, different processors were expected to communicate hierarchically. With the development of minicomputers, the advantage of peer-to-peer computing became clear: any node can talk to any other node. All the major computer companies are now building this capability into their systems; this makes it simple to configure and reconfigure resources on the network.

Peer-to-peer information access is a major challenge. It is one thing to be able to connect computers on the network, but it is quite another to support interoperability between dissimilar operating systems. In addition, even though client-server computing is allowing us to reach any other node in a network with ease, we face major hurdles in interfacing multiple applications. Certainly as the technology has evolved over the last five years, networking within and between companies is becoming easier.

Over the years companies have developed hundreds of applications on different computers. As we network these computers, the natural tendency is to want to interface the applications as well, so that we can share common information. Unfortunately, applications written at different times have used different naming conventions. One of the biggest problems that we face is that various applications may use different words to mean the same thing, the same words to mean different things, or different shades of meaning for the same words.

The most significant change that peer-to-peer networking brings is in the way that people in the enterprise interact with one another. The superior-subordinate relationship of the steep hierarchy assumes that a higher level is an indication of superiority. It may indicate superiority in rank, but it does not guarantee superiority of knowledge.

If we can begin to envision the resources of the enterprise arranged in a large circle, or in multiple circles, as was discussed in Part 1, it will be easier to think of tapping into the resident knowledge, wherever it may reside, as we form multiple task-focusing teams. Each of the functions becomes a resource from which talented people can be drawn together. The experience at Eastman Chemical and the writings of Sally Helgesen should give added support to this change.

In the industrial era, as teams are formed, the members are sometimes told to "protect our department's interest." Moreover, members of the teams often compete with one another to show how clever they are. At times it may be necessary to have every department equally represented on megateams. These behaviors inhibit effective teamwork, because as team members put one another down, they become mired in the politics of the organization and do not actively contribute to the success of the project.

Suppose instead that we were told by our managers to do our best, that we really wanted to learn from one another, and that each team had only those resources needed to get the task done. The quality of work within and between teams would be greatly enhanced.

Peer-to-peer networking assumes that there will be teamwork of teams. Small, well-defined and well-staffed teams will meet with one another periodically to share their learning, insights, and challenges. We will cross-fertilize one another's efforts. We will develop a rhythm of meetings that allows us to work on the particular, without losing sight of the larger context. And as the team members work together and learn from one another, we will be refreshing and renewing our knowledge and visions. This is what we mean by dynamic teaming.

In order to fully appreciate the dynamic teaming process, we have found it necessary to distinguish between "teams" and the "teaming" process. Most people think they know all about teams because they have played on sports teams. Unfortunately, there is a major difference between most sports teams and dynamic business teaming.

In sports teams the rules are known, the roles predefined, and the task is to beat the other team. In dynamic teaming we evolve the rules as we go, the roles are fluid, and the task is to collaborate with other teams. James Carse has captured this distinction extremely well in his book *Finite and Infinite Games*.[4] Similarly, we can learn from Watterson's *Calvin and Hobbes*. "Calvin ball" has only one rule: the game cannot be played twice with the same set of rules. The genius of this insight is that in dynamic teaming we are focusing on co-creation among and between the members of the team and with other teams. There cannot be clear rules for creativity, because it lives at the intersection of the expected and the unexpected, just as laughter does, although the insights from previous games can be codified and serve as a resource to be drawn upon as needed.

Moreover, we must realize that the rules of the market and technology are continually changing, as Dan Burrus so eloquently points out in *Technotrends*.[5] Therefore, the minute we feel comfortable and smug in our companies is the time we should start worrying. At one time a computer maker could spend $50 million to build a board shop, yet as the technology has collapsed into silicon, well over a billion dollars is needed for a new semi-conductor plant. In essence, the rules of business are continually being rewritten and then rewritten again—Calvin ball in action.

Peer-to-peer knowledge networking allows us to pull people together to work cross-functionally on market opportunities, instead of parsing the various aspects of those opportunities into stiff and rigid steep hierarchies, as the dialogue in Part 1 indicates. This allows us to size up a problem's patterns and make this learning available to others in our company.

Peer-to-peer knowledge networking does not homogenize people into bland commonality. Instead, it sharpens our perceptions of one another's talents and abilities. We learn to value differences and to build upon each other's strengths. We become more important as individuals as we participate on multiple teams, because our knowledge and talents are sought by the other members. We learn to shift from a culture of devaluing to one of valuing in which we can seek out and build upon one another's competencies.

Our natural leadership abilities are challenged and nurtured when we are continually being asked to assume leadership or support others' leadership. Each team needs a talented project leader. Over time this role will rotate to different people. I may be the project leader on one team, while on another I actively support another's leadership.

New arrangements of local- and wide-area networks are making possible dynamic peer-to-peer collaboration between people, processes, and companies—within and between companies. Applications can be run through the network, putting the power of the mainframe on the desktop. Text and graphics can be shared in new ways. People can work interactively, passing information back and forth in an iterative manner while developing ideas, instead of becoming bogged down in turf warfare and in managing the sequential handoffs of paper-based systems.

Peer-to-peer networking assumes that as we network, we generate value based on our thinking, observing, knowledging, and envisioning. Managers, professionals, and employees are no longer cogs that must mesh together, as in a machine in a steep hierarchy—we are knowledge contributors and decision points, or nodes, within the network.

H. Chandler Stevens describes this shift to networking in a short poem:

I'd rather be a node in a network
Than a cog in the gear of a machine.
A node is involved with things to resolve,
While a cog must mesh with cogs in between.[6]

As we picture ourselves as nodes or decision points within the network, we will sense our own empowerment. Empowerment is not like carrying a credit card; it must come from within to be effective.

Peer-to-peer knowledge networking assumes that people are not superior or inferior; each has something of substance to add to the overall output. This assumption contradicts the Greek notion of the inferiority of human work. On the contrary, work brings excitement and challenge and is the basis of growth.

A peer-to-peer model of networking requires a different coordination strategy from that of the traditional hierarchical organization; otherwise, indecision will rule the day. As people make decisions in a networked environment, there has to be some commonality of context. We need to understand how our own activities are going to fit into a larger whole and how to draw upon common information resources—knowledge—so that we can see significant patterns, adding value through our own insights and wisdom. The work in holonics, fractals, and agility has brought more understanding to these processes.

Knowledge networking does not eliminate the hierarchy; it just recasts its role and function. Companies still need some levels of authority. There are times when decisive leadership from the top is necessary. But executives of the flatter hierarchy move away from our preoccupation with the prerogatives of decision making. Instead, we find we get better results when we actively listen to our teams, ask challenging questions, define the context for the teams, and build our resources.

We also need to be in touch with one another in meaningful ways so that we can deal with complexity and act decisively in support of the larger organization. This suggests that "being in touch" is more than just being able to reach another person on the network; instead, it implies that the integrative process is multidimensional and continuous. It is a process which helps put us in touch with ourselves and one another, our thoughts, feelings, capabilities, and aspirations. As we connect at a deeper level, we find the inspiration, insights, and courage to be bolder in our creative endeavors.

The Integrative Process

In a modern enterprise, people and processes are not set in concrete; they are virtual resources, available when called upon. Constant adjustments are necessary as the enterprise responds to ever-changing customer expectations, market conditions, government regulations, competitor activities, and supply strategies. In a fluid environment, as teams are configured and reconfigured, the challenge is to continually "reach out and touch" the thinking of others in order to identify and act upon significant patterns. This assumes that our organizations will indeed master the art of self-organization, self-teaming, and self-focus within the larger context of the opportunity.

In fact, seeing the significant patterns together as teams is the challenge of any enterprise. Too often, different departments see portions of a pattern and act as if they have seen the whole. Technical networking provides us with the connectivity across functions that we need in order to see, reflect upon, and act on these patterns together.

The integrative process requires us to be in touch with the key patterns inside and outside the enterprise. It involves perception, judgment, and the will to act: this is why the role of people is very important. The integrative process is not something that is fixed; it requires continual dynamic reconfiguring of ideas, people, processes, and resources, the process we call knowledging. The fractal metaphor helps us to better visualize this process.

Among the most critical ingredients of the integrative process are the knowledge and values that those in the enterprise accumulate over the years. This knowledge makes it possible to see, interpret, and act upon significant patterns. Unfortunately, this knowledge is woefully underutilized in most enterprises because of the internal logic of steep hierarchies, whose accounting and reward systems have no way to value it.

Traditional management strategies are out of place in a networked enterprise. They do not encourage workers and professionals to build learning capabilities or to develop the ability to see significant patterns and align resources rapidly.

This is why the use of the word "integrated" creates a false sense that one arrangement will serve for all time. Business ideas evolve, technologies evolve, capabilities evolve, and people grow in their understanding and knowledge, so it makes little sense to develop hard-and-fast walls between functions, operations, or people. To be successful we need to spend time getting to know the human capabilities, experiences, knowledge, and values of the others in the enterprise.

New developments in organizational development (OD) theory are aiding in this process. Instead of thinking that the task is to figure out a needed change, unfreeze the organization, institute the change, and then refreeze everything, OD now supports continuous change.[7]

What is important is not just the storage of bits and bytes on hard disks connected by networks; it is the knowledge of the people in the enterprise and our ability to bring this knowledge to the task of seeing, interpreting, and acting decisively on significant patterns. This is why we call our new age the early knowledge era, rather than the information era. In this era, work recaptures its natural meaning.

Work as Dialogue

What is work? We began our discussion of automation with the Greek attitude toward labor and work. This described not what work *is* but one culture's attitude toward it. In this section, a more fundamental examination of work itself is in order.[8]

Work is part of our everyday experience, yet it can be elusive in its meaning: we know what it is—until we are asked! Of course, it is exertion, what we get paid for, the result of our efforts, being in operation like a machine, and the application of energy to accomplish an altered state of affairs. But what is the essential character of work?

The answer to this challenging question is critical, because our attitudes toward work and its organization have shaped the context in which we perform every day. Does "Work is exertion" tell me what it is? Does "Work is what we get paid for"?

"Work is being in operation like a machine"? "Work is a measure of energy applied"? "Work is the result of the effort"? Only partially!

In the industrial era, there seem to be three notions that have shaped our thinking about work: (1) it is effort or travail, (2) it is being in operation like a machine, and (3) it is what we get paid for. Why should these three definitions predominate? As the industrial era began, Newtonian physics was still the rule, with its orderly universe operating like clockwork. As early as Descartes, the machine was the major reference model. People were fascinated by figuring out how the pieces fit together. They also had to content themselves with receiving compensation for giving up their time to work for someone else.

In the industrial context, these notions fit nicely with the idea of the division and subdivision of labor. Each activity was to fit into the larger whole like a cog in the gear of a machine. The natural task was to become expert at the routines so that the enterprise operated like a well-oiled machine.

No wonder the need to introduce bureaucracy and routine has been a major management challenge in the industrial era. Certainly the automationists have accepted these ideas and want to use CIM to perfect their vision.

The "physics" of organizations continues to rely more on the outdated notions of Newton than on the newer principles of Heisenberg and Einstein. Even though the rigor and determinism of Newtonian physics has given way to the indeterminacy of Heisenberg or the nonlinearity of the new physics of chaos, we are still trying to build into our manufacturing and service organizations the same mechanical routines. Margaret Wheatley's excellent book, *Leadership and the New Science*, explains this shift extremely well.[9]

Such experts as Drucker, Beer, Trist, Peters, Briggs, and Peat speak of the turbulence, the uncertainty, and the chaos of the environments in which our firms operate.[10] Nevertheless, we have not really understood the new physics from an organizational perspective. This is unfortunate, because it means that we continually misappropriate our technology and human resources, trying to arrange them in configurations that are inappropriate for the tasks at hand.

Human energy remains bottled up in organizational structures that allow little room for true human creativity. A new wave of management literature speaks of human empowerment: Waterman's *The Renewal Factor* and Kanter's *The Change Masters,* as well as a growing discussion on high-performance systems.[11] In Chapter 7 we covered other literature that speaks to this point.

Let us return to the question at hand: *What is work?*

When you and I work, we are involved in a *process* of doing something in time. We are engaging in a series of acts that have a pattern, in much the same way that a piece of music consists of a series of notes arranged in a particular pattern. The creations of the pattern become the *products* of the effort. Work then involves *processes* and *products* (Figure 10.5).[12]

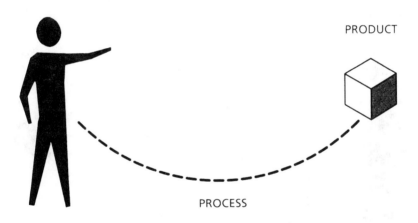

Figure 10.5 **Work involves process and product**

In the process of working, we are giving expression or form to our visions (the future which is in the now), enhanced by our knowledge (the past which flows with us). The quality of the process of giving expression is very much dependent upon our ability to listen to the themes being expressed and to respond accordingly. Our work is also dependent upon our ability to envision and actively sort out what we know (knowledging). In other words, our ability to listen (present), see (future), and remember (past) must play together in the process of work.

The product of the effort embodies the thoughts and ideas of the process. The result is the *expression*—literally, "pressing out." That which is inside us presses out. We give birth to new arrangements, new patterns, new conditions. When we see what we have done, we may be either inspired by its quality or depressed that it does not match our vision and knowledge of what it might have become.

We can see both the process by which we express ourselves and the product of that expression (Figure 10.6). As we see what we have done and how we have done it, we can choose to repeat the process or to improve and alter it, thereby altering the resulting product. We do this all the time. The process may be building, scheduling, writing, researching, coordinating, or arranging. The products may be widgets, schedules, reports, research findings, task team efforts, or meetings.

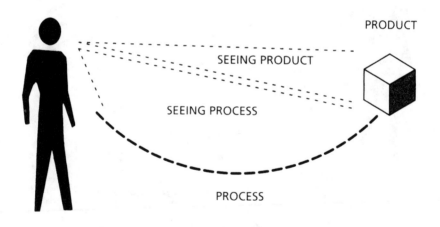

Figure 10.6 **"Seeing" the process and product**

Work has a more fundamental meaning than whether we get *paid* for our time, one of its classic definitions. There is human engagement and expression in work, wonder and uncertainty, and a striving to give expression. As we press out these ideas in ourselves, the excitement of discovery, exploration, and accomplishment seasons our work experience.

We grow as we are able to master a process and see the results of the effort embodied in the product.

The traditional concept of work in the industrial era has little understanding of this simple and natural process. Instead, people are expected to fit into a small portion of a larger process, a job. We are trained to do something and are told not to deviate from the established procedures. Our visions are considered unimportant and liable to get in the way. Our knowledge is of little real value. Instead, we are to put ourselves in a predetermined setting and perform our rote skills.

This system is based not on trust but on distrust. In fact, many of the activities in our industrial-era enterprises are there not to add value but to check and double-check whether people have been performing their assigned tasks. Distrust is a natural corollary of the division and subdivision of labor; it is built right into the fabric of our organizations and cannot be overcome by exhortations to be more trustful.

There is a significant difference between work in which we are engaged—listening, envisioning, and remembering—and work in which we are just doing what we are told. Most jobs in industrial-era companies are defined in ways that make it hard for both the worker and manager to see the entire process. Industrial-era jobs do not give people a clear understanding of the nature of the product. A significant part of the process and the product is locked into a black box, out of sight of the individual contributor (Figure 10.7).

Is it any wonder that workers take a short-sighted approach to the process and the product? Changes made to their part of the process may not be compatible with other portions of the process, with downstream consequences that surprise everyone. As a result, process and product configuration management is a difficult and thankless task in many organizations.

Work then is an activity involving a process of expression and an evolving product. The existence of a product sets up an anticipation pattern of how the product may vary in the future. Once something is created, we wonder how it may be improved. The product is not an isolated entity but the statement of an effort at a particular point in time. It is, in essence, an invitation to *dialogue*.

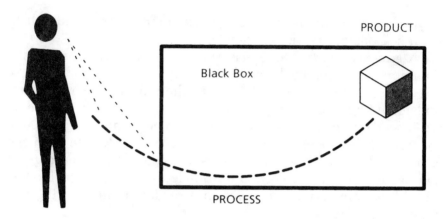

Figure 10.7 **Portion of process and product hidden**

For example, companies may produce a product, then vary it in subsequent product offerings. If the product hits a responsive chord, there is a sense of excitement as new versions are brought to market. For example, Lotus set an expectation pattern in motion with Lotus Notes; the product has grown since then through additional iterations.

What is the value of a well-executed process? What is the value of a well-designed product? Both can bring satisfaction, recognition, and a completeness to the effort that both challenges and inspires. This is also part of the dialogue.

In producing something, from a musical score to a bookshelf, we see the process and the product not in isolation but within the larger horizon of our visions and knowledge. Our mastery of the process and the resulting product inspire us to want to use our skills, vision, and knowledge to bring out variations on the product by varying our techniques. This is really a *self-dialogue,* combining vision and knowledge in a dialogue with ourselves and others. When we are engaged in a process that is creative, innovative, or experimental, what we are learning becomes available for future efforts. As we master the process, we find our vision broadened and we are encouraged to create bolder visions (Figure 10.8).

Notice the integrative process involved in work. We need to be dynamically in *touch* with our envisioning and knowledging as the

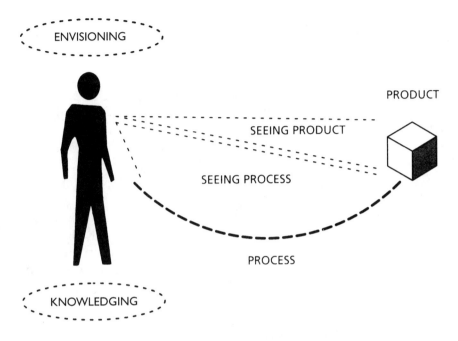

Figure 10.8 **Work as dialogue: using envisioning and knowledging to shape process and product**

product is being developed. Before we can make something, we envision what is to be made. This vision is of a future state of affairs, but it is very much here in the present as it guides us in our projects.

A vision without knowledge is unrealizable. Knowledge gained from past study, training, and experiences becomes a resource that stays with us. Our visions and our knowledge come from two sources: (1) our own experiences, training, and studies; and (2) the collected experiences and knowledge of the culture of which we are a part, whether they were gained at home, in school, or through the media. As we reach out and share experience, knowledge, and visions with one another, we are involved in human networking. This is more than simply connectivity between people; in a concrete sense it involves our ability to interrelate our vision and knowledge in a creative manner.

Networking is not only an individual process; it also involves the person in a community of others. Too often engineers will get fancy in a new design rather than using listed parts and techniques. This creativity can unnecessarily add to inventory and introduce complexity into the manufacturing process. Engineers should stay in touch with the material and manufacturing constraints of their organization. This is the dynamic side of the integrative process, of being in touch with not only one's own vision and knowledge, but also with the vision and knowledge of the larger organization, which may be articulated in its strategic plans, budgets, market analyses, engineering standards, and operating norms.

Work involves not just one process and one product, but a continual process of producing many products and variations on these products. Feedback from the process is important in order to improve it; feedback from the use of the product will add knowledge and vision as the next version is developed and produced.

Work is an iterative process, never conducted in a vacuum. Instead, it is very much a creative process when it is viewed as a whole. When work's wholeness is stripped away, as it is in so many industrial-era jobs, the worker or professional feels like a prisoner in the present, without the right to have a vision or recognition for the knowledge that he or she has accumulated over the years.

Notice the creative elements in the work process. As we make, build, write, or coordinate, something is created. We are also adding to our vision and knowledge. We create in our minds the possibility that we can do something similar to what someone else may have produced. This becomes part of our vision and adds to each individual's knowledge.

Work is a *transitive* verb: we make something.

Work can also be a *reflexive* verb: we make ourselves as we work. We make ourselves as individuals and we make our companies as organizations. We also participate in the creation of one another's companies as we collaborate on joint projects.

Our envisioning and knowledging are being enriched. Our work is also creative for others because it challenges or adds to their visions and knowledge.

In its essence, work is a *form-bestowing activity*.[13] It empowers. It not only forms products, it also informs the worker (envisioning and knowledging) and informs or inspires others (their envisioning and knowledging). The actual product produced is only one aspect of the overall work effort (Figure 10.9).

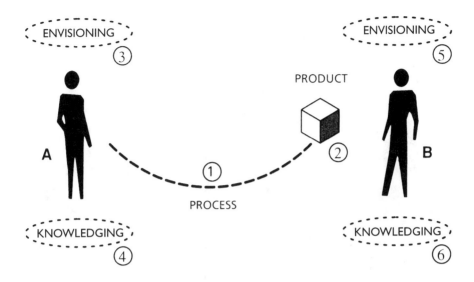

Figure 10.9 **Work as dialogue with self and others**

As shown in Figure 10.9, work is a multifaceted activity. We (A) are producing not just one item but six. We are involved in a process (1) that results in a product (2). We see the process and product, and it inspires our vision (3) and adds to our knowledge (4). Another person (B) also sees what was done and the resulting product, which adds a dimension to this person's envisioning (5) and knowledging (6).

We (A) gain recognition not only through seeing our own process and product, but through the process and product being seen by the other person (B). We may discuss the process and the product with someone else and together see aspects that neither of us had seen individually. We learn together and add further information to our knowledge. This is work as dialogue.

Suppose we are craftspeople who have mastered an entire process. What happens if this process is divided into a number of steps (Figure 10.10), as in Adam Smith's pin-making factory? The worker (A) loses an overview of the entire process. The product is also hidden by the fragmentation in the process. Work ceases to be a dialogue; instead it becomes drudgery.

There is no excitement, no wonder. There is nothing that inspires people's vision or adds to their knowledge. And there is no

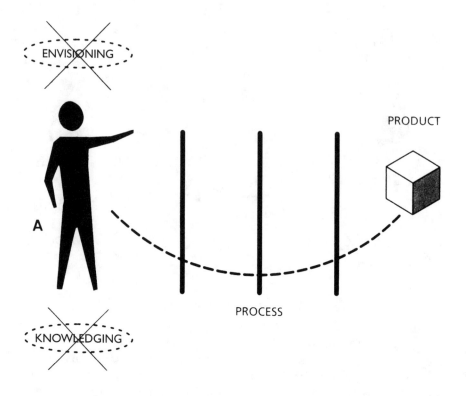

Figure 10.10 **Production process cut into tiny steps**

meaningful recognition, because it is hard to see what any individual has contributed creatively.

In fact, what is desired in this system is not creativity, but conformity to the established procedures. Supervision will be needed to make sure that these people conform to the company's procedures and goals. Workers are told to leave their envisioning and knowledging capabilities at home and just follow the process instructions. These people are out of touch with the *wholeness* of the operation. They are no longer involved in an integrative process but in a fraction of a process.

The whole strategy of the industrial era has been to fragment the work process so that few can see the overall process. Time and motion studies, the industrial engineer, and work standards are concrete embodiments of this approach, this fragmentation with which we are presently struggling as we seek to empower one another. Little wonder that under these conditions people feel "stupefied," to use Adam Smith's word. This is the Achilles' heel of the industrial era, its tragic flaw.

Seeing and responding to patterns is the process of dialogue. Work, in fact, is a continual dialogue with a vision of what is to be made, knowledge of how to make it, and the creative results of a combination of the two in active engagement with the elements of the mind and nature. Work cannot be understood apart from a fresh look at the nature of human time.

Human Time[14] and Timing

As the industrial era progressed, timing increased in importance. The time clock, the stopwatch, the run time of machines, and the timing of activities became ever more important.

Ten to thirty years ago, the concern was cost: get cost out of the product. Today time is the concern: get time out of the product. Timing is even more critical today in terms of time-to-market, windows of opportunity, and cycle time. The automobile companies want to bring new cars to the market in one to three years instead of the historical four to six years. Cycle times in computers are constantly decreasing: the CPM systems of the 1970s ran at 4.7 MHz, while newer workstations run at 90 to 300 MHz.

With our preoccupation with clock time, we have overlooked a dimension of time that is equally critical—human time. Human time is an essential part of what it is to be human. Clock time assumes a past, present, and future, each separate from one another. Human time assumes that the past and future are integral to the present. There is a wholeness of time from the human perspective. Meaning is discovered. Yet clock time has given us the impression that there is a separation between our past and future.

Clock time is omnipresent. It is easy to think about. It is obvious. It is everywhere we look. We have assumed that clock time is the only type of time that there is. This is a fatal mistake. Perhaps in this we have also been captive to "either/or" thinking.

It is not surprising that the industrial era and the modern timepiece have grown together. In any enterprise, events must be synchronized. When one activity depends on another, proper coordination is essential. Precision has become even more critical in the computer world, where activities have to be timed to the microsecond. In terms of time as synchronization, the clock is essential to coordinate a large variety of activities. It lets us divide events into several categories—those that come first, second, and so forth. Would the division and subdivision of labor be possible without it? Hardly. But what is clock time?

Is not clock time a series of moments? Past, present, future: these are the three parts of time. But how do they relate?

We think of clock time in spatial terms. This simple model has shaped our thinking in a more profound manner than most of us realize. It leads to the following assumptions:

*The **past** is left behind. There is physical separation.*

*The **future** has not yet arrived. There is physical separation.*

If the past is left behind and the future has not yet arrived, we have access only to the now. We are disengaged from the past and the future. There is a physical separation between us and the past and future. The only thing that really matters is the present.

The past is behind us, so it is best forgotten. If something is done poorly, there is always an opportunity to correct and improve it. It is best to try to forget what has been done and get on with the activities at hand.

The future is still to come; its shape can be influenced when it gets here. Planning is the way to try to shape and influence it. Therefore, it is only proper to engage in long-range or strategic planning as a way to decide how to allocate resources. But at the same time, because the future is out there, separate and distant, if we do not plan as carefully as we should, we can always correct things when the future becomes the present, or so we suppose.

In short, conventional wisdom tells us that the past has been left behind us, the present is now, and the future is way out ahead of us. Typically, we mark time by the hands on the clock. The minute hand points to the present, the now. What is behind the hand is the past, and what is to come is the future.

We view time with the use of a spatial model because of the convenience of showing "before" and "after." This spatial view of time gives us the impression that the present is all we have access to. Does Figure 10.11 correctly represent clock time?

Have we now answered the question: "What is time?" It would seem so, unless someone were to ask, "How long is the present?"

The length of the present should not be difficult to calculate, or is it? Using this century as an example, we know that ninety-six years have gone and there are three to come, so the present must be this year. But we know a month has gone and ten are on their way. So, of course, it is this day. Perhaps. But fifteen hours have gone and there are eight to go, so it must be this hour, this minute, this second, this nanosecond, this picosecond, this . . . and so on.[15]

Could it be that the present is so infinitesimally short that it does not really exist? Or is the present so minute that it is trivial? If so, we really live either in the past or the future—but that does not seem right. So what is clock time?

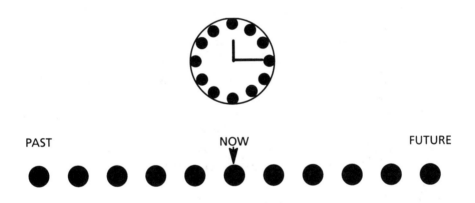

Figure 10.11 **Clock time**

St. Augustine once said that he knew well what time was—that is, until someone asked him.[16] He was reacting to Aristotle's notion that "time is the number of movement in respect to before and after."[17] Figure 10.11 represents Aristotle's definition in a spatial manner. Time is a series of moments that can be numbered in relation to those that have come before and those that will come after. Is this clock time?

Yes, as we understand clock time, Aristotle's definition is perfectly adequate. And from a pragmatic point of view, it works! It allows us to coordinate and synchronize events most efficiently. But it has not answered the question of the length of the present.

William James's *Principles of Psychology*, published in 1885, describes some studies he conducted to determine people's perceptions of how long the present seemed. He concluded that the present is typically perceived to be twelve seconds, a figure that suggests attention span rather than time itself. But James also said something much more significant: "The past flows with us."[18] These two ideas, the span of attention and the idea that the past flows with us, are the keystones in understanding human time.

When we are designing a new part, identifying a new metallurgic process, or defining a new service, our span of attention encompasses a now that lasts twelve seconds or one hour—time during which our immediate attention is focused on the activity at hand. But the designing or developing process does not occur in a vacuum. We call upon knowledge gained in past studies and through experience to shape the product or process. Those things that we studied in the past stay with us as a resource.

Technically, it is our anticipation of the future and remembrance of the past that are present in the now with us. The discussion of work as dialogue illustrated this point (see Figure 10.8). The design of products and the creation of services are done because we anticipate in the present their expected future implications for the marketplace.

Examples of the past flowing with us abound in our companies. Engineering drawings are still around. Invoices, part numbers, process routings, and customer profiles are still with us, as are data on purchases, inventory usage, maintenance work orders, process settings, and order transactions. This information may be well ordered and readily accessible, or it may be like Fibber McGee's closet, piled high with the door forced shut.

Individuals, like companies, also have information that flows through time: training, education, experiences, or notes in a little black book. This information may be more or less readily available, depending on how well it was grasped, categorized, and arranged in memory.

The future is not really *out there*; like the past, it is very much here in the present. An enterprise's future is determined by its expectations, shared vision, values, and norms. But whether these elements are clear, or a jumbled mess, they are very much a part of present reality.

Human time can be more clearly understood by examining our perception of music. Music is a series of notes, one following another. In terms of clock time, at any point in a symphony we are listening to a single note or chord. Notes already played have been left behind. Notes not yet played are still somewhere out in the future. But is this really the way we experience music?

When we listen to music, each note seems to sink down into our consciousness, allowing us to grasp patterns and themes; we grasp its meaning (Figure 10.12). Suppose we are listening to Beethoven's Fifth Symphony. If we were to hear the first three notes, would we know the theme? No. But when we hear the fourth note, suddenly the pattern becomes clear: dit, dit, dit, dum!

What happens to the first three notes when we hear the fourth? They are not left behind, as they should be in clock time, but instead sink down in our consciousness as, in human time, we grasp the pattern and meaning. At this point, our sense of expecta-

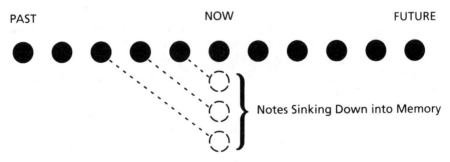

Figure 10.12 **Perceiving the pattern of music in human time**

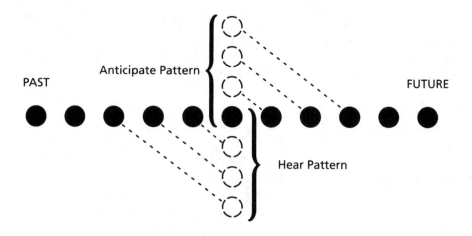

Figure 10.13 **Anticipating the patterns to come in human time**

tion is awakened. We anticipate that future notes will have some relationship to those just heard (Figure 10.13).

Certainly clock time is an important backdrop for human time, but notice how in human time we grasp patterns that have occurred in clock time and begin to anticipate patterns that will occur in the future. Remembrance of the past and anticipation of the future are immediately present in human time.

Indeed, without this human capability, Beethoven's Fifth would be just a jumble of notes. But we know from experience that it is anything but a jumble. The Fifth is brilliantly built upon the first four notes. At times our anticipation is confirmed; at other times it is surprised. This is what gives it its delight, and what involves us in the piece in a meaningful and significant manner: our natural ability as humans to retain what we have heard, perceive significant patterns, and anticipate those to come.

Isn't this what an experienced machinist does as he operates a drill press? Changes in the pitch of the drill signal a pattern that the machinist recognizes, so a dull drill is changed. Unless he anticipates what can follow the pitch change, he will not take timely action. A skilled financial advisor can pick up patterns in the market, even if they are faint and diffused, and give sound advice.

The Past: Living Remembrances (Knowledging)

Our ability to grasp significant patterns in music, as well as in other experiences, is a function of our previous learning, experience, and familiarity with a given subject. We draw upon this experience and knowledge to help interpret and understand these patterns. For example, if we have learned to play the piano, studied composition, or played in a band, that knowledge can help us to hear the themes in Beethoven's Fifth Symphony (Figure 10.14).

The availability of knowledge depends upon how well we have mastered the piano lessons or composition classes. Experience with a band would also help. If we paid attention and discovered patterns in our activities, our ability to match those patterns with the ones at hand would be greatly enhanced. By knowing Beethoven's Fifth, we have a greater appreciation for Gershwin, and we can understand what Miles Davis and Oscar Peterson are trying to expand upon in their music. There is a lesson in this: Live in the past, the present is too late!

Of course, we cannot live in the past, but what we do in the present becomes part of the past, which flows with us. Thus the present is the portal into the past. If we have sorted out and arranged our thoughts and experiences, they can become a resource to help us live more effectively in the present. If we have done a slipshod job, the past can be an anchor weighing us down rather than a buoy keeping us afloat.

Like individuals, companies also live in human time. Those companies that have sorted out their engineering standards (a pattern), their parts-listing schemes (another pattern), and their classification and coding of drawings (still another pattern) know the value of these resources in the present. Those who have not will find themselves adding new parts, increasing inventory, and generally adding to the complexity of their operation because they did not live wisely. These are the knowledge bases that Nonaka and Takeuchi discuss in their "hypertext organization."[19]

Notice how little thought we typically give to our company's *legacy*, the knowledge that is distributed among file drawers, in hundreds of different databases, and in the hands and eyes of our experienced professionals. It is this legacy that is really the key asset of an enterprise. Unfortunately, our accounting friends have not found an effective way of auditing and valuing it. If they had,

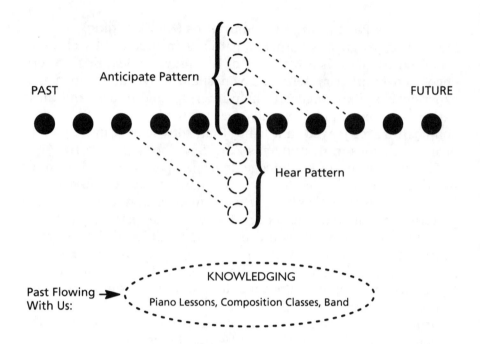

Figure 10.14 **Drawing upon knowledging to see and anticipate patterns**

we would quickly understand how important past actions are to our present reality.

To some, the legacy is a two-edged sword. Our accumulated knowledge is valuable because we can use it to discover new patterns—the source of learning and the basis for more knowledge. But we must continually arrange and rearrange it in significant patterns to use it. This takes time and energy; however, if we just throw things into the hall closet, the mess will live on to haunt us.

Many companies feel burdened by their old ways of doing things. They wish they could simply leave their outmoded policies and procedures behind and start fresh. Unfortunately or fortunately, the past flows with us. The only way to deal with it is to reinterpret it, to rearrange the patterns, and to sort out the twisted jungle of "ways of doing things." This book, in fact, is an example of an attempt to reinterpret the past and sort it out.

Since the first edition of this book, the idea of living remembrances has become even more important, especially in light of the discussion of core competencies and capabilities. (I tend to think of capabilities as usable competencies.) Capabilities are grounded in knowledge and experience that flows with us from the past into the present. They are a portable wellspring upon which we can continually draw.

Our anticipation of future patterns will be very important to the way we attend to the present. If we envision starting up a new product line in the custom semiconductor sector, wholesale banking, or custom valves, the steps we take today will largely determine its future outcome.

The Future: Living Anticipations and Aspirations (Envisioning)

Think again of the music analogy. The skill and care with which we listen to Beethoven's Fifth is conditioned not only by our past

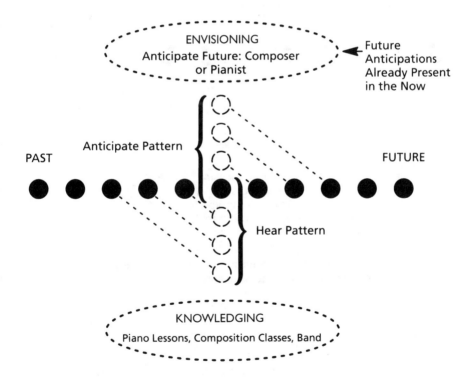

Figure 10.15 **Future envisioning influences ability to see and anticipate patterns**

knowledge, but also by our anticipation or aspiration of becoming a conductor or concert violinist or having a nice dinner after the performance. Our future vision is very much in the present, an important factor in the attention we give to the Fifth or any other activity (Figure 10.15).

Music is meant to be not only listened to but also played. A pianist envisions a piece while she or he is playing. Through the creative process, the texture of the piece is expressed and enriched

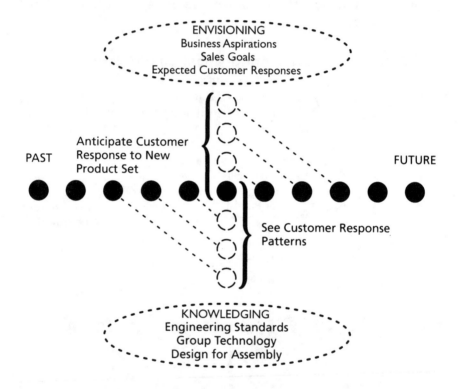

Figure 10.16 **Enterprise's business envisioning and knowledging help it to see customer response and anticipate future responses**

by the pianist's knowledge and skill. This vision is what motivates his or her attention to the piece. But what is envisioned may also be a piece of music brought up from memory. The dialogue between the envisioned piece and the actual keyboard performance is where the performer's creativity is expressed.

What is true for an individual is also true for an enterprise. Its ability to see patterns of responses from customers, to anticipate trends, and to draw upon its own collective knowledge in light of its business vision will influence its competitive success in the market. The better the enterprise is able to draw on these resources, business visions, and knowledge and attend to emerging patterns, the more likely it is to be a significant participant in

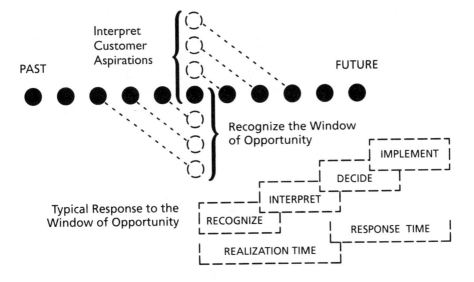

Figure 10.17 **Response process to window of opportunity**

the market (Figure 10.16). This is especially true today because the windows of opportunity come in all shapes and sizes and at random times; therefore, discerning patterns becomes even more challenging.

The enterprise must become more flexible, agile, and in tune with the market signals; otherwise it will miss many opportunities. Figure 10.17 illustrates the typical product decision cycle.

The process of recognizing the patterns that indicate the opening of a window of opportunity usually takes time. Then the signs have to be interpreted, and decisions must be made and implemented. It is not enough for only one function of the organization to "see" the patterns: most of the functions must identify the appropriate responses almost concurrently, given the capabilities and constraints of their organizations. They must make sure that there is alignment between the signals of the market and the capabilities and resources of their company. We have all run into a situation where marketing and sales have sold something that does not exist, with no idea as to whether it can be produced. Engineering takes it on as a challenge, and manufacturing rises to the occasion to beat the odds. Quality function deployment (QFD), a method of sorting out customer expectations, is helping to remove the ambiguities in this sequential approach.[20] (In the five years since writing this I have come to understand that it is not just anticipation of what will happen, but our aspirations that will help shape the future. Our aspirations are our contribution to the shaping of this future, as Dan Burrus and C. K. Prahalad and Gary Hamel point out.)

The functions must grasp, understand, and jointly interpret the many and various marketplace experiences of actual and potential customers. Rather than developing a wide variety of products to meet different operating conditions, it makes more sense to develop a robust design that can operate over a wide range of conditions. For example, one part of Japan runs its electricity on sixty cycles, the other part on fifty cycles; a product to be used there must be capable of operating in both zones.

Listening to the market is certainly much more complex than listening to one piece of music. In fact, it may be more like listening to ten or twelve different pieces at once. Without good statistical sampling techniques and QFD, it is hard to unscramble the significant patterns.

The interpretation of customer expectations (and customer aspirations) can be further complicated if there is inadequate alignment between the functions' visions and their knowledge. If there is no agreement about the business's mission or critical success factors, each function will look at customer patterns from a different perspective. This leads to a key set of questions: What is adequate alignment between visions? How is it achieved? Who is responsible for bringing it about? A corollary set of questions deals with core alignment of functional knowledge. What is minimal alignment of this knowledge? How is it developed and achieved?

How much effort does it take? (I now understand that we need to focus on our customers' aspirations. What are they trying to do with their customers? These aspirations provide the seeds of opportunities around which to organize our capabilities with those of our suppliers and customers.)

The alignment process is critical for management if the functions are to see and respond quickly to customer signals as the windows of opportunity are opening (Figure 10.18).[21]

Paul Lawrence and Davis Dyer's landmark study, *Renewing American Industry*, points out the varying temperaments of the functions that make them tend to pull in different directions.[22] For example, engineering loves complexity, whereas finance prefers simplicity. Marketing is generally unconstrained in its interpretation of market needs, while manufacturing is strongly constrained by its existing equipment.

Typically, marketing determines customer needs, translates them into specifications, and hands off the information to engineering, which designs the product. The product designs are then given to manufacturing or process engineering to produce. Once the product has been sold, service is responsible for supporting and maintaining it. Notice that all these activities occur in sequence.

On the other hand, suppose that the various functions work together in an iterative manner from day one to review the marketing product, process, and service considerations. Will the final outcome meet the customer's expectation better? Will the product be robust in design and easily serviceable? Will the designs have picked up the pattern of themes of multiple customers? Will the product also reflect the proper customer aspirations? In short will it be in tune with the market? More often than not, the answer will be yes.

There are already examples of concurrent or simultaneous engineering in which design and manufacturing engineers are developing next-generation products and processes together in an iterative process.[23] Each function is able to explain its visions and constraints to the other. Other companies have combined marketing and product development in an attempt to get quicker and better alignment. Still others are doing co-engineering between two separate companies: as one company designs its new product, the

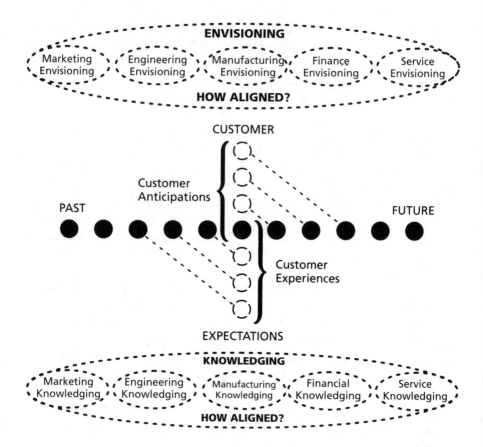

Figure 10.18 **Alignment of envisioning and knowledging**

second company develops the process for building it. These efforts cut the length of the product cycle.

Often companies use project management for cross-functional coordination. Project management will be critical to human networking because the dialogue between the functions is iterative and parallel; this capability makes it possible for the companies to take decisive and well-timed actions that strengthen their market presence.

The interplay between work as dialogue, human time, and timing is what gives a company its strength because it can team and re-team its capabilities to profitably seize market opportunities. An enterprise's interaction with the market is not just passive listening; it is listening to and playing the music at the same time, the way jazz musicians pick up a theme and work with it. The theme aligns their vision; then each musician interprets the theme based on his or her individual knowledge. As they play, they inspire and challenge each other to new combinations, new modes of expressing themselves around the basic theme; yet they play with emotion and discipline because of long hours of practice.

The same thing can happen within a company that listens to the themes of the marketplace. As the functions learn to work in parallel, they improve their timing, reduce cycle time, and improve quality and time-to-market. The alignment of their vision and knowledge allows them to discern significant market patterns, and their individual abilities add creativity and uniqueness to their response as they shape their market strategy, product design, process strategy, and service capabilities concurrently. Often finance and personnel are also involved in these efforts. In working together as cross-functional task teams, each function considers the constraints under which the other functions operate, often finding ways around some of them and avoiding unnecessary engineering change orders.

Figure 10.19 illustrates the dialogue possible when the different functions are in touch with their aligned visions and knowledge and can act decisively. Communicating on a peer-to-peer basis, the team can quickly resolve issues and maintain market rhythm. By identifying and chartering well-composed, cross-functional, task-focused teams, they can recapture in a "crafts-team" many of the virtues that once characterized the craftsperson.

No one person can master all the intricacies of a complex set of operations, but a well-developed team can. This is what Drucker was suggesting in his *Harvard Business Review* article.[24] Making pins or shoes is something an individual craftsperson can do alone. But electronic or discrete parts manufacturing requires more skill and knowledge than any one person can master. Modern insurance and banking require many different technical capabilities. We need to be able to draw on the multiple talents in an enterprise to put together virtual task-focusing teams.

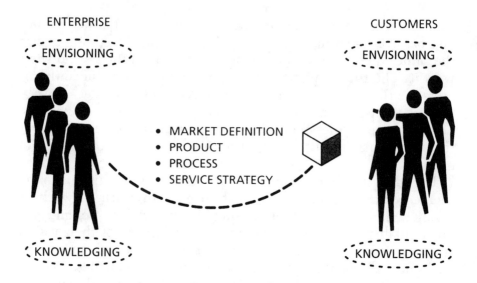

Figure 10.19 **Task-focusing team developing concurrently its response to customer aspirations**

Virtual Enterprising and Dynamic Teaming

There are two concepts from the world of computer science that may be of help in our activities: multiplexing and virtual memory. "Multiplexing" refers to the parallel transmission of more than one message over a single line. Humans can multiplex their attention from one project to another—that is, they can shift their focus from one task to another in short order.

The word "virtual" is defined as "being such in force or effect, though not actually or expressly such." "Virtual" has the connotation of being unreal, yet a virtual resource is very real. Something that is virtual is an available and adaptable resource. The concept of "virtual memory" has made it possible for computer systems to run much larger programs than their physical memory would allow by swapping blocks of information into and out of random access memory as needed. As far as the program is concerned, the entire program and all its data are fully accessible, if not in physical fact, in virtual fact. Companies such as Hewlett-Packard, Digital Equipment Corporation, and IBM have used this concept effectively in their computer operating systems.

Now, how do we take these concepts and apply them organizationally? We may have to move to virtual teams in virtual organizations, teams that can multiplex their focus, in order to shepherd multiple projects through the organization.

Virtual Enterprising[25]

In steep hierarchies, assignments are hard-wired with fixed areas of responsibility. The hierarchy assumes that someone else knows what everyone should be doing and that assignments can be made all the way down the chain of command. The functions are predetermined and people are stuffed into the appropriate slots. Such an organizational structure lacks the flexibility, adaptability, and agility to respond to the multiple demands put on organizations today. On the other hand, when people are seen as resources with capabilities available to support others, rather than as owners of narrowly defined boxes, they become virtual resources.

Virtual enterprising is a process through which companies team their capabilities, building upon their ability to define and redefine multiple cross-functional teams (Figure 10.4) as needed. These teams may include not only members of the company, but also people from vendor or customer companies. Virtual enterprising relies more on the knowledge and talents of people than on their functions. Managers, professionals, and workers can multiplex their attention to multiple projects with different sets of project members during the course of a day, month, or year. At one point, they can be dealing with operational questions, a short time later they are working on planning exercises, and then they may shift to personnel matters. They can also see the interconnections between these seemingly different disciplines. Moreover, these teams do not need to be co-located.

Research studies indicate that geographically dispersed teams can often work as effectively as co-located teams, if not more so. A dispersed group must communicate more explicitly, requiring clarity of thought, whereas co-located groups often tend to communicate haphazardly. Dispersed groups also periodically find ways to communicate face to face.[26]

The virtual enterprising process is an evolution of what some have called "open organizations." It is really not an accident that there should be so much interest in the International Standards Organization's Open Systems Interconnection (OSI) networking models and X/Open, an industry coalition dedicated to stimulating the development of portable software. Whereas the industrial-era model tried to cover all contingencies with bureaucracy, policies, procedures, job descriptions, and departmental charters, the new understanding is to create a common core, extending it as the need arises. UNIX, for example, is built around a clearly defined kernel that can easily be extended.

If we hope to use this flexibility, we must not define the enterprise in spatial terms, as the hierarchical organizational chart does. Instead, we should use the principles of human time as an organizing principle for allocating responsibilities.

It is also important to understand the idea of work as dialogue in conceptualizing the operation of the enterprise. People need access to their own visions and knowledge as well as to the core vision and knowledge of the virtual teams. These resources are what allow the people in the enterprise to maintain their individual and team focus, see significant patterns, and respond accordingly.

The hierarchical model assumes that the main task is to divide up the production operations and assign persons rigidly to take care of individual functions. In contrast, virtual enterprising treats groups of activities as projects, with teams working in an iterative and parallel manner to form a collage of teams. The management of the virtual enterprises then supports the teamwork of teams.

Virtual teams arise through assignment and volunteers. They are intentionally kept as small as possible, making it easier to get work done. They do not need to have representatives from all the functions, because the interplay of the teams ensures focus and coordination. The teams can deal with multiple challenges, from assessing market changes to championing new product development using approaches such as QFD. These teams are expected to first clarify their own assignment so that there is focus within the group, then to tackle the assignment. They are also expected to undertake projects in such a way that their learning adds to the larger enterprise. Time-to-market is made possible through time-to-learn.

Enterprises deal concurrently with multiple themes. Major and minor themes are played out at the same time, as well as noises and background static that may divert attention from the key themes. Some themes or patterns are picked up by one group and others by other groups. Groups are challenged to see the interrelationships between the various themes, because they may provide some very important clues as to the best market, product, or service response.

We are involved in a process that is more than passively listening to music or to themes from the market. We are also participants in the process, creating themes of our own that influence those of others in the marketplace, whether they are customers or competitors. This is part of work as dialogue; when an enterprise creates a product, it also creates in the vision of a competitor the possibility of creating a similar product. There is a great deal of room for active involvement in this process by all participants.

Dynamic Teaming as Task-Focusing Teams

Drucker writes of "task-focused teams." It is better to speak of "task-focusing teams," because each team will have to do its own focusing, rather than relying on an external executive. These teams need to be self-organizing, self-aligning, and self-responsible. Top management might establish certain parameters, articulate an organizing metaphor, or identify organizing principles, but the more detailed focusing will be done by the teams themselves.

The primary objective of task-focusing teams—dynamic teams, as we have been calling them—is to discern the themes coming from the market, from the competition, from suppliers and partners, and from within their own company. They must then design products, processes, and service strategies to support the products throughout their life cycles. By working together, on a peer-to-peer basis, they can iterate possible solutions until they develop a mature and market-ready plan.

These dynamic teams are the crafts-teams of the enterprise. They embody work as dialogue, using human time and a strong sense of market timing.

Interrelating the Five Conceptual Principles

The five conceptual principles—peer-to-peer knowledge networking, integrative process, work as dialogue, human time and timing, and virtual enterprising and dynamic teaming—are clearly interrelated. They are summarized in the next two figures, which are two-dimensional spatial representations of a very dynamic process of expression and dialogue.

The networking of vision and knowledge allows virtual enterprises and dynamic teams to see the patterns of the present and to express their own patterns. Knowledge networking involves drawing upon visions and knowledge to develop quality actions in the present, in concert with a team. These teams of professionals are

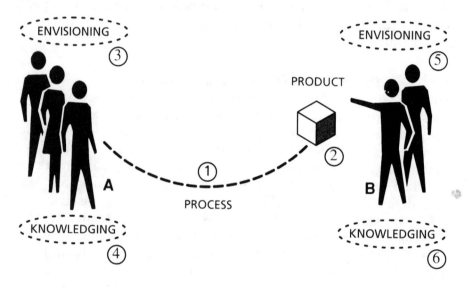

Figure 10.20 **Virtual enterprising and dynamic teaming**

charged with recognizing, interpreting, deciding, and implementing responses to windows of opportunity that will meet both the customers' expectations and the teams' enterprise vision (Figure 10.20).

Virtual enterprise and dynamic teams (A) define, develop, and run the process (1), which produces the products (2). The teams draw on their individual and collective knowledge (4), then design and produce the products in dialogue with their visions (3), which provide the context within which to focus their activities.

The customers (B) see the product (2) and the way it was produced (1) as exemplified in the process. As they think of how it may be used, they access their knowledge (6) and consult their visions (5) of what they would like.

Notice that there is communication among and between the virtual team members (A) as they listen to and anticipate the expectation patterns of the customers (B). This puts them in dialogue with the market. The virtual team members communicate in the present, tap into their individual and collective knowledge, and enter into dialogue with their visions. This is knowledge

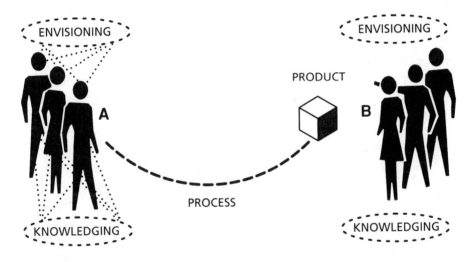

Figure 10.21 **Virtual team and knowledge networking**

networking (Figure 10.21). They are individually and collaboratively envisioning the possible, drawing upon their knowledge capabilities and experience (knowledging) as a way to shape the process and make the product.

While the dynamic team members (A) may use their technical networking infrastructure to work in parallel on the project, they must also tap into their own experiential knowledge, knowledge of their company, and knowledge of their culture—that is, public scientific knowledge. The dynamic team members also have access to their own personal visions, the visions of their group, the visions of their company, and the visions of their culture to inspire them in their work.

Knowledge networking represents a dialogue with the past, which flows with us; the present, in which we act; and the future, which is also in the present. The quality of this dialogue determines the appropriateness of the processes and products produced by the virtual team. This dialogue is more than just a cognitive exercise; it involves our values and emotions. They play an important role in tempering our envisioning, knowledging, and acting.

The five principles can only work together if there is strong leadership throughout the enterprise. If people at all levels rise to the occasion, they can help to define the enterprise's vision and add to its knowledge base. Strong leadership will be especially important on the multiple task-focusing teams. As we enter the knowledge era, virtual enterprises will shift focus from "control" to "commitment," from "monitoring" to "motivating," and from "commanding" to "conducting."

Leadership involves conducting, coaching, and mentoring: a conductor brings forth the best talents of an orchestra; a coach builds capabilities and confidence; and a mentor shapes talent. Knowledge-era enterprises are a composite of orchestras, basketball teams, and jazz combos. Perhaps they are more like jazz combos, because the rules are often more fuzzy and ambiguous than those governing an orchestra or a basketball game. Jazz combos know the basics, but they can take a theme and innovate creatively.

A new management strategy is needed for the knowledge era— one that can pick up on the themes of the market, technology, and human visions, and intertwine them into a score that catches the market's attention. Instead of "management by command" we move to "management as dialogue," where we foster strategy dialogue with our business partners. If work is dialogue, so is management. If managers, professionals, and workers are resource centers with knowledge that can be tapped, the challenge is to involve and focus their efforts. By working together, we can empower one another. We can master the confusingly complex, because we are using an elegantly simple model based on work as dialogue and human time: knowledge networking.

Evidence is mounting that this is the way to go. Computer-based networking technology with fiber optics of 100+ megabytes per second is making entirely new organizational structures possible; studies in neural networking and chaos are helping to move us beyond the machine model of organizations;[27] the research of Jessica Lipnack and Jeffrey Stamps of The Networking Institute shows the power of geographically distributed teams;[28] and the groupware scholarship of Robert Johansen shows the power of teamwork.[29] There are other indications that the time is right for a shift to human networking.

A new generation of professionals is growing up with the technology of networking. Natural clusters of interest arise spontaneously on computer bulletin boards and conferencing networks. User groups are pulling together people from diverse backgrounds around common themes of interest. People are networking not because they are told to, but because of natural interests. They are initiating relationships rather than waiting to be assigned to a particular spot.

Some of the seeds of change were planted years ago. Hayward Thomas, former president of Jensen Industries and former plant manager at Frigidaire, redefined Frigidaire's manufacturing organization in the late 1950s. He used round organizational charts resembling medieval chain mail, where many small steel rings are interlocked to build a structure of great strength.[30] Frigidaire's large factory used hundreds of small teams working as a coordinated whole. Unfortunately, the experiment was not sustainable because Frigidaire was changed by General Motors, which wanted to recentralize operations in a hierarchical manner. But other companies, such as Procter & Gamble and Heinz, have a long tradition of using small teams with great effectiveness.

Today design engineers are working together with manufacturing or process engineers across town or around the world. They can call on materials specialists in a third location to help cost their projects. Marketing can participate as part of the team in the development of new product ideas. These groups, working together from diverse locations, can design, build, and market products and services to meet real customer needs. Each function is a resource available to work in parallel with other resources in a give-and-take mode, iterating ideas back and forth on the network.

In a similar manner, investment banking or insurance companies pull together teams from across their companies to work on multiple issues. These changes are empowering individuals, teams, and enterprises in new and creative ways. Ultimately, professionals at all levels will find empowerment through self-empowerment. When we realize that we are the authors of our own work and when we can thrive on the tension between our vision and knowledge, we will find empowerment.

There is a clear transformation occurring from the industrial era to the knowledge era. The next chapter looks more closely at the key shifts implicit in this transition.

CHAPTER

11

CONFUSINGLY COMPLEX TO ELEGANTLY
SIMPLE ENTERPRISES

What if our CEO were to tear up our organizational chart and ask us to redefine basic relationships, as happened in Part 1? Could we put the confusing complexity of our present organization aside and develop an elegantly simple core understanding of its basic relationships?

How do we move from second-generation steep hierarchies to fifth-generation knowledge networking? How do we overcome the complexity of industrial-era organizations and discover the simplicity of the knowledge era? How do we initiate such a transition?

Certainly the transition cannot be bought from a systems integrator. True, there are companies that can install local- and wide-area networks, interface one application with another, and help develop a unifying data architecture. But the real transition comes only when we look more deeply at the conceptual frameworks in which we operate. In order to break out of the confining quarters of second-generation management, we will need to shift our attitudes and approaches. Figure 11.1 shows the focus of this chapter.

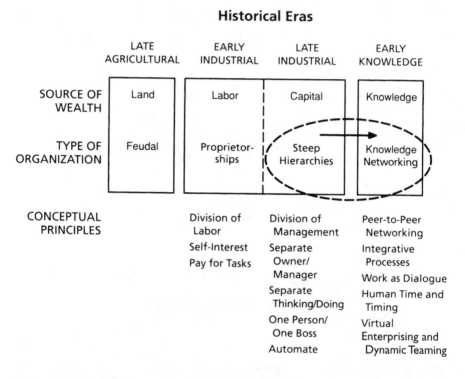

Historical Eras

	LATE AGRICULTURAL	EARLY INDUSTRIAL	LATE INDUSTRIAL	EARLY KNOWLEDGE
SOURCE OF WEALTH	Land	Labor	Capital	Knowledge
TYPE OF ORGANIZATION	Feudal	Proprietor-ships	Steep Hierarchies	Knowledge Networking
CONCEPTUAL PRINCIPLES		Division of Labor	Division of Management	Peer-to-Peer Networking
		Self-Interest	Separate Owner/ Manager	Integrative Processes
		Pay for Tasks	Separate Thinking/Doing	Work as Dialogue
			One Person/ One Boss	Human Time and Timing
			Automate	Virtual Enterprising and Dynamic Teaming

Figure 11.1 **Chapter focus: the transition from steep hierarchies to knowledge networking enterprises**

If they are to form an acknowledged basis or core understanding, the knowledge-era conceptual principles must strike a chord of intuitive acceptance. Is it more natural to work as superiors and subordinates or peer to peer? Is it more natural to hide in a box or to serve as a knowledge resource in a network? Is it more natural to follow orders that we do not fully understand or to engage in work as a dialogue, which encourages us to use our envisioning and knowledging? Is it more natural to try to mesh our activities in a synchronized set like clockwork or to have access to an understanding of the company's vision and collective knowledge? Is it more natural to struggle with the inflexibility of automated processes or to participate in the discovery process as part of a task-focusing team? Can we, in our companies, initiate our own discovery process as did our friends in Part 1?

The Basics: Space and Human Time

The industrial and knowledge eras have different starting points. The industrial era is built on a spatial model of reality, while the knowledge era rests on an understanding of the interplay between human time and clock time.

Space is an easier metaphor to understand. It is easier to see what is up and down, back and front, left and right. It is easy to show relationships between things and people using spatial diagrams. This is why the organizational chart is so seductively simple. It gives us the illusion of understanding how the organization works. It is much harder to see changing relationships over time, because no spatial diagram can easily capture what is going on. Yet our humanness unfolds itself in time, not space. We live in human time, at the intersection of our envisioning and knowledging. It is our dreams and remembrances that fuel our activities and give them content and texture. It is the tension between the two that motivates us.

The transition from a model based on spatial relationships (lines and boxes) to one based on time (human time and clock time) is the essence of the transition. There is a newness and an oldness to this transition, because in some ways we are recapturing the involvement and engagement of the farmer and craftsperson of the pre-industrial era.

The farmer was very much engaged in a dialogue with the land, the seasons, and the weather. Vision and knowledge, timing and action, were woven into the fabric of the farmer's life. A craftsperson was engaged with materials and processes, visions and knowledge, customer reactions and feedback. But in the industrial era, fragmentation of processes has denied many access to their knowledge and visions. Dialogue has stopped. For all the goods and services the industrial era has provided, there is a tragic side. It has arranged patterns of relationships in such a way that it has made it extremely difficult for us to experience the full range of who we are in our work life. We are stuffed into little boxes and only given half the script, yet punished for not acting according to the full script. The good news is that when we see the short-sighted stupidity of the A, B, C triad explored in Chapter 3, we will understand that there is another way of being with one another. The knowledge era will allow us, once again, to recapture a fullness of life not possible because of the assumptions of the industrial era. And if we can really understand the new possibilities of co-creation, it is likely that we will be able to rebuild our economy on knowledge. As people feel valued, they will find new incentives to enhance their own capabilities and those of their colleagues and this can lead to a new and very significant burst of economic activities.

In the knowledge era, we plant our ideas in the fields of technology; our craftspersons have become part of a cross-functional, task-focusing virtual crafts-team in a network of teams. Envisioning, knowledging, and a sense of timing are as important today as they were centuries ago. Our teaming is not just within our companies but between companies, through virtual enterprising. Our teaming is not just static, locking ourselves in teams much as we have been locked in tiny boxes; instead, it is a dynamic process of teaming and re-teaming. And our teaming is built on our respect for one another's competencies and aspirations. This knowledge networking is essential to our ongoing success.

Transition in Management Models

Figure 11.2 suggests some of the elements involved in the transition to human networking. We will first work our way around the outside of the box, then look more specifically at the transition between management models. Although the discussion may give the impression that we are engaged in an "either/or" dialogue, this is not the intent; the contrasts are sharpened to bring the alternatives into relief.

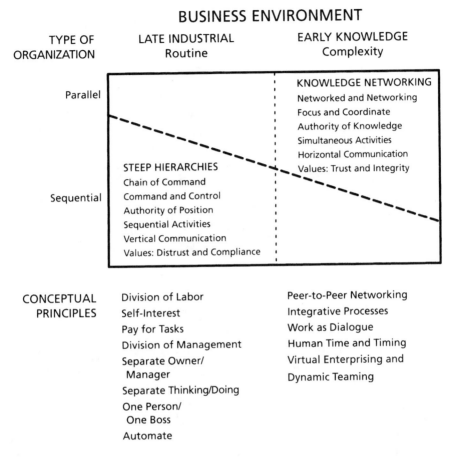

BUSINESS ENVIRONMENT

TYPE OF ORGANIZATION	LATE INDUSTRIAL Routine	EARLY KNOWLEDGE Complexity
Parallel		KNOWLEDGE NETWORKING Networked and Networking Focus and Coordinate Authority of Knowledge Simultaneous Activities Horizontal Communication Values: Trust and Integrity
Sequential	STEEP HIERARCHIES Chain of Command Command and Control Authority of Position Sequential Activities Vertical Communication Values: Distrust and Compliance	

| CONCEPTUAL PRINCIPLES | Division of Labor
Self-Interest
Pay for Tasks
Division of Management
Separate Owner/
  Manager
Separate Thinking/Doing
One Person/
  One Boss
Automate | Peer-to-Peer Networking
Integrative Processes
Work as Dialogue
Human Time and Timing
Virtual Enterprising and
Dynamic Teaming |

Figure 11.2 **Transition from steep hierarchies to knowledge networking**

Figure 11.2 suggests a number of interrelated themes raised in previous chapters. They include:

1. The transition from the *industrial* era to the *knowledge* era

2. The transition from *routine to complexity*

3. The transition from *sequential* activities to *parallel* iterative activities

4. The transition from industrial-era *conceptual principles* to those of the knowledge era

5. The *management shifts* in structure, control, authority, and communication

The diagonal line in Figure 11.2 is not drawn from corner to corner. Knowledge networking enterprises will still have hierarchical authority structures, although they will be much flatter. This hierarchy will not perpetuate the debilitating A, B, C triad discussed in Part 1, but will work to coach and mentor, building upon one another's capabilities.

Some activities will continue to be sequential and routine. It is not a question of "either/or" but "both/and." There will still be some division and subdivision of labor, with certain tasks remaining narrowly defined. Top management will still have overall responsibility for the strategic direction of the enterprise, and vestiges of the chain of command and automation will survive.

Navigating the Transition

The transition from steep hierarchies to networking enterprises does not involve moving or even eliminating the boxes. This has been management strategy for decades: when something does not work, move the boxes, decentralize or centralize.

What is the source of the drive for change? Does it start with the CEO and management committee? Possibly, but often they are too preoccupied with "big issues," such as capital investment decisions, to really understand what is going on within the organization. Does it come from middle management? Unlikely, because even though they see the issues, they do not have the power to implement the change. Does the information systems community lead the charge? Probably not, because they are too tied to the technology to have adequate leverage with the organization.

The next transition will probably come through a coalition of interested parties within the enterprise. Ideally, this coalition should include key persons from engineering, manufacturing, finance, service, information systems, personnel, human resources, organizational development, and other interested parties. In many companies the unions will have a major role to play in helping to facilitate the change. But the transition will not arrive simply because we have computerized our steep hierarchies.

Terry Winograd and Fernando Flores, in their book *Understanding Computers and Cognition*, have questioned our blind belief in the power of the computer.[1] Their book reminds us that without understanding the "whole picture," the gestalt or the organizing pattern, a computer application is extremely limited. For example, attempts to capture an expert's knowledge in an expert system are limited, because it is one thing to identify a specific sequence of steps captured as rules, but it is quite something else to identify the whole context in which an expert thinks. An expert has power because he or she can see the multiple relationships in an event and adjust for new contingencies and unexpected changes.

This leads us back to a consideration of Figure 11.2. We will take each of the five points that we have mentioned and discuss them in relation to the transition process.

Transitioning from the Industrial Era to the Knowledge Era

We have two choices: stay within the industrial-era mindset and computerize our steep hierarchies, or refocus our thinking toward the integration that is possible through human networking. The first choice will not overcome our organizational bankruptcy. The second choice will add value to past investments and increase future investments.

It is often said that the purpose of CIM is to get the right information to the right people at the right time to make the right decisions. Certainly this is a real and important process, but there is more to do than just create, move, store, and process this information. It is the human element that is able to see the Pareto charts, the histograms, the customer profiles, and the business graphics, and to understand how the patterns interrelate. Because we can grasp the organization's vision and understand its history, we know what to look for. It is the larger context, derived from human time, that makes it possible to see the patterns, even the fuzzy and obscure ones. Certainly as we experience the World Wide Web on the Internet and build corporate-wide webs, we will be able to better process these ideas, insights, and opportunities.

Our automationist mentality has led us to think that we can capture everything in databases. Although databases are becoming indispensable to modern business, the human capability to see and act on patterns related to the larger context and mission of the organization is an essential complementary capability. It is our human knowledge bases that are our real assets. We need a strategy that recognizes and appreciates our human capability to see and anticipate, to expand our visions and share them, and to learn and capture this learning as a shareable resource within the enterprise. This is why time-to-learn is as significant as time-to-market, if not more so.

When we refer to human capabilities and the human element, we are not advocating a humanistic approach. Too often people want to build "niceness" into an organization and encourage "participation" because it is the right thing to do. What often happens, however, is that these philosophies are superficially applied to industrial-era organizations. Even Maslow's "hierarchy of needs" and McGregor's "Theory X and Theory Y" are not adequate because they have not come to terms with the underlying assumptions of the industrial era.[2] McGregor pointed us in the right direction, although Maslow had little empirical foundation for his theories.

In the knowledge era, people will not necessarily be nice to one another. It is more important to have honest and open dialogue about the real issues, patterns, challenges, technologies, and business opportunities of the enterprise. There will still be politics, distrust, misunderstandings, disagreements, and fights over scarce resources at budget time. Trust must be won through the integrity of those in the company. If people understand the company's vision, it is because there is openness and honesty. If the enterprise learns to learn from its experiences, it is because it has interest in the thoughts and ideas of its members and not just self-interest.

The transition to the knowledge era is not a transition to a utopian or humanistic paradise. It puts people in touch with real problems and challenges, although with a more holistic understanding of their context. This is part of the alignment process, the discourse through which real understanding arises. People in the knowledge era are expected to be tempered by a realism that is capable of seeing the patterns of the past, the present, and the future.

We constantly stand at the "intersection of the timeless with time," to use T. S. Eliot's phrase.[3] We must use our ability to see and hear the patterns of the music, whether it is played in the marketplace of the business world or the laboratories of the scientists. We are also called upon to make our own music in order to capture the market's attention.

The transition from the superficiality of the industrial era to the humanly demanding knowledge era challenges us to confront ourselves as people in new and exciting ways. As Ken Olsen suggested, we may find that being in touch with our creativity, our knowledge, and our motivation has a profound value in and of itself, as well as affecting the bottom line.[4]

Transitioning from Routine to Complexity

When the future is much like the past, organizing for routine makes a great deal of sense. But when curve balls, unexpected tunes, and kaleidoscopic technological changes are the order of the day, a strategy for dealing with complexity and variety is in order.

The real siphon of a company's profits is not work-in-process (WIP) but decisions-in-process (DIP). It is those countless little decisions that are made half-heartedly or not at all that sap the strength and inspiration of an enterprise. Many good ideas are put on hold so long, waiting for the politics to settle down, that when their day comes, they look like flat tires. Decisions-in-process have to be made even when boundaries are fuzzy and information is scant.

It is not a coincidence that we should be experiencing a birth of widespread interest in the subject of chaos. James Gleick's *Chaos: Making a New Science* attempts to make available to the average person the intricacies of fractals.[5] The challenge is to find the patterns in chaos. The beauty and regularity in the irregularity of the Mandelbrot set is most intriguing. It is not surprising that Tom Peters should have named one of his books *Thriving on Chaos*.[6] In a related vein, there is growing interest in "fuzzy set theory": working with patterns that are not easily distinguishable.

How often have we heard, "If only we knew what the customer really wanted"? The concept of "the customer" is an abstraction.

This customer is really a composite of many different customers with wide-ranging needs who reflect a variety of aspirations and interdependencies. Often it takes perceptive marketing to discern the faint, fuzzy, visible patterns. We also need a good sense of timing so that we can act decisively at the right moment. A company cannot be successful being dead right at the wrong time. Too much, too late hardly pays the rent.

It is for these reasons that enterprises need honest and open dialogue. The truth is often buried in the confluence of a variety of human perceptions. Only through the give-and-take of hard dialogue can it be discovered. This is why organizations that rely on the authority of knowledge, rather than the authority of position, often succeed where others fail. For example, Digital Equipment Corporation has a culture that values the notion of "push-back." When someone makes a statement or takes a position, others are expected to push back until the truth of the matter is discovered. It does not matter what rank the person has. Without respect for the truth of the matter, it is hard to deal with complexity. A push-back is not a put-down, but signifies an openness and a willingness to stick with the issue until the truth is known. Other organizations call this "peeling the onion," or the "five-why routine." These are examples of the authority of knowledge.

The transition, then, from routine to complexity is a transition in attitudes, perceptions, and expectations. It is not a black-and-white issue, but should be thought of as a continuum. Some companies characterized by a great deal of routine can continue to be very effective in narrowly defined market niches. Many others long for the old days when they could run economic order quantity (EOQ) formulas, instead of having to worry about lot sizes of one.

Transitioning from Sequential to Parallel

Working sequentially isolates people and processes from one another. Each function has its role to play but lacks an appreciation of the constraints that the other functions live under. It is easy to blame another function for not understanding or failing to carry out instructions, especially if one is removed from the other function's daily worries.

We have built an educational feeder system that contributes to the fragmentation of the enterprise. Engineering schools provide engineers. Industrial engineering departments supply IEs. Many manufacturing engineers come up through the ranks, although this is changing now. Those in finance live in, and come from, their own worlds. Marketers have their own pedigrees, and so it goes. It is very rare to find an effective interdisciplinary program feeding the manufacturing industry.[7]

As we begin to work more in parallel through such efforts as concurrent engineering, a new set of dynamics is initiated. This does not mean simply that the functions operate concurrently, but that they work together. Spatial or temporal proximity is not essential, thanks to the power of networks and common windowing formats.

Working in parallel requires more discipline than working sequentially. In a sequentially run company, there are usually old-timers at the interfaces who are wise and seasoned enough to translate the output of another department into the idiom of their own. They are the unsung heroes of our corporations, the ones who have ensured that "as designed" and "as built" bear some resemblance.

Companies such as Delco-Remy are rediscovering concurrent engineering. This idea, developed in the 1950s but lost in the centralization trend of the 1960s, is now being rejuvenated. Design, manufacturing, and industrial engineers are working shoulder to shoulder to design both products and processes. This leads to easier-to-manufacture designs and better-quality processes. This is only the start in the trend toward working in parallel, elbow to elbow or over a network.

We also find that companies are beginning to work in parallel. As one company designs a new automobile, its equipment contractor is concurrently designing the transfer line upon which it will be built. The second company can do this only because it has prepared itself over the last ten years by unifying its database, building discipline into its organization, and moving to a project management approach. This allows the contractor to change the design of its transfer line dynamically as the automaker's new designs emerge. This development is significant because it is the only way that new-car cycle times can be cut from five years to two or less.

Companies experiencing the challenges of electronic data interchange (EDI) are only now beginning to create webs of networks that will eventually allow them to work together in parallel. It is becoming easier to send orders and invoices electronically; the real challenge will be to transmit the geometry, typology, tolerances, and forms and features to the supplier community electronically. Technical data interchange (TDI) is being developed under the banner of Product Data Exchange Specification, which is to become the International Standards Organization's STEP (Standards for the Transfer and Exchange of Product model data) standard. The use of an increased networking bandwidth between primes and subcontractors will explode, perhaps exponentially. The U.S. Department of Defense's (DOD) Computer-aided Acquisition and Logistics Support (CALS) system, now known as "Commerce at Lightening Speed," is helping to speed this process along. The DOD has asked that, after 1990, its prime contractors supply it with design specifications in digital rather than paper form, or allow it access to the primes' databases with this information in it.

The signs are clear that we are moving more quickly than most realize toward working in parallel. It will require a different mindset: one that is willing to examine the assumptions underlying the industrial era and contribute to developing a new set of principles.

Transitioning the Conceptual Principles

Thomas Kuhn, in *The Structure of Scientific Revolutions*, discusses the process and role of paradigm shifts or mindset changes.[8] We are at the threshold of such a shift today. But there is no guarantee that we will make the shift satisfactorily. It is not inevitable. It will depend upon our own perceptiveness, intuition, integrity, and creativity. So much of the future must be created by us through our own efforts.

We can no longer afford the petty isolation of sequential work built on the division and subdivision of labor and management. Simplistic self-interest, taking our box on the organizational chart as something that we own exclusively, will go the way of the buggy whip. As Drucker suggests, we need new pay and reward systems that will nurture and grow individual and collaborative knowledge resources.[9] Bureaucracy has a role, but it is much more limited. We need to be both thinkers and doers to become simultaneous leaders and followers—mentors, teachers, and learners—as we work together on self-focusing task teams, using automation within a reasoned context. If we can change the focus of the exercise and put people into the center of the equation, we will pull in the appropriate technology to help us get the work done.

Transitioning to New Structures

Drucker, Davis, Nolan, Zuboff, Nonaka, McMaster, Peters, Burrus, and others suggest that the "new organization" will require new structures with different control, authority, communication, and accountability strategies. Now that we have worked our way around the outside of Figure 11.2, let us look at the two lists within the figure, comparing the differences between steep hierarchies and human enterprise, point by point (Figure 11.3).

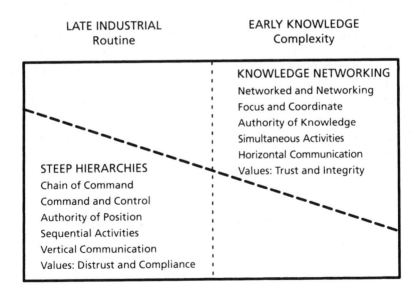

Figure 11.3 **Management shifts**

"Chain of Command" to "Networked and Networking"

Henri Fayol's fourteen principles are based on his experience as the managing director of the Comambault mining company in France in the early part of this century.[10] At about the same time, Taylor was developing his theories of "scientific management." Taylor focused on the shop floor and worked up, while Fayol began with the board of directors and worked down. As Taylor developed a strategy for defining and directing direct labor, Fayol theorized about planning, organizing, commanding, coordinating, and controlling management's responsibilities.

These ideas were ideal in a time when markets changed slowly, many companies were geographically isolated, and the introduction of new technology progressed at a modest rate. They are no longer adequate in an era of global markets, geographical integration, and accelerating technology.

Today, the mere existence of a networked infrastructure in an organization does not guarantee that the organization will leverage its resources. An extensive road, telephone, and telegraph system makes it possible to communicate, but it does not ensure that we will communicate meaningfully.

Networking is an ongoing process of reaching out and getting in touch with others to get tasks done. As we become nodes in a network—knowledge resources—we tap into this available knowledge and our effectiveness increases. Instead of being confined by the chain of command, we can go directly to sources of knowledge, whether they are inside or outside the enterprise.[11]

When a friend joined Digital, he was told a good news–bad news story. The good news was that he had 120,000 people working for him. The bad news was that they did not know it. It was up to him to figure out how he could best network himself and build working alliances.

"Command and Control" to "Focus and Coordinate"

The steep hierarchy has a command and control structure, with orders originating at the top. To take initiative, a worker or professional lower down in the organization must first get his or her boss's blessing. Knowledge and wisdom are supposedly embodied in the years of experience represented by those at the top.

This thinking has been based on the "calculus of importance": the higher up in the organization, the more important the person, as measured by number of direct reports, budget approval authority, and access to the power centers. Too often this model degenerates into not what but whom a person knows.

The irony is that managers grow skillful at giving orders but never learn to ask perceptive questions or listen carefully. A question is considered a sign of ignorance unbefitting one's rank in the organization. This attitude stifles significant communication. It is a hundred small decisions made throughout a company that cause it to earn or lose money, rather than the occasional "important" big decision coming from on high. But if the culture does not support careful listening prompted by probing questions, the enterprise will atrophy.

Network enterprises with fewer levels of management face significant new challenges: How do we ensure that all levels of the enterprise are focusing on the key critical issues? How do we ensure coordination between interrelated efforts? How do people get rewarded when there are fewer levels?

A team's focus will depend, to a great extent, upon understanding its context. The enterprise's vision and knowledge base provide this context and become important determinants in the focusing process. As teams come to understand this context, they will do their own focusing. Karl Weick's *The Social Psychology of Organizing* has a wonderful description of self-directing teams.[12] As parts of their tasks are solved, the teams shift their focus to other business opportunities and interrelated aspects. The power of the task-focusing team lies in its freedom to shift its focus as needed, to zoom in on particular aspects of an opportunity and zoom out to see the whole picture.

In organizations that use multiple task-focusing teams, the teams will need to interact, like the themes in a well-developed piece of music. Part of a team's responsibility is to help grow the enterprise's vision and knowledge base; the team's learning becomes a valuable resource for other task-focusing teams.

As these teams learn to interact effectively, they will gradually become the lifeblood of the organization, their fast-paced activities giving flexibility and agility to the enterprise. Task-focusing dynamic teams are not the same as autonomous or ad hoc teams. The concept of the autonomous team suggests a disconnect between the team's efforts and the life of the larger organization. As the Sociotechnical Systems community was developing its approach, it found it necessary to carve out some space for its team—to operate, free from the traditional constraints, assumptions, and bureaucracy of the steep hierarchy. The term "ad hoc" suggests teams that are not an integral part of the working organization, merely afterthoughts designed to correct malfunctioning systems. They are provisional and transient.

Membership on task-focusing teams may be provisional, but the use of teams is structured into the daily operation of the enterprise. Thus teams need clear discipline, well-established expectation patterns, and project management skills to guide them as they sort out multiple interrelated activities, timing their efforts to achieve desired ends. In fact, Tom Peters and others are arguing that our companies will live more and more with temporary project teams. This makes it even more important to understand that our workplaces are no longer an aggregation of narrowly defined functions, but a pulsating community of capabilities that can easily be teamed and re-teamed around concrete market opportunities.

We need not only coordination but increased collaboration. Interestingly enough, the word "collaboration" can more readily be used today. It is an excellent word, but for too long it carried the burden of the *collaborator* connotation. Our companies will come alive as they become communities of talented individuals who can easily collaborate with one another, building upon one another's talents and capabilities. We will gradually come to understand that the power of collaborative intelligence and people, working together, can generate value by combining one another's raw ideas, and not just add value to raw materials.

"Authority of Position" to "Authority of Knowledge"

Within steep hierarchies, position and authority are defined by boxes and lines: the higher up the position, the more powerful it is. The prerogatives of position legitimize an arbitrary attitude with subordinates. Superiors need not listen; they merely monitor and control subordinates.

Given narrowly defined tasks, subordinates are supposed to know what to do. They are not required to be creative, only to accept the rules of the game, knowing that it is only a matter of time before they advance to the next rung. As the steep hierarchies are delayered, what happens to the subordinates' aspirations? With fewer layers, promotions come more slowly. Are people content to wait longer to advance? What happens to morale and motivation?

Authority of position works well for organizing routine tasks, but can it handle complexity? Customer needs do not come in Lego-like packages. The development of the next-generation disk drive involves physics, chemistry, engineering design, and process control, all at the same time. The logic of the market requires enterprises to use their cross-functional and cross-company knowledge resources to develop an overall response strategy.

Authority of knowledge is fast becoming more important for success in the marketplace. This is not knowledge doled out in tiny bits like currency, but knowledge available to all. As steep hierarchies are replaced by multiple task-focusing teams, the individual's knowledge becomes both more important and more accessible, and a lack of knowledge can no longer be hidden behind the walls of organizational boxes. People quickly learn who has knowledge and who will share it. They are the ones who become key players on task-focusing teams. This is why Skandia, Dow, ABB, and other companies are paying much more attention to their knowledge assets and intellectual capital resources.

The organization that believes in authority of position is likely to want to automate and computerize as many processes as possible, giving top management access to executive-decision support systems. As Winograd and Flores remind us, we can only automate and computerize specific information that we have acquired in the past.[13] We cannot automate or computerize the context—that is part of our human understanding.

Enterprises based on the authority of knowledge are messy. Neither knowledge nor tasks come in neatly wrapped packages. One person's knowledge overlaps with others'. Some people have deep resonance in their knowledge, others are fast learners, and still others turn off their thinking sets.

Authority of position is based on defining and arranging assignments so that even those with the least common denominator of knowledge have a reasonable chance of success. By overeducating a person, then underutilizing his or her talents, companies hope that the assigned tasks will get done. But an organization built on the authority of position is a slow learner because the barriers of the rigid structure act as learning baffles. Good learning does not go on between levels, since superiors are "supposed to know," even if they do not. Too often we find the pretext of knowing, rather than genuine knowledge. This attitude is quickly becoming a luxury most companies cannot afford; it is unrealistic to expect people at all levels to know more than their subordinates.

On the other hand, if the enterprise is built on the authority of knowledge, we must take one another seriously and discover what others really know. Managers must get to know their subordinates' capabilities, aspirations, and experiences. This will also require a greater appreciation of individual differences. In fact, we are only beginning to understand what it means to value differences in background, tradition, education, gender, and age.

Knowledge is more than just knowing something. It comes in a variety of forms:

Know-how—procedures that get things done
Know-who—key resources to call upon
Know-what—the ability to discern key patterns based on
    knowledge
Know-why—understanding the larger context, the vision
Know-where—where things can and should happen
Know-when—a sense of rhythm, timing, and realism

Much of this knowledge will remain in the heads of those in the enterprise, although significant portions can be captured and sorted into applications, databases, and procedures. For example, the discipline of classifying and coding engineering drawings makes group technology possible. Phase review procedures coordinate orderly cooperation between functions. Customer profile databases help in customizing products and services.

Most manufacturing companies work hard to increase inventory turns. How many companies even give a second thought to "knowledge turns"? Not many. In my studies from around the world, I have found that on a potential scale of 100, most companies score from 7 to 1. The best scores have come from India.

Knowledge turns is defined as our ability to build upon the other's capabilities, divided by the level of distrust. The "other" can be the other person, the other functions, the other line of business, the supplier, the customer, or the customers' customer.

"Sequential Activities" to "Simultaneous Activities"

A great deal has already been said about the shift from the sequential to the parallel, concurrent, or simultaneous mode of operation. The challenge is to develop a culture that supports the establishment of core teams that are free to draw on knowledge resources wherever they are found, within or outside the enterprise.

Enterprises will be successful if these teams are able to customize 20 percent of the product, leveraging the 80 percent that has already been developed. Through the use of group technology, parametric design, manufacturability rules, expert systems, and service considerations, we should be able to effectively utilize already existing resources.

"Vertical Communication" to "Horizontal Communication"

The shift to horizontal communication should be an obvious one, especially as we see people not as turf-owners but as knowledge resources within the network. There will still be vertical communication, of course, but the predominant communication will be horizontal in nature as the core task-focusing teams leverage knowledge wherever it may be in the enterprise.

Horizontal communication in a networked environment is freer and more fluid, with few bureaucratic barriers; it also facilitates serendipity, where key patterns may be unexpectedly discovered. Perhaps a request from one team to another will provide a clue to the pattern the other team is trying to discern. If we see our work as dialogue, we will stay open to discovery, observe the interplay of multiple patterns, and achieve our visions.

In light of the new dialogue in Part 1, we should be talking about conversation and dialogue and not "communication" or "discussions." The word "dialogue" will take on increasing importance in our companies as we realize that it is significance and meaning that we seek, and not just satisfaction. Without understanding the larger context and what it means, we will have a hard time adequately teaming our capabilities.

"Distrust and Compliance" to "Trust and Integrity"

Distrust seems built into steep hierarchies. The fragmented structure breeds mutual distrust among functions. It is common to hear people complain of how another department throws information over the wall. Robert Hall, together with a group from the Association for Manufacturing Excellence, has been studying the "functional silo" problem.[14]

Manufacturing must double-check the drawing it just received from engineering. Sales feels it must recount the inventory because it does not believe finance's numbers. These activities do not add value to the product, just cost, but they are endemic to too many enterprises.

In the knowledge era, trust and integrity are critical. When people work closely together as resources in a network and as members of task-focusing teams, it quickly becomes obvious who can be trusted and who cannot. Do we share our thinking, our visions, and knowledge with those whom we know will misuse them?

Digital expects its people to "push back" until the truth is known; each person is expected to "do the right thing." Hewlett-Packard asks its plant managers to locate their offices right on the plant floor, where they are easily accessible. These policies engender honesty, trust, and openness. But these values are fragile and hard-won. A few key people can easily torpedo a climate of trust and integrity without even realizing what they have done.

Integration efforts are delicate and easily disrupted, especially if the atmosphere of trust fizzles. I know of instances in which companies that had made remarkable strides toward CIM had their efforts turn sour almost overnight when management was changed or the company was bought.

Technology by itself is hollow; this is why the integrative process must involve both technology and values. Even if the company controllers cannot assign a quantitative value to trust and integrity, these qualities are no less significant to the enterprise.

Just because we cannot touch or count them does not mean that they are not real.

Two Examples of the Transition: Managing with Blurry Boundaries

Consider two examples of the shift in thinking that we will need as we enter the knowledge era. The first example is from the United States, the second from Denmark. They illustrate the thought patterns that move a company to a new understanding of its business.

Jim Lardner, vice president of John Deere and Company, has suggested the need to reduce a company's "complexity index."[15] He was reflecting on the real experience of Deere as it ran into difficulties trying to computerize and automate its Waterloo, Iowa, tractor works in the early 1980s.

Lardner realized that Deere had to reduce the confusion, contradictions, and inconsistencies that had crept into its processes over the years. Rather than building high-bay storage and automated work-in-process tracking systems, why not get rid of the WIP? Rather than pushing material through the plant, why not go to a Just-in-Time pull system? Rather than inspecting quality at the end of the line, why not design for robustness and get control over the processes so that quality would be ensured?

These changes required an elegance and sophistication that could not be bought from an outside vendor. Deere initiated its own efforts to reduce its complexity index. Its CIM, JIT, and Total Quality efforts simplified procedures while developing a more elegant understanding of how the various processes fit together and interact. Deere came to appreciate the interrelatedness of a wide variety of factors.

As companies attempt to unravel specific problems, serendipity can play an important role, as a second example shows. A Danish textile manufacturer was faced with the onerous task of taking yearly inventory. Traditionally, workers unrolled all the bolts of cloth and measured them. This was tedious and time-consuming.

This Danish company explored ways to measure the thicknesses of the bolts to compute their length, but found that some were wound more tightly than others and the widths of the cores varied. They reasoned that if they could get the core makers to standardize their cores, they could weigh the bolts and thereby compute the length. They then started bar coding the bolts. This made it possible to put bar code readers at the wholesale warehouses, giving them an indication of downstream consumption and allowing them to cut their inventory by fine-tuning production to market demands.[16]

What started out as an annual inventory measuring issue led ultimately to a more elegantly simple way of doing business. As the company followed the thread of the problem through its own organization and to its distribution network, it found that many departments needed to adjust their procedures. It also discovered that it operated within a web of networked and interrelated issues and opportunities.

These examples are echoed in many other manufacturing and service enterprises. Banking finds itself in a web of networked interrelationships, as do insurance companies, distribution supply houses, and mining companies. The Japanese trading companies, the *Sogo Shosha*, are masters at working in a web of interrelationships.

We cannot afford to continue playing the superficial power games that sap the strength from so many enterprises. Unfortunately, our educational systems have been more successful in pitting one student against another than in creating conditions under which students can learn to learn from one another in networking enterprises.

Some may argue that human networking requires too much of people. They are not interested in doing anything more than getting a fair day's pay. We have been conditioned well by the industrial era to expect little from our narrowly defined jobs. But attitudes are changing. Jack Welch, Jr., chairman and CEO of General Electric Company, has explained that GE's drive to downsize and delayer is targeted not primarily at cutting costs but "at liberating, facilitating, [and] unleashing the human energy and initiative of our people." Cutting out the layers of management removes "all the dampers, valves and baffles" that have stifled human creativity.[17]

Downsizing and delayering, by themselves, do not release human creativity. Executives need to be as accomplished in building people up and putting them in touch with themselves and one another as they are in tearing down walls and removing layers of management.

The confusing complexity of the industrial era's steep hierarchy is due primarily to its superficial appreciation of human creativity. It is an artificial construct, useful in its time but fast becoming a lumbering dinosaur in an era where lean, agile, action-oriented enterprises are a necessity. The transition to the elegantly simple idea of the knowledge era requires an understanding of human time and work as dialogue. We must release the pent-up human energy in our enterprises.

Figure 11.4 summarizes the model of the knowledge networking enterprise. Virtual, task-focusing teams are interacting with suppliers of finances, people, materials, and technology. They are also dialoguing with distributor networks and with customers. Their efforts, held together by their envisioning and knowledging, are responsive and quick.

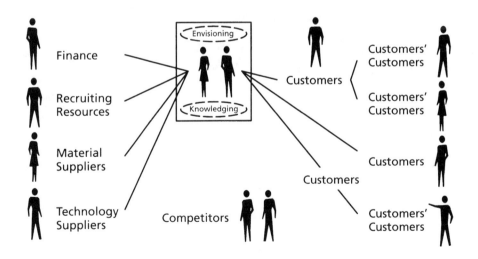

Figure 11.4 **Knowledge networking enterprises**

The transition to fifth-generation management is a process of leading and responding to people and opportunities. It is very much a human-centered process because it recognizes our natural ability to develop visions, to remember, and to act decisively. It involves us in the excitement of virtual enterprising, dynamic teaming, and knowledge networking. These processes thrive when open and honest dialogue is present. The final chapter presents ten practical considerations for managing more integrative and elegantly simple enterprises.

CHAPTER

12

MANAGING KNOWLEDGE NETWORKING

Frank Giardelli, CEO of Custom Products and Services, is able to send shock waves through his staff by tearing his organizational chart in half. Our journey from the confinement of the steep hierarchies to the spaciousness of human networking has been a slower and more deliberate process. We have had to work our way through the Smith/Taylor/Fayol bottleneck. We now face a new challenge. How do we manage fifth-generation enterprises?

The old rules of thumb no longer apply. Instead of worrying about commanding and controlling the enterprise, we must now focus and coordinate multiple task-focusing teams within and between companies. How will we build a climate of trust and openness? How will we learn to build upon the unique strengths of our people? And how will we engender accountability and learning?

Fifth-generation management is not something we are easily taught. It has to come from within, as a result of discovering the power of our own insights, emotions, and ability to see new patterns. We are not only listening to the music; we are the music. This final chapter focuses on ways we can use the new source of wealth—knowledge—to build effective knowledge networking enterprises (Figure 12.1).

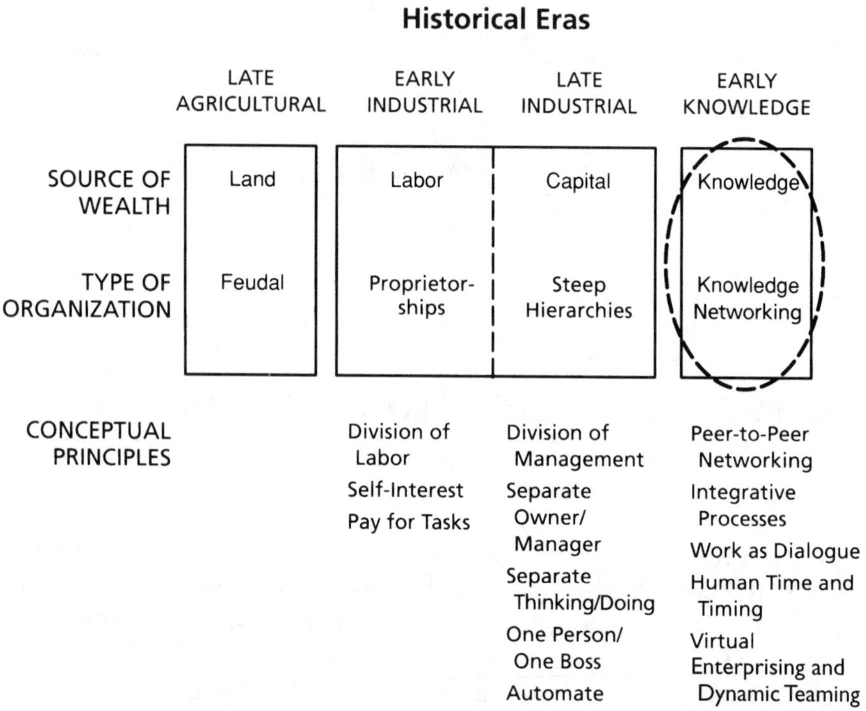

Historical Eras

	LATE AGRICULTURAL	EARLY INDUSTRIAL	LATE INDUSTRIAL	EARLY KNOWLEDGE
SOURCE OF WEALTH	Land	Labor	Capital	Knowledge
TYPE OF ORGANIZATION	Feudal	Proprietor-ships	Steep Hierarchies	Knowledge Networking
CONCEPTUAL PRINCIPLES		Division of Labor Self-Interest Pay for Tasks	Division of Management Separate Owner/Manager Separate Thinking/Doing One Person/One Boss Automate	Peer-to-Peer Networking Integrative Processes Work as Dialogue Human Time and Timing Virtual Enterprising and Dynamic Teaming

Figure 12.1 **Chapter focus: managing knowledge networking**

We find that management by question is much more effective than management by command. Questions engage us in the matter at hand. They put us at the intersection of our envisioning and knowledging, human time and clock time. Questions spark growth, insights, and clarity; it is this creativity that gives an organization its long-term viability.

In knowledge networking, not everything is entirely new. Some of the hierarchical organization remains. There are still boards of directors: presidents, vice presidents, and directors. There are still managers, professionals, and employees. Collective bargaining still exists. The wage and hour laws are still a part of the environment. Departments continue, people still have individual assignments, and there is still dull and boring work. What is new is that we have learned to work with "both/and" instead of "either/or" thinking. We are able to manage the routine and team for the non-routine.

There is, however, a qualitative difference between the industrial and knowledge eras. Organizations are much flatter. They are networked and networking. The president, vice presidents, and others are working much closer together as teams. They are coaches and mentors. The quality of human interaction is much higher. Women are likely to find that they are particularly well suited for management responsibilities in these networking enterprises. In fact, more companies will move women into management ranks because it makes good business sense; they often have excellent networking skills.

Instead of working sequentially in isolated departments or isolated companies, cross-functional and cross-company capabilities are combined to work on large and small projects in parallel through task-focusing teams and through teamwork of teams. Costing is done by project rather than by burdening direct labor. The enterprise internalizes the capability of continual learning. People are expected to teach and learn from one another on an ongoing basis. There is more discipline in these organizations. Instead of bureaucracy, the enterprise is held together by the excitement of actively responding to ever-changing market opportunities. Instead of just creating a vision of how a company wants others to see it, it needs to collect its customers' visions, the statement of their aspirations. It can then use its talents to enhance the capabilities of these customers so that they can better reach their aspirations.

The wealth-creating capacity of the enterprise is based on the knowledge of its people, their capabilities, and their aspirations. Much of this knowledge is only accessible through people, while other knowledge may be captured and embedded in application programs, databases, expert systems, neural networks, processes, and procedures. The creativity of the organization and its capacity to add value and generate value come through the intersection of its envisioning (the future made present), its engagement in the present, and its knowledging (the past made present).

If indeed the wealth-creating capacity of the enterprise is in its people and their capabilities and aspirations, we should examine the practical considerations required for leveraging this capability.

Ten Practical Considerations

The following ten considerations are not ordered by priority, but are interrelated. They should help us build knowledge networking into enterprises. An enterprise must be able to:

1. Develop envisioning capabilities so that the context is readily visible for the task-focusing dynamic teaming

2. Develop functional centers of excellence

3. Develop a technical networking infrastructure that is easily reconfigurable

4. Develop a data-integration strategy

5. Develop the ability to identify and track multiple task-focusing teams within and between companies

6. Develop learning, relearning, and unlearning capabilities

7. Develop norms, values, rewards, and measurements to support task-focusing dynamic teaming

8. Develop the ability to support the teamwork of teams

9. Develop and grow the knowledge base

10. Extend task-focusing virtual enterprising to include suppliers, partners, distributors, and customers

These ten considerations are designed to support the conceptual principles of the early knowledge era: peer-to-peer networking, integrative process, work as dialogue, human time and timing, and virtual task-focusing teams (Figure 12.2).

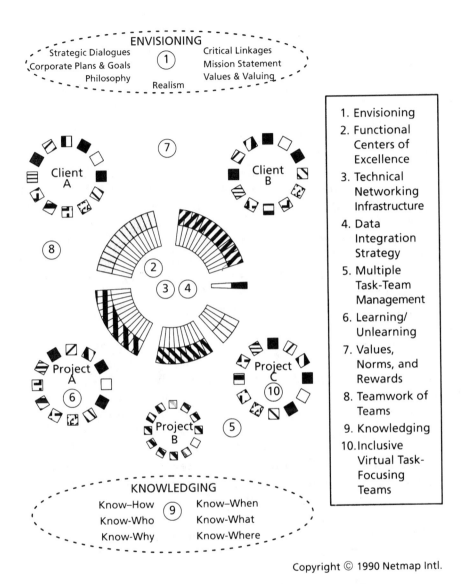

ENVISIONING
Strategic Dialogues   Critical Linkages
Corporate Plans & Goals   Mission Statement
① Philosophy   Values & Valuing
Realism

1. Envisioning
2. Functional Centers of Excellence
3. Technical Networking Infrastructure
4. Data Integration Strategy
5. Multiple Task-Team Management
6. Learning/ Unlearning
7. Values, Norms, and Rewards
8. Teamwork of Teams
9. Knowledging
10. Inclusive Virtual Task-Focusing Teams

Client A ⑦ Client B
⑧
② ⑧
③ ④
Project A ⑥ Project B ⑤ Project C ⑩

KNOWLEDGING
Know–How   Know–When
Know-Who ⑨ Know-What
Know-Why   Know-Where

Figure 12.2 **Ten practical considerations**

1. Envisioning Capabilities and Aspirations

Envisioning provides the context that guides the multiple task-focusing teams. These teams build upon the capabilities within and between companies. They are organized to address concrete customer aspirations, as embodied in concrete opportunities or to undertake specific projects. They may be composed of all internal resources, or include professionals from customer and supplier companies.

The company's envisionings are a composite of several elements: strategic dialogues, plans, goals, missions, critical linkage factors, philosophy, and values and valuing, tempered with market realism. As a company engages in strategic dialogue with its customers and suppliers, it develops an overall direction which is then translated into concrete plans, goals, and missions. The critical linkages between capabilities, wherever they may occur, is made. The company's philosophy and values provide the operating norms, and its ability to value capabilities and aspirations provides the substance with which to work.

Well-chosen corporate goals can help to coordinate efforts in areas that cut across traditional functional boundaries. Stretch goals can be particularly effective in providing focus by measuring customer satisfaction, on-time delivery, problem-free installation, and cycle-time reduction. Goals may include internal measures such as inventory turns, process quality, reduced engineering change orders, or data quality.

The company's philosophy and values help define its spirit. Often these are simple, direct statements that can be captured on one or two pages. They usually include references to customer satisfaction, the importance of correct relationships, and the value of all employees. They may also include references to the importance of valuing differences and the necessity of honesty and integrity.

Critical linkage factors, like critical success factors, are factors that bind the enterprise cross-functionally for success. For example, quality consciousness cannot be owned by one department. Others may refer to CLFs as mission-critical business processes. An order entry and management function cuts across many boundaries. In addition, many companies also develop architectures for materials, finance, and quality that must be linked together to be complementary and mutually reinforcing.

The often-overlooked element in a vision is its realism. It is easy to get carried away when "the rubber meets the sky." Realism works both ways. Timidity is as much of a trap as blind enthusiasm. This is where the enterprise's sense of timing and rhythm is so critical; it must be able to pace itself. It is too easy to become intoxicated with success, just as it is to become overly melancholy in defeat.

Good envisioning comes from within the enterprise, not just from the top. If managers, professionals, and workers are not involved, the vision will seem irrelevant. In the best envisioning, there is an active dialogue between the higher-level visions and specific capabilities. Often teams of engineers, marketers, service technicians, or manufacturing engineers will have ideas that can give generalized visions specific reality.

Virtual task-focusing teams should be expected to periodically challenge and enrich the enterprise visions, based on their specific work. This will help to keep the visions current and fresh. Real visions have meaning as they are realized in particular designs, products, processes, and services.

2. Functions: Centers of Excellence

As we shift from working sequentially to working in parallel with cross-functional teams, each person's knowledge and abilities will be even more significant. Therefore, the traditional functions must select the best people available and invest time and money to keep their knowledge on the cutting edge of their fields. It will be more critical than ever for professionals in functional departments to have both excellence in their own knowledge and a mastery of the procedures, standards, and operating norms of their group.

The functional department heads will need to work closely with the human resource department in hiring, promotion, and career development, as well as in training, education, and learning-support programs to keep their people current in their areas of discipline. These department heads should get to know their people and their aspirations, dream capabilities, and uncertainties. Instead of being seen as bosses, they should build mentoring and coaching relationships with their people. One way to do this is to invite individuals to keep a reference description of their backgrounds, interests, and capabilities in an accessible database. These references can then be easily searched when putting together task teams. This approach allows us to see people in a new way. Instead of beginning with narrowly defined job descriptions, we can begin with richer and more varied self-definitions of personal interests and capabilities. It is through close personal contact that department heads will be able to help nurture and develop their professional resources.

These functional centers of excellence—marketing, sales, engineering, manufacturing, finance, personnel, and human resources—are resource centers. There will no longer be high walls encircling a functional department's turf; instead, managers, professionals, and workers in the centers will be available to participate in a variety of individual and team efforts. This enhances the networking process, encouraging these professionals to compose well-balanced teams.

3. The Technical Networking Infrastructure

We need to create virtual teams regardless of the location of individual people. Physical and temporal proximity is of less importance when the enterprise has a well-designed and flexible technical networking capability. Electronic mail, computer note files, voice mail, distributed databases, integrated services digital network (ISDN), the Internet and World Wide Web, and a host of proprietary communication systems are adding richness to the world of networking. As these networks grow and evolve, nodes will be added, moved, and removed.

Enterprise networking will link both internal and external resources. Closer internal linkages are being forged between marketing, engineering, manufacturing, finance, and service. Working digitally, products and processes can be designed concurrently and simulated even without a physical prototype. Bills of material can be stripped out and sent to the manufacturing resource planning (MRP II) system, while information on the product's physical characteristics is sent to numeric control (NC) equipment, and other information is sent to technical publications.

Externally, enterprises are expanding their electronic data interchange (EDI) networking capabilities to include technical data interchange (TDI). The aerospace and automotive companies are leading in these efforts, but many other industries, from banks to service companies, will become involved over time.

Technical networking develops through several stages. First, connectivity and interoperability are established; then professionals and applications are interfaced. Gradually, common user interfaces and common reference architectures are developed to provide more integration. As the technical networking infrastructure is developed, new horizons open in the use and deployment of internal and external resources. We find ourselves working in a web of interrelationships, some of them complex and delicate. In order to communicate well both within the enterprise and between enterprises, we pay more attention to the way we define products, processes, and services.

4. Data Integration Strategy

In the discussion in Chapter 8, we explored the "shades of meaning" problem, the questions involving language ambiguity that face companies as they attempt to computerize their steep hierarchies. Simply put, our languages use terms that can be very ambiguous. When computers were first used, the challenge was to conserve memory and CPU cycles. Now that memory and CPUs are relatively inexpensive, the challenge has shifted to "meanings management."

We now recognize how important it is to define a limited core set of data elements that can be used by all the different functions. Hewlett-Packard, a recognized leader in this regard, has carefully defined twenty to thirty core elements that cut across the enterprise. Many different functions use these same elements.

The tools and techniques for data integration are available. Computer-aided software engineering (CASE), computer-aided data engineering (CADE), data dictionaries, relational databases, and object-oriented databases help focus efforts toward the development of core data architectures. Instead of locking the data within each application, more and more companies are developing a shareable and extensible data architecture. This makes it possible for different applications to use the same core data.

We can standardize our tools and procedures, and we can ask the task teams to identify core data elements that can be added to the enterprise data dictionary and merged into the core data architecture. Over time, we can then expand our data architectures, developing consistent and agreed-upon meanings for the key terms. How do we start this process?

We begin by listing all existing applications and grouping them by function. Then, using a Netmap-like technology, we identify existing patterns of interfacing between these applications, flagging the translators. We then develop a list of twenty key items our enterprise needs, such as "part," "assembly," "project," "tolerance," "location," and "vendor." We choose ten key applications and see how these terms are defined, not only in the official data dictionary, but more importantly, in the context of the application, including attributes. This effort usually reveals a wide variety of definitions for the same or similar terms. It is the shades of meaning in these applications that make nightmares of many translation projects. People can deal with ambiguity in language; computers cannot. Once our enterprises understand our spaghetti-like interfacing of applications and the different flavors of the definitions, we can begin to simplify our data architectures. This can be a daunting undertaking, but well worth the price, as shown by Ingersoll Milling Machine's success. In the 1970s, Ingersoll developed a common and shareable data architecture for multiple applications. This is integration. Most of our companies are still lost in the jungle of interfacing applications.

5. Multiple Task Team Management
As we switch from steep hierarchies to the use of multiple task-focusing teams within and between companies, we will need to give these teams visibility and support. Unfortunately, in steep hierarchies, task teams often remain invisible to those who are not involved. Professionals and managers feel torn between their involvement on these teams and the work for which they normally get rewarded. This process needs to be reversed.

By aligning the organization in a circle, it is possible to show the clustering of multiple teams, as in Figure 12.2. With the appropriate windowing software, it will be possible to see the organization with its teams in one window, a list of themes that they are working on in another, a list of participants in a third, and the project status in a fourth.

The teams should be responsible for defining their goals, purpose, and mission—together with their project plan—in a shareable database. Teams can then scan various other activities to ask for help or share insights. Task teams will need to be brought together periodically so that they can exchange progress notes, clarify themes, focus on critical issues, and struggle with knotty problems. The teams need a rhythm to their meeting schedules in order to keep their work focused and on track. As these teams share their work, they will be aligning their efforts with the enterprise's visions and knowledge base.

The vitality of our enterprises is becoming more people- and team-dependent. We must put more time and effort into building sound and flexible team organizations, using all that we have learned from employee involvement, sociotechnical systems, participative management, organizational development, and team building to increase our team management capabilities. When people know that they have visibility for their participation in these activities, it is likely that they will put more of themselves into the effort, especially if the reward and measurement systems are also adjusted appropriately.

The use of centers of excellence together with multiple task-focusing teams means that both technical and human resources can be used more effectively and efficiently. It becomes a manageable virtual environment, based on human knowledge and capabilities. This approach can also generate rapid learning.

6. Learning, Relearning, and Unlearning

Traditional steep hierarchies focus primarily on training and education. A third component must be added: learning, relearning, and unlearning. In order to maintain self-generation and knowledge growth, we will need to become much more effective learners. As we sort out experiences, impressions, and past learning, we relearn the key lessons. In the unlearning process, some old ideas are discarded.

Typically, when people participate in teamwork, they want to prove how much more clever they are than the others. For this competitive attitude we can thank our schools, where students are pitted against one another, vying for the teacher's accolades. Rarely are students taught how to learn from one another.

We are good at tearing down each other's ideas, not building them up. Moreover, learning is often impeded because we are afraid that if we give away our good ideas, someone else may get credit for them. Simply put, we have a lot of cultural baggage to overcome, or unlearn, if we hope to nurture a learning capability within our organizations.

If we hope to be successful in rapidly changing markets, our teams must spot the right patterns early by listening and learning, then responding quickly. We are dependent on one another's knowledge, insights, and experience to cut through the fuzzy and ambiguous clouds shrouding possible market opportunities. Sustained responsiveness requires that group learning be captured and applied to other efforts. Unfortunately, many project teams fail to retain their knowledge as they proceed through the project. At the end of the effort, when they have disbanded, much of what they have learned evaporates into the ether. As we become more sophisticated in our expectations of task teams, we periodically will ask them to share their learning with other teams, thus contributing to the knowledge resources and envisioning of the enterprise.

Some may object that this approach is too idealistic, that it will not work in the real world. People have learned to be very careful in sharing ideas. Their emotional scars are a reminder of how brutal some experiences can be. Certainly these experiences cannot be discounted.

As long as we are preoccupied with the idea of possession, we will limp along. On the other hand, if we can begin to understand the nature of human time and the importance of envisioning and remembering, we will gain a new perspective. Instead of seeing group participation as a power struggle, we will come to appreciate the human-growth aspects of work.

A simple change of norms can open up new possibilities. For example, if each time I participate in a group I actively try to learn two or three new things from the others in the room, I put myself into a learning mode. I gain—as do the others, because they feel listened to. One of the greatest rewards in life is to feel listened to. This is the basis of recognition, something we all seek. As we learn to listen carefully to one another, we are doing two things— learning, and affirming others as people. Unlike the Greeks' idea of work, our work is as rich as our leisure. As we grasp the nature of work dialogue and of human time, active learning will become an essential part of everyday life.

7. Values, Norms, Rewards, and Measurement Systems

It is easy to install a technical networking infrastructure within an enterprise. It is harder to shape new values and norms, and to support them with the proper reward and measurement systems. How do we manage the shift?

- The industrial era used the dexterity of the hand to grow. We need to build upon the dexterity of the mind.

- In the industrial era the past was a throwaway. In the knowledge era the past is a source of insight and knowledge that flows with us.

- The industrial era assumed that the future was far ahead. The knowledge era finds the future contained in the present, through our aspirations and active envisioning.

- Envisioning and knowledging were of minor importance to the industrial era. They are everything in the knowledge era.

- The mechanical model predominated in the industrial era. Today it is being replaced by a biological and organic model. Instead of gears meshing together, we appreciate minds growing.

Having worked in a machine shop, Frederick Taylor knew how work groups set their own quotas. He realized that the only way to break this process was to set up a planning office that would define a fair day's workload. This led to his idea of separating thinking from doing, which resulted in his scientific management theory.

However, if visibility and accountability are built into the system, Taylor's concerns are no longer problems. Instead, top management can stimulate, inspire, and challenge the teams, releasing much of the pent-up energy that is wasted in so many of our enterprises. Instead of beginning with a machine-like organizational model, we need a free-form approach that supports knowledge networking, using our envisioning and knowledging abilities.

Values are a particularly important component of the envisioning. They are not gained through a training course or through wall posters, but are nurtured and grown over time through personal interaction. Trust and openness reflect the attitudes of top management as well as those of everyone else in the enterprise. These values grow slowly, yet they can disappear almost overnight. The fact that Digital employees are expected to "do the right thing" is a sign of trust in the employees—and a measure of management's integrity, honesty, and wisdom. Values come alive as verbs. This is why it is critical that we quickly evolve our corporations from cultures of distrust and devaluing to cultures of valuing and trust. As people feel genuinely valued, they will reveal so many more talents and the company will be that much richer in assets.

General Georges Doriot, whose venture capital firm invested the initial $70,000 in Ken Olsen's idea for Digital's interactive computer, was fond of stressing the importance of "generosity." By this General Doriot meant the willingness to give other people their due, to give them space to express themselves, and to listen carefully for the seed of an idea in what they are saying. Attitudes like this build trust, openness, and integrity.

Each enterprise determines the constellation of values that it deems important; there is no prescribed list. But as new norms emerge, we are able to see who has integrity and who misuses information. We know who listens and who strangles thought. We know who shares knowledge and who hides behind a position of authority. We know who is able to share leadership and who holds on to it. In fact, good leadership will also display excellence in learnership. Leaders of the future will be able to ask exceptional questions as a way to deepen and focus others' efforts.

Now we need to redefine our rewards and measurements to catch up with the times. When we think of rewards, we usually think first of monetary rewards. In doing so, we accept the Greek notion of work as punishment: if we give up our time to do something we do not like, then we should be rewarded handsomely.

Although these rewards will continue to be important, they will be complemented by another dimension of reward, that of quality human interaction. It can be very exhilarating to participate on a dynamic team that encourages human growth. There is reward in being listened to and challenged by our peers and reward in the sheer joy of accomplishment. This helps to bring out the best in us. Participation in a community of co-creation is itself a powerful motivator and reward, especially when we believe in the significance of the overall effort. This is why Stephen Covey's principle-centered leadership approach is so appreciated.[1]

As we align ourselves in virtual enterprises or dynamic teams, we will be interacting peer to peer rather than superior to subordinate. The former supports growth; the latter kills inspiration. Perhaps the heads of centers of excellence will have the final say on rewards, but peer reviews will probably play a growing role in the reward process. This process will remain quite subjective, but its success will depend on the integrity of one's peers and on the heads of the centers of excellence, rather than on one's "boss." Since more rewards will be given for contributions to the team success and fewer for isolated individual firefighting, incentive systems will need to be adjusted accordingly. Cost accounting will tailor its systems around programs and projects rather than burdening direct labor. Much work remains to be done in this area.[2]

8. Teamwork of Teams

In the rhythm of the enterprise's work, some products or services are being born, others are maturing, and still others are being phased out. As different teams pursue their objectives, they will inevitably overlap with one another; this is natural and wholesome. Instead of envisioning the organization as mutually exclusive boxes, we should think of overlapping teams and overlapping companies, like Venn diagrams. This happens both within the company between functions and between companies (Figure 12.3).

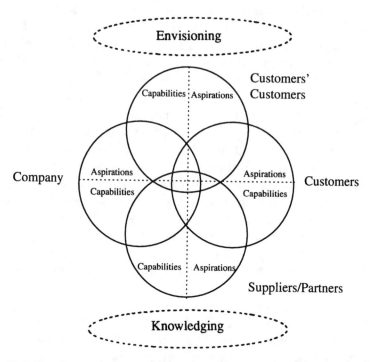

Figure 12.3 **The Virtual Enterprising and Dynamic Teaming of Capabilities and Aspirations, nurtured by collaborative Knowledging and Envisioning**

Once the enterprise installs its network and begins networking with other companies directly or through the Internet, it can pull teams together across geographical distance and time zones. We do not have to share the same office space; in fact, using extended networks, teams can include key people from supplier or client companies. Ingersoll Milling Machine has mastered this capability in a large project with an automobile maker.[3] Its project team includes engineers from the car company who work side by side with its team in design and building efforts.

Some companies use "management by event" as a powerful focusing technique. Professionals like to rise to the occasion; given an opportunity to show their worth, they often surprise even themselves. The enterprise can periodically stage events in which the task-focusing teams are asked to help grow the enterprise vision based on work that has been done.

Our challenge is to facilitate the teamwork of teams. Just as each task team has a rhythm of its own, so too there is a rhythm in the work between teams. A team developing a new iron reduction process may be dependent upon the developments of another team working on plasma arcs. (This idea is not new; the success of the industrial revolution was made possible by concurrent developments in many interrelated disciplines, from fluid dynamics to metallurgy.) A technical networking infrastructure and shareable core data will help facilitate the interchange of themes between work teams.

Earlier I suggested that virtual task-focusing teams are like jazz combos. Each combo is capable of taking a theme and adding value to it in unique and individual ways. It can toss a theme to another combo to see how the other combo works with it. Its unique tempo, rhythm, and articulation can challenge and inspire the other combos or task teams.

9. Knowledging Capabilities

Networking enterprises are much freer in form than steep hierarchies. They are held together not by rigid bureaucracy but by shared visions and common knowledge resources, the most valuable of which are in people's heads. We humans have a wonderful knack of recombining what we have learned to find new ways to solve problems—for example, we may combine an understanding of metallurgy, electrical flux, and test results to discover why a particular type of disk drive fails. We can look at a situation in the larger context. Unlike computers, we can work with vague clues, fuzzy patterns, and ambiguous data.

Relational and object-oriented database technology makes it easier to dynamically reconfigure computer-based memory, but this technology is limited. On the other hand, if an enterprise captures 30 percent of its core knowledge in a consistent and shareable manner and in an understandable data architecture, then a partnership between people and processors can be quite powerful. Group technology has been a wonderful teacher of how to classify and code drawings and processes. Just-in-Time has helped us sort out basic relationships both within our organizations and with our suppliers.

We need tremendous discipline in the care and nurturing of our enterprise knowledge bases. We must be ready for the costs of maintaining both our legacy systems and new ones. As individual and team learning is codified in engineering standards, classification and coding systems, operating techniques, applications, data dictionaries, and customer profiles, an invaluable resource is developed. What teams in one plant learn in mastering surface-mount technology can benefit other plants in the same company. These bases are critical, as Nonaka and Takeuchi point out.[4]

Even if accountants have difficulty valuing the know-how represented in the knowledge base, it is a key resource for the enterprise and the source of new business visions. Mastery of unique knowledging capabilities gives the enterprise market differentiation. Therefore, task teams should be expected to not only solve the tasks at hand, but also to contribute to the knowledge base and to augment the shared business vision. The measurement and reward systems should acknowledge this added contribution.

10. Inclusive Virtual Task-Focusing Teams

As we learn to think beyond the four walls of our own enterprise, we can configure our task teams to include representatives from suppliers, partners, distributors, and customers. Just like internal resources, these people are virtual resources. For example, a product development team may include two representatives from a customer organization whose presence adds to the team's understanding of real-world customer expectations.

This approach also helps the enterprise involve the customer in delivery of the product or service. When automatic teller machines involve the consumer directly in the operation of the bank, the bank wins in two ways: it makes money from this extension of its service, and it reduces its own clerical staffing needs.

Concluding Thoughts

We can either remain prisoners in the boxes and lines of our organizational charts or experience the challenge of working and teaming together in virtual enterprises, dynamic teams, and through knowledge networking, as explored in Part 1. We can either live by clock time, as prisoners of the present, or be inspired and nurtured in human time as we network our envisioning (the future that is present) and knowledging (the past that flows with us). We can either look up to our bosses and down on our subordinates or engage as peers in a dialogue about the significant themes challenging our enterprises.

We can flounder in the separation of thinking and doing or engage in the integrative process of continual creativity. We can remain isolated from one another or seek out the capabilities and aspirations of one another as individuals or through teams to get on with the work. Look again at the historical eras and the changes they have brought. The transition to networking enterprises is not inevitable; it is up to us to bring it about. We can either remain in a transaction mode, looking to just satisfy needs, or we can redefine our realities, learning ways to co-create together.

Our new source of wealth is more a *capability* than a *possession.* Knowledging, our human ability to discover, interrelate, and respond to patterns of opportunities on an ongoing basis, gives us a new mastery over time and improves our timing. As we network and team with one another, we are able to act decisively and overcome the fragmentation of the industrial era. Through this shift, we gain a new sense of accountability toward one another, a new sense of excitement, and a new sense of co-creativity.

Think back over the previous chapters and substitute the concepts of "envisioning" and "knowledging" (capabilities) for the words "vision" and "knowledge" (something possessed). These changes should underscore the significance of "work as dialogue" and "human time and timing" as key factors in putting the functions in touch with one another. This process can never be automated or computerized, although it can be supported by computers and networking.

No system by itself can overcome the fragmentation in our steep hierarchies. Only as people start to reach out and network with one another will this fragmentation be overcome. It will not always be easy, because old attitudes live on in strange ways. In fact, it is natural to expect that we will encounter many "gotchas" along the way. People who have a hard time listening and learning from one another will have difficulty working in cross-functional teams or between companies. Top management may be slow in learning to accept ideas from below. Teams will go off in different directions in an uncoordinated manner because the rhythm of the organization is not well established. Without many rungs on the career ladder, some managers will not know how to gauge relative success. Companies will just plain miss market signals, get behind the technology curve, and misinterpret developments. We will still have to contend with people's darker sides. These are all elements we will encounter and will have to deal with in one way or another. Will these "gotchas" be fatal? Probably not, if we are clear about where we are going and what needs to be done; otherwise, there will be those who want to retreat to the comfort of the steep hierarchy where the stovepipes are warm and cozy.

Other management challenges deal with accountability, focusing and coordinating, and learning. It should be clear by now that accountability comes through envisioning. Envisioning and knowledging also help the multiple virtual task-focusing teams to focus and coordinate their efforts. And as we break out of the web of industrial-era conceptual principles, we will be able to build into the daily life of our enterprises the practice of continual learning. Just as athletes learned to rethink the way they high jump, we can redefine the way that we work together. We have only one life; why tolerate a way of working that demeans our capabilities and denies us our aspirations?

Dan Infante, former vice president of Digital Information Systems, has captured the spirit of fifth-generation management when he writes: "A good place to work is one which engages the whole person—his or her thoughts, feelings, and, yes, even aspirations. It is a place which values diversity, and sees peoples' uniqueness as the seed of new ideas and possibilities." In addition, he believes that "A good place to work is where people feel at ease collaborating cross-functionally and feel empowered to make decisions that are right for the organization."[5]

Ken Olsen's vision of this elegantly simple organization is realizable, especially as we work more in parallel, in multiple dynamic teams. We can learn to use our education and knowledge to motivate and inspire one another, as they did for Custom Products and Services, Inc., in Part 1. Fifth-generation management is not only a possibility; it is a necessity in order to build the foundation for the next economy, one based on knowledge as the new source of wealth. As we learn to *generate value* through the active valuing of one another's capabilities and aspirations, we will discover the excitement and flow of virtual enterprising, dynamic teaming, and knowledge networking. Indeed, we will know that we are on the way when our language changes and we start using *with* more than *for* and we do not just talk about the importance of values (nouns), but we actively value (verb) one another. May we have the same courage shown by Frank Giardelli and his colleagues as they risk letting go of the old organizational model so that they can spring to new heights of understanding and creativity.

Good luck on your journey toward the wholeness of knowledge networking in elegantly simple enterprises. Please keep a log that you can share; learning is an ongoing process for us all. I hope the visions expressed in this book will speed you on your way, and I would like to learn from your experiences, both successes and failures. Both are important as we learn together. Please send me a note on the net: csavage@ix.netcom.com.

AFTERWORD

By Daniel Burrus

In Watterson's comic strip, Calvin and Hobbes, they occasionally play "Calvin Ball." The game has only one rule, it can never be played twice with the same set of rules. Survival in Calvin Ball is not holding onto the old set of rules; thriving comes by continually co-creating a new set, a process I explored in *Technotrends*.

Why is it so hard to continually let go of the tried and true and innovate instead? The familiar is comfortable, the unexpected is intimidating. Yet we live amongst sets of swirling, pulsating, and chaotic technological developments, which, in their own ways, are continually redefining the rules of the game.

Why do little Calvin and his sidekick Hobbes understand this so much better than most of us? Why do we worry so much about how much to "change" (noun), when life is itself a kaleidoscopic process of continual "changing" (verb)?

In *Fifth Generation Management, Co-creating through Virtual Enterprising, Dynamic Teaming, and Knowledge Management*, Charles Savage works many of these same underlying themes as I do in *Technotrends*, but from an organizational perspective. I might focus more on ways new technologies, such as genetic engineering, digital electronics, and intelligent networks, are shaping our business environment, whereas Charles focuses on the essential nature of work and human time. Even though our starting points are different, we are certainly kindred spirits when it comes to the underlying values we both believe in, such as the role of synergy, collaboration, and co-creation.

Instead of just protecting the canvas of the past, we both are excited about ways to paint in the opportunities of the future. Most of what life can be, it is not yet. It is up to us to inspire one another as individuals and companies to unleash our collaborative creativity. Charles helps us understand how we blend the color and texture of one another's ideas through virtual enterprising, dynamic teaming, and knowledge networking.

We do not put asset numbers on ideas, but it is these raw ideas which are refined on the canvas of the possible which provide our ever-changing products and services. Today our language still focuses us on the processes of transforming raw materials into finished goods. But underlying this is the process of transforming raw ideas into powerful products and saleable services. As Charles points out, the Industrial Era has focused on mining limited natural resources, whereas the Knowledge Era ushers in the possibilities of mining unlimited human resources, our minds.

The Industrial Era gave us an economy of scarcity, where we had to protect and control. The Knowledge Era is providing a platform to create the economy of abundance, based on non-scarce ideas, which through dynamic collaboration, can grow into inspirational arteries which nurture even more creativity. The Industrial Era was dependent on a well tuned infrastructure, while the Knowledge Era is dependent on vibrant "infostructure."

This infostructure is dependent not just on advances in computer based technology, from parallel processing to the World Wide Web on the Internet, but it is also dependent on a shift in our attitudes or mindsets. In the first part of *Fifth Generation Management*, Charles uses the analogy of high jumping. People reach higher levels because they are willing to rethink their mindsets. On the Web, people are valued not because of a fancy title or big car, but because of the quality of their interaction. It is not communication or discussion, but quality conversation and dialogue which count. Questions are more valuable than statements, because they nurture exploration and discovery.

Our tools are changing. In the Industrial Era we used heavy hammers to break apart the earth to free its riches. In the Knowledge Era we use probing questions to uncover the underlying patterns of thought, the new riches. The one breaks apart, the other helps weave fragments of tiny ideas into larger actionable patterns.

Indeed, in the Industrial Era we could only deal with complexity by breaking it apart, often to such an extent that we lost an understanding of the whole or the compelling context. In the Knowledge Era, as Charles points out, we are again comfortable with complexity, seeing its parts and its wholes at the same time. Fractals, holonics, agility, and hypertext organizations are metaphors which help us to begin to master the new paradigm, the dynamic interplay of the whole and the parts. This makes it possible to shift from the value chain to the valuing cluster, as Charles points out, where business becomes a strategic dialogue among and between our companies and our suppliers, customers and customers' customers, truly a process of co-creation.

Rather than protecting the past, we need to bring the playfulness of Calvin and Hobbes to the canvas of the possible. Instead of confirming rules, we need liberating roles, through which we not only create products and services, but we co-create ourselves and our cultures. Charles helps us move from the stifling "boxes and lines" model to the synergy of overlapping circles. He helps us rediscover the nature of human work, playful work, creative work, and co-creative work which is continually shaping our future and yet is never complete. The seeds of the economy of abundance, based on the mining of minds, of teaming capabilities and building off aspirations, are planted. How can we nurture their growth, because they are our growth?

Emerging trends in technology pry us loose from our blind bondage to yesterday's way of doing things. Can we seize the moment and experience the deep resonance of the dialogue of work? Can we discover ways to more effectively engage in the present, because we can mine the past and envision the future? Certainly, Charles has helped us to speak the new language in simple terms which bring value to what we do and who we are. By actively valuing one another as individuals and companies, our natural co-creative capabilities can blossom forth. We can leverage the intellectual capital already in our companies, a resource we have hardly begun to tap.

We are indeed on the threshold of a new infrastructure of understanding which will make the emerging infostructure a rich resource of minds out of which to build a vital Knowledge Era economy. This economy will not be built by a few barons of industry, but by us all, you and I and our colleagues in the world, because we have moved beyond our simplistic commutative attitudes and learned to value one another's capabilities and listen for one another's aspirations. Charles has pointed us in the right direction, but it is up to us now. The possibilities are exciting, but can we seize the opportunities?

—Daniel Burrus, author of *Technotrends*

CHAPTER NOTES

Foreword

1. Sherrin Bennett and Juanita Brown, "Mindshift: Strategic Dialogue for Breakthrough Thinking," in *Learning Organizations: Developing Cultures for Tomorrow's Workplace*, ed. Sarita Chawla and John Renesch (Portland, OR: Productivity Press, 1995).

Chapter 3. Wednesday

1. Debra Rogers, president of Entovation International, Inc., has servicemarked the concept "Innovating with Customers" as she has understood the new model of teaming that is emerging. Boeing, in developing the 777, included representatives from United and other airlines on the design team, a real example of innovating with one's customers.

Chapter 4. Thursday

1. Dr. Arun Gairola, VP Technology, ABB Holding, Mannheim, Germany.

Chapter 6. Introduction: The Past and Future

1. Stephen Grossberg, "Nonlinear Neural Networks: Principles, Mechanisms, and Architectures," *Neural Networks* 1, no. 1 (1988): 17–61.

2. Robert G. Eccles and Dwight B. Crane, *Doing Deals: Investment Banks at Work* (Boston: Harvard Business School Press, 1988).

3. Margaret Wheatley, *Leadership and the New Science: Learning About Organization from an Orderly Universe* (San Francisco: Berrett-Koehler, 1992) and Sally Helgesen, *The Web of Inclusion: A New Architecture for Building Great Organizations* (New York: Doubleday Currency, 1995).

4. Ikujiro Nonaka and Hirotaka Takeuchi, *The Knowledge-Creating Company: How Japanese Companies Create the Dynamics of Innovation* (New York: Oxford University Press, 1995). An excellent description of the project teaming and learning processes. Nonaka and Takeuchi are adding a rich and different perspective to the work begun by Peter Senge in *The Fifth Discipline*.

5. Ibid.

6. Edward A. Feigenbaum and Pamela McCorduck, *The Fifth Generation: Artificial Intelligence and Japan's Computer Challenge to the World* (Reading, MA: Addison-Wesley, 1983).

7. I once asked Beth Reuthe, president of Maine Tommow, who has managed production plants for both Bendix and Digital, about her approach to management. She told me a story of how she helped one of her key managers get in touch with his inner self. Although formerly a workaholic, he started spending more time with his family and in community service. She noted that he became much more effective at the plant. As I reflected on the story, I realized that the industrial-era approach has never encouraged us to get in touch with our own selves, with our feelings, our thoughts, and our aspirations. Instead, it has wanted us to "do what we're told." If we are going to listen to others at a deeper level, we are going to have to quiet down and listen to ourselves at the same time.

8. Eric Teicholz and Joel N. Orr, *Computer Integrated Manufacturing Handbook* (New York: McGraw-Hill, 1987), 1.4–1.5.

9. See the discussion of the "A," "B," "C" triad in Chapter 3.

10. Peter Drucker, "The Coming of the New Organization," *Harvard Business Review* 66, no. 1 (January–February 1988): 47. For an expansion on this article see Peter Drucker, *The New Realities: In*

Government and Politics/In Economics and Business/In Society and World View (New York: Harper & Row, 1989), 173–252.

11. Ken Olsen, "Presentation at the Annual Meeting of Digital Equipment Corporation, Boston, November 6, 1986," in *Digital Equipment Corporation Second Quarter Report 1987* (Maynard, MA: Digital Equipment Corp., 1987): 4.

12. Paul Kidd, "Technology and Engineering Design: Shaping a Better Future or Repeating the Mistakes of the Past?" *IEEE Proceedings* 135, no. 5 (May 1988). See also: Kidd, *Agile Manufacturing: Forging New Frontiers* (London: Addison-Wesley, 1994).

13. Kazuto Togino, "A Global Programming Language and Orchestration of the Execution of Jobs and Tasks," National Research Council Canada, Symposium on Manufacturing Application Languages, June 20–21, 1988, Winnipeg, Manitoba.

Chapter 7. Five Generations of Computers and Management

1. Gerhard Friedrich of Digital Equipment Corporation, together with the Industrial Liaison Program of MIT, organized a conference in May 1985 called "Managing the Transition to the Fifth Generation." Following the conference a videotape was produced entitled "Fifth-Generation Management."

2. Edward A. Feigenbaum and Pamela McCorduck, *The Fifth Generation: Artificial Intelligence and Japan's Computer Challenge to the World* (Reading, MA: Addison-Wesley, 1983), 17.

3. See reference to John von Neumann in *Computer Basics: Understanding Computers*, ed. Russell B. Adams and Donald Cantley (Alexandria, VA: Time-Life Books, 1985), 62–63.

4. Charles M. Savage, *Fifth Generation Management for Fifth Generation Technology* (Dearborn, MI: Society of Manufacturing Engineers, 1987), 3.

5. Adam Smith, *The Wealth of Nations* (London: Penguin Classics, 1987).

6. Frederick Winslow Taylor, *Scientific Management* (New York: Harper and Brothers, 1947), 24.

7. Henri Fayol, *General and Industrial Management*, trans. Constance Storrs (London: Pitman, 1949), 24. His fourteen points are as follows:

   1. Division of work (specialization belongs to the natural order)
   2. Authority and responsibility (responsibility is a corollary of authority)
   3. Discipline (discipline is what leaders make it)
   4. Unity of command (men cannot bear dual command)
   5. Unity of direction (one head and one plan for a group of activities having the same objectives)
   6. Subordination of individual interest to the general interest
   7. Remuneration (fair, rewarding of effort, reasonable)
   8. Centralization (centralization belongs to the natural order)
   9. Scalar chain (line of authority, gangplank principle)
   10. Order (a place for everyone and everyone in his or her place)
   11. Equity (results from a combination of kindliness and justice)
   12. Stability of tenure of personnel (prosperous firms are stable)
   13. Initiative (great source of strength for business)
   14. Esprit de corps (union is strength)

8. Ibid.

9. According to Leslie Berkes, Netmap International has completed over 250 studies undertaken to discover the real structure of organizations—that is, the structure created by individuals in carrying out their vital tasks. These studies have been conducted in major international Fortune 500 corporations across a variety of industries, large privately held companies, government agencies, nonprofit groups, and service firms. Across all these studies fewer than 20 percent of formally designated managers proved to be key to the vital task networks. See also John J. Galloway, "Revealing Organizational Networks," Annual Conference of Australian Communications Association, Sydney, July 1987; John J. Galloway and Anne Gorman, *Going Places: How to Network Your Way to Personal Success* (Sydney: Allen and Unwin, 1987); and Donald G. Livingston and Leslie J. Berkes, "Netmap: An Innovative Diagnostic Tool," *Journal of Managerial Psychology* 4, no. 4 (1989): 7–14.

10. Stanley M. Davis and Paul R. Lawrence, *Matrix* (Reading, MA: Addison-Wesley, 1977).

11. Davis, *Future Perfect* (Reading, MA: Addison-Wesley, 1987), 86. See also Fred V. Guterl, "Goodbye, Old Matrix," *Business Month* (February 1989): 32–38.

12. Davis, *Future Perfect*, 87.

13. Digital Equipment Corporation, in recognizing the growing gap between technology and the organization, has done pioneering work in developing ways to intertwine the development of a company's *business, technology,* and *human resources.* See Dennis O'Connor and Wendy Wilkerson, *Guide to Expert Systems Program Management* (Maynard, MA: Digital Equipment Corp., 1985).

14. Stephen Covey has awakened many to the need for principle-centered leadership in his writings and speaking.

15. William Bridges, in the lead article in *Fortune* of September 19, 1994, suggests that "jobs" are an artifact of the industrial era and have outlived their usefulness. He elaborates on this theme in his recent book, *Jobshift: How to Prosper in a Workplace without Jobs* (Reading, MA: Addison-Wesley, 1994).

16. Thomas Stewart, "Your Company's Most Valuable Asset: Intellectual Capital: New Ways to Build It and Measure It," *Fortune* (3 October 1994).

17. Winfried Sihn, Stefan König, Rita Kristof, "Aktives Ideenmanagement (AIM)—Dienstleistungen kreativer gestalten" [Active idea management (AIM)—service providing through creative approaches] in Hans-Jürgen Warnecke, *Aufbruch zum Fraktalen Unternaehmen: Praxisbeispiele für neues Denken und Handeln* [Breakthrough to the fractal enterprise: practical examples for new thought and action] (Berlin: Springer-Verlag, 1995), 95–112.

18. Ikujiro Nonaka and Hirotaka Takeuchi, *The Knowledge-Creating Company: How Japanese Companies Create the Dynamics of Innovation* (New York: Oxford University Press, 1995).

19. Shoshana Zuboff, *In the Age of the Smart Machine: The Future of Work and Power* (New York: Basic Books, 1988). Zuboff has raised the discussion of computer-based technology to a higher level of understanding. She has provided an insightful look at the impact of computers in the factory, bank, and office. According to Zuboff, "informating" is qualitatively different from automating. Automa-

tion removes the human element; informating, on the other hand, involves the individual in new and exciting ways. Although it suggests a process, "informating" connotes information, something that is already known in the past. "Knowledging," on the other hand, draws both on what is known and on our ability to envision what has not yet come into being.

20. Joseph Harrington, Jr., *Computer Integrated Manufacturing* (1973; reprint, New York: Robert E. Krieger Publishing Co., 1979); Jay Galbraith, *Designing Complex Organizations* (Reading, MA: Addison-Wesley, 1979); and Daniel Bell, *The Coming Post-Industrial Society: A Venture in Social Forecasting* (New York: Basic Books, 1973).

21. Peter Drucker, "The Coming of the New Organization," *Harvard Business Review* 66, no. 1 (January–February 1988): 47; Davis, *Future Perfect*; Richard Nolan, Alex J. Pollock, and James P. Ware, "Creating the 21st Century Organization," *Stage by Stage* 8, no. 4 (Lexington, MA: Nolan, Norton and Co., fall 1988): 1–11.

22. Drucker, "The Coming of the New Organization," 45.

23. Ibid., 50.

24. Ibid., 53.

25. Davis, *Future Perfect*, 89.

26. Nolan, Pollock, and Ware, "Creating the 21st Century Organization."

27. Ibid., 1.

28. Ibid., 2.

29. For more information, contact the IMS Promotion Center, Tokyo, Japan, phone: 81-3-5562-0331, fax: 81-3-5562-0310.

30. Arthur Koestler, *The Ghost in the Machine* (London: Hutchinson & Co., 1967).

31. Jeffrey Stamps, *Holonomy: A Human System Theory* (Seaside, CA: Intersystem Publications, 1980).

32. Hans-Jürgen Warnecke with Manfred Hüser, *The Fractal Company: A Revolution in Corporate Culture* (Germany: 1992; reprint, New York: Springer-Verlag, 1993).

33. Warnecke, *Aufbruch zum Fraktalen Unternehmen.*

34. Ibid., 97. (Translated from the German text). Incidentally, in a study of innovative companies in the United States, Europe, and Latin America, I found that they consciously got away from using the word "employee." In its place they used "co-worker" (Oticon in Denmark), "associate" (Wm. Gore & Associates in the United States and Semco in Brazil), and "member" (Johnsonville Foods in the United States). See Joan Lancourt and Charles M. Savage, "Organizational Transformation and the Changing Role of the Human Resource Function," (New York: *Compensation and Benefits Management,* Volume II, Number 4, Autumn, 1995).

35. Manfred Hüser and Ralf Kaun, "Wer wa(a)gt, gewinnt—Wägetechnik nach Kundenwunsch von der *Mettler-Toledo GmbH*" [Whoever weighs, wins: weighing technology according to customer wishes from Mettler-Toledo] in Warnecke, *Aufbruch zum Fraktalen Unternehmen,* 315–337.

36. Conversations with Len Allgaier of General Motors, Richard Engwall of Westinghouse, Rick Dove of Paradigm Shift, and Roger Nagel of Lehigh University.

37. Rick Dove, "Lean & Agile: Synergy, Contrast and Emerging Structure," Defense Manufacturing Conference '93 (December 1993).

38. James Womack, Daniel Jones, and Daniel Roos, *The Machine That Changed the World* (New York: Rawson Associates, 1990).

39. Steven Goldman, Roger Nagel, and Kenneth Preiss, *Agile Competitors and Virtual Organizations: Strategies for Enriching the Customer* (New York: Van Nostrand Reinhold, 1994).

40. Paul Kidd, *Agile Manufacturing: Forging New Frontiers* (London: Addison-Wesley, 1994).

41. Presentation by Ted Goranson at the April 1995 Agility Forum in Atlanta, Georgia.

42. Patricia Moody, "Take Down the Walls! Building World-Class Customer, Supplier Partnerships," AME (Association for Manufacturing Excellence) *Target* (AME's periodical news service) (September 1992).

43. C. K. Prahalad and Gary Hamel, *Competing for the Future: Break-through Strategies for Seizing Control of Your Industry and Creating the Markets of Tomorrow* (Boston: Harvard Business School Press, 1994).

44. Daniel Burrus with Roger Gittines, *Technotrends: Twenty-four Technologies That Will Revolutionize Our Lives* (New York: Harper Business, 1993).

45. Nonaka and Takeuchi, *The Knowledge-Creating Company.*

46. Ibid., 10–11.

47. S. K. Chakraborty, *Managerial Effectiveness and the Quality of Worklife: Indian Insights* (New Delhi: Tata McGraw-Hill, 1990).

48. Nonaka and Takeuchi, *The Knowledge-Creating Company*, 169 ff.

49. Sally Helgesen, *The Female Advantage: Women's Ways of Leadership* (New York: Doubleday Currency, 1995). [This book was first published in 1990.]

50. Helgesen, *The Web of Inclusion: A New Architecture for Building Great Organizations* (New York: Doubleday Currency, 1995).

51. Ibid., 20. [Note: Margaret Wheatley in *Leadership and the New Science* also sees organizations in terms of the particle/wave metaphor.]

52. Ibid.

53. The meeting held in Cambridge, MA, in July 1995 included Sherrin Bennett, Leif Edvinsson, David Isaacs, Karen Fox, David Marsing, Gordon Petrash, George Por, Hubert St. Onge, Adriana Triana, Eric Vogt, Alan Webber, and myself.

54. Margaret Wheatley, *Leadership and the New Science: Learning About Organization from an Orderly Universe* (San Francisco: Berrett-Koehler, 1992).

55. Dee W. Hock, "The Chaordic Organization: Out of Control and Into Order," in *World Business Academy Perspectives* (Washington, DC: World Business Academy, 1994).

56. Thommy Haglund and Leif Ögård, *Livs Långt Lärande: En Arbetsmodell för kompetensutveckling och för att Skapa en Lärande Organisation* [Life long learning: a working model for competency

development and for creating a learning organization] (Uppsala: Konsultförtaget AB, 1995).

57. Tom Peters, *Liberation Management: Necessary Disorganization for the Nanosecond Nineties* (New York: Macmillan, 1992) and *The Tom Peters Seminar: Crazy Times Call for Crazy Organizations* (New York: Vintage Books, 1994).

58. James Quinn Brian, *Intelligent Enterprises: A New Paradigm for a New Era* (New York: The Free Press, 1992); Charles Handy, *The Age of Unreason* (Boston, MA: Harvard Business School Press, 1989); Gifford Pinchot and Elizabeth Pinchot, *The End of Bureaucracy and the Rise of the Intelligent Organization* (San Francisco: Berrett-Koehler, 1993); and James O'Toole, *Leading Change: Overcoming the Ideology of Comfort and the Tyranny of Custom* (New York: Jossey-Bass, 1995).

59. Jessica Lipnack and Jeffrey Stamps, *The Networking Book: People Connecting with People* (New York: Routledge & Kegan Paul, 1986) and *The Team Net Factor: Bringing the Power of Boundary-Crossing into the Heart of Your Business* (Essex Junction, VT: Oliver Wight, 1993).

60. Michael D. McMaster, *The Intelligence Advantage: Organising for Complexity* (Newton, MA: Butterworth-Heinemann, 1995).

61. George Por, "The Quest for Collective Intelligence," in *Community Building: Renewing Spirit and Learning in Business*, ed. Kazimierz Gozdz (San Francisco: New Leaders Press, 1995).

62. Thomas Stewart, "Intellectual Capital: Your Company's Most Valuable Asset, New Ways to Build It and Measure It," *Fortune*, Oct. 3, 1994.

Chapter 8. Computerizing Steep Hierarchies: Will It Work?

1. George J. Hess, "Computer Integrated Manufacturing—How to Get Started" (presentation at AUTOFACT Conference, Detroit, MI, 14–17 November 1983 [unpublished]).

2. Adam Smith, *The Wealth of Nations* (London: Penguin Classics, 1987).

3. Alfred D. Chandler, Jr. and Herman Daems, *Managerial Hierarchies: Comparative Perspectives on the Rise of the Modern Industrial Enterprise* (Cambridge, MA: Harvard University Press, 1980), 16.

4. Ibid., 3.

5. Ibid., 9.

6. Paul R. Lawrence and Jay Lorsch, *Organization and Its Environment* (Cambridge, MA: Harvard University Press, 1967).

7. John T. Ward, *The Factory System* (New York: Barnes & Noble, 1970).

8. These include Dan Ciampa, *Manufacturing's New Mandate: The Tools for Leadership* (New York: John Wiley & Sons, 1988); Thomas G. Gunn, *Manufacturing for Competitive Advantage: Becoming a World Class Manufacturer* (Cambridge, MA: Ballinger, 1987); Robert W. Hall, *Attaining Manufacturing Excellence* (Homewood, IL: Dow Jones-Irwin, 1987); Robert H. Hayes and Steven C. Wheelwright, *Restoring Our Competitive Edge: Competing through Manufacturing* (New York: John Wiley & Sons, 1984); Rosabeth M. Kanter, *The Change Masters: Innovation and Entrepreneurship in the American Corporation* (New York: Simon & Schuster, 1983); Paul R. Lawrence and Davis Dyer, *Renewing American Industry: Organizing for Efficiency and Innovation* (New York: The Free Press, 1983); Raymond E. Miles and Charles C. Snow, "Organizations: New Concepts for New Forms," *California Management Review* 28, no. 3 (spring 1986): 62–73; Tom Peters, *Thriving on Chaos: Handbook for a Management Revolution* (New York: Alfred A. Knopf, 1987); Robert B. Reich, *The Next American Frontier* (New York: Times Books, 1983); Robert H. Waterman, *The Renewal Factor: How the Best Get and Keep the Competitive Edge* (New York: Bantam Books, 1987); and Shoshana Zuboff, *In the Age of the Smart Machine: The Future of Work and Power* (New York: Basic Books, 1988).

9. Eric Teicholz and Joel N. Orr, *Computer Integrated Manufacturing Handbook* (New York: McGraw-Hill, 1987), 1.4–1.5.

10. Reich, *The Next American Frontier*, 96.

11. James Lardner, "Integration and Information in an Automated Factory," *Proceedings of the AUTOFACT 1984, Anaheim,*

CA (Dearborn, MI: Society of Manufacturing Engineers, 1984).

12. George C. Homans, *The Human Group* (New York: Harcourt Brace Jovanovich, 1950).

13. David Stroll, private correspondence with author, 27 October 1989.

Chapter 9. Steep Hierarchies: Breaking Free

1. Adam Smith, *The Wealth of Nations* (London: Penguin Classics, 1987), 1.

2. Bernard Mandeville, *The Fable of the Bees*, ed. Phillip Harth (Baltimore, MD: Penguin Books, 1970).

3. Smith, *Wealth of Nations*, 234.

4. Ibid., 112.

5. Charles Babbage, *On the Economy of Machinery and Manufacturers* (1832; reprint, New York: Augustus M. Kelley, 1963).

6. Ibid., 173.

7. Edward Mason, *The Corporation in Modern Society* (New York: Atheneum, 1970); and Adolf A. Berle and Gardiner C. Means, *The Modern Corporation and Private Property* (New York: Harcourt, Brace & World, 1932).

8. Alfred D. Chandler, *The Visible Hand: The Managerial Revolution in American Business* (Cambridge, MA: Harvard University Press, 1977).

9. Stanley M. Davis, *Future Perfect* (Reading, MA: Addison-Wesley, 1987), 140.

10. Stratford P. Sherman, "The Mind of Jack Welch," *Fortune* (27 March 1989).

11. Frederick Winslow Taylor, *Scientific Management* (New York: Harper and Brothers, 1947).

12. Ibid., 38.

13. Ibid., 31.

14. Robert B. Reich, *The Next American Frontier* (New York: Times Books, 1983).

15. Claude S. George, Jr., *The History of Management Thought*, 2nd ed. (Englewood Cliffs, NJ: Prentice-Hall, 1972).

16. Lyndall Urwick, "Organization as a Technical Problem," in *Papers on the Science of Administration*, ed. Luther Gulick and Lyndall F. Urwick (New York: Columbia University, Institute of Public Administration, 1937), 51.

17. James D. Mooney and Allan C. Reiley, *Onward Industry!* (New York: Harper and Brothers, 1931), 37.

18. Paul R. Lawrence and Jay Lorsch, *Organization and Its Environment* (Cambridge, MA: Harvard University Press, 1967), 167.

19. Jay Galbraith, *Organization Design* (Reading, MA: Addison-Wesley, 1977).

20. Chester Barnard, *Functions of the Executive* (Cambridge, MA: Harvard University Press, 1938).

21. Ibid., 128.

22. Herbert Simon, *Administrative Behavior*, 3rd ed. (New York: The Free Press, 1976).

23. Reich, *The Next American Frontier*, 134.

24. Peter F. Drucker, *The Frontiers of Management* (New York: Dutton, 1986), 220–221.

25. George J. Hess, "Computer Integrated Manufacturing—How to Get Started" (presentation at AUTOFACT Conference, Detroit, MI, November 1983 [unpublished]).

26. Douglas McGregor, *The Human Side of Enterprise* (New York: McGraw-Hill, 1960).

27. Aristotle, *The Politics of Aristotle*, Bk. I, Ch. IV, §3, ed. and trans. Ernest Barker (New York: Oxford University Press, 1958).

28. Eric Teicholz and Joel N. Orr, *Computer Integrated Manufacturing Handbook* (New York: McGraw-Hill, 1987).

29. Adriano Tilgher, *Homo Faber: Work through the Ages*, trans. D. Fisher (Chicago: Regency, 1965).

30. Bill Lawrence addressing the Automation Forum, a group sponsored by the National Electrical Manufacturers Association, during a visit

to the Texas Instruments plant in Sherman, Texas, on 23 March 1988.

31. Joseph Harrington, Jr., *Computer Integrated Manufacturing* (1973; reprint, New York: Robert E. Krieger Publishing Co., 1979), 6.

32. Ibid., 7.

33. Harrington, *Understanding the Manufacturing Process* (New York: Marcel Dekker, 1984).

34. U.S. Air Force, Integrated Computer Aided Manufacturing, *ICAM Program Prospectus* (Dayton, OH: Air Force Materials Laboratory, Wright-Patterson Air Force Base, 1979).

35. David A. Marca and Clement L. McGowan, *SADT: Structured Analysis and Design Technique*, with a foreword by Douglas T. Ross (New York: McGraw-Hill, 1988).

36. Dan Appleton, *Introducing the New CIM Enterprise Wheel* (Dearborn, MI: CASA/SME, 1986).

37. Ibid.

38. John Hall, President, Marshall Aluminum Products, Cerna, CA, and former Chairperson of the CASA/SME Technical Council, phone conversation with author, 14 September 1989.

39. ESPRIT, Project No. 688, CIM/OSA, *A Primer on Key Concepts and Purpose* (Brussels, Belgium, 1987), 4.

40. Harrington, *Computer Integrated Manufacturing*, 6.

41. Tom Peters, *Thriving on Chaos: Handbook for a Management Revolution* (New York: Alfred A. Knopf, 1987).

42. Radovan Richta, *Civilization at the Crossroads: Social and Human Implications of the Scientific and Technological Revolution*, trans. Marian Slingova (Prague: International Arts and Sciences Press, 1968).

43. Nolan, Norton, and Co., "Computer Integrated Manufacturing Payoff Working Group," an unpublished working group report, 25–26 March 1987.

44. Shoshana Zuboff, *In the Age of the Smart Machine: The Future of Work and Power* (New York: Basic Books, 1988), 310.

Chapter 10. Human Networking: Self-Empowering

1. C. K. Prahalad and Gary Hamel, "The Core Competence of the Corporation," *Harvard Business Review* (May–June 1991).

2. "Cords of Change," *World* (Chicago: Peat Marwick, summer 1988). Interview discussion with Alvin Toffler, Leslie Berkes, and others.

3. Ibid.

4. James P. Carse, *Finite and Infinite Games: A Vision of Life as Play and Possibility* (New York: The Free Press, 1986).

5. Daniel Burrus with Roger Gittines, *Technotrends: Twenty-four Technologies that Will Revolutionize Our Lives* (New York: Harper Business, 1993).

6. H. Chandler Stevens, *The Network Notebook* (Washington, DC: National Science Foundation, 1978).

7. Peter B. Vaill, *Managing as a Performing Art: New Ideas for a World of Chaotic Change* (San Francisco: Jossey-Bass, 1989) and Marvin R. Weisbord, *Productive Workplaces: Organizing and Managing for Dignity, Meaning, and Community* (San Francisco: Jossey-Bass, 1987).

8. Charles M. Savage, *Work and Meaning: A Phenomenological Inquiry* (unpublished Ph.D. Thesis, Boston College, 1973).

9. Margaret Wheatley, *Leadership and the New Science: Learning About Organization from an Orderly Universe* (San Francisco: Berrett-Koehler, 1992).

10. Stafford Beer, *The Heart of the Enterprise* (New York: John Wiley & Sons, 1979); Tom Peters, *Thriving on Chaos: Handbook for a Management Revolution* (New York: Alfred A. Knopf, 1987); Peter Drucker, "The Coming of the New Organization," *Harvard Business Review* 66, no. 1 (January–February 1988): 45–53; Eric Trist, "The Evolution of Sociotechnical Systems: A Conceptual Framework and an Action Research Program" (Toronto: Ontario Quality of Working Life Center, Occasional Paper No. 2, June 1981); and John Briggs and F. David Peat, *Turbulent Mirror: An Illustrated Guide to Chaos Theory and the Science of Wholeness* (New York: Harper & Row, 1989).

11. Robert H. Waterman, *The Renewal Factor: How the Best Get and Keep the Competitive Edge* (New York: Bantam Books, 1987) and Rosabeth M. Kanter, *The Change Masters: Innovation and Entrepreneurship in the American Corporation* (New York: Simon & Schuster, 1983).

12. I first realized the richness of the work process while reading some fragments from the writings of the young Marx while he was heavily under the influence of Hegel. See Loyd Easton and Kurt Guddat, eds. and trans., *Writings of the Young Marx on Philosophy and Society* (New York: Anchor Books, 1967), 281.

13. Savage, *Work and Meaning.*

14. The section on human time has been inspired by Edmund Husserl, *The Phenomenology of Internal Time-Consciousness*, ed. M. Heidegger and trans. J. S. Churchill (Bloomington: Indiana University Press, 1969). I am using "human time" to refer to Husserl's idea of "internal time-consciousness." See also William James, *Principles of Psychology*, vol. 1 (New York: Dover Publications, 1950).

15. St. Augustine, *Confessions*, trans. R. S. Pine-Coffin (Baltimore: Penguin Books, 1961).

16. Ibid., 157.

17. Aristotle, *Physics*, 218b9, in *Selections*, ed. W. D. Ross (New York: Charles Scribner's Sons, 1955), 122.

18. James, *Principles of Psychology*, 613, 643.

19. Ikujiro Nonaka and Hirotaka Takeuchi, *The Knowledge-Creating Company: How Japanese Companies Create the Dynamics of Innovation* (New York: Oxford University Press, 1995).

20. Raymond M. Fortuna, "A Primer on Quality Function Deployment," *CIM Review* (The Journal of Computer-Integrated Manufacturing Management) 5, no. 1 (fall 1988): 49–54. See also William Eureka and Nancy Ryan, *The Customer-Driven Company: Management Perspectives on QFD* (Dearborn, MI: ASI Press, 1988).

21. Charles F. Kiefer and Peter Stroh, "A New Paradigm for Developing Organizations," in *Transforming Work*, John D. Adams, ed. (Alexandria, VA: Miles River Press, 1984).

22. Paul R. Lawrence and Davis Dyer, *Renewing American Industry: Organizing for Efficiency and Innovation* (New York: The Free Press, 1983).

23. See series of articles on simultaneous engineering in *Manufacturing Engineer* 101, no. 3 (September 1988).

24. Drucker, "The Coming of the New Organization."

25. Jan Hopland of Digital Equipment Corporation first suggested to me that the concept of virtual memory has an analogy: the virtual enterprise. See also Jan Hopland and Charles M. Savage, "Virtual Teams and Flexible Enterprises," *Digital Technical Management Education Program News* 3 (July 1989) and "Digital Equipment Corporation: The Endpoint Model," Harvard Business School case study, 1988. [This case includes reference to "virtual integration."]

26. Jessica Lipnack and Jeffrey Stamps, *The Networking Book: People Connecting with People* (New York: Routledge & Kegan Paul, 1986); Jeffrey Stamps, *Holonomy: A Human System Theory* (Seaside, CA: Intersystem Publications, 1980); and Jessica Lipnack and Jeffrey Stamps, *How Groups Think* (Waltham, MA: Networking Institute, 1988, unpublished).

27. Stephen Grossberg, "Nonlinear Neural Networks: Principles, Mechanisms and Architectures," *Neural Networks* 1, no. 1 (1988): 17–61; and Briggs and Peat, *Turbulent Mirror*.

28. Lipnack and Stamps, *How Groups Think*.

29. Robert Johansen, *Groupware: Computer Support for Business Teams* (New York: The Free Press, 1988).

30. Hayward Thomas, personal correspondence with the author, 26 January 1989.

Chapter 11. Confusingly Complex to Elegantly Simple Enterprises

1. Terry Winograd and Fernando Flores, *Understanding Computers and Cognition: A New Foundation for Design* (Reading, MA: Addison-Wesley, 1987).

2. Douglas McGregor, *The Human Side of Enterprise* (New York: McGraw-Hill, 1960) and Abraham Maslow, *Toward a Psychology of Being* (Princeton, NJ: D. van Nostrand, 1968).

3. T. S. Eliot, *The Complete Poems and Plays: 1909–1950* (New York: Harcourt, Brace & Co., 1952), 136.

4. Ken Olsen, "Presentation at the Annual Meeting of Digital Equipment Corporation, Boston, November 6, 1986," in *Digital Equipment Corporation Second Quarter Report 1987* (Maynard, MA: Digital Equipment Corp., 1987), 4.

5. James Gleick, *Chaos: Making a New Science* (New York: Viking Penguin, 1987).

6. Tom Peters, *Thriving on Chaos: Handbook for a Management Revolution* (New York: Alfred A. Knopf, 1987).

7. One of the pioneers in helping to change the fragmentation of our academic institutions has been Nathan Chiantella, who for several years administered an IBM grant program designed to encourage more effective interdisciplinary programs at our technical colleges and universities. He was also instrumental in initiating the Society of Manufacturing Engineers' Industry and University Leadership and Excellence in the Application and Development of CIM (LEAD) award programs. We owe a lot to people like Mr. Chiantella for their vision and accomplishments. They are helping to put people in touch at the universities and in industry.

8. Thomas S. Kuhn, *The Structure of Scientific Revolutions*, 2nd ed. (Chicago: University of Chicago Press, 1970).

9. Peter Drucker, "The Coming of the New Organization," *Harvard Business Review* 66, no. 1 (January–February 1988): 50.

10. Henri Fayol, *General and Industrial Management*, trans. Constance Storrs (London: Pitman, 1949).

11. Jessica Lipnack and Jeffrey Stamps, *The Age of the Network: Organizing Principles for the 21st Century* (New York: John Wiley & Sons, 1994).

12. Karl E. Weick, *The Social Psychology of Organizing*, 2nd ed. (Reading, MA: Addison-Wesley, 1979).

13. Winograd and Flores, *Understanding Computers and Cognition.*

14. Robert W. Hall and the AIM Study Group on Functional Organization, "Organizational Renewal—Tearing Down the Functional

Silos," AME (Association for Manufacturing Excellence) *Target* (AME's periodical news service) 4, no. 2 (summer 1988).

15. James Lardner, "Integration and Information in an Automated Factory," *Proceedings of the AUTOFACT 1984, Anaheim, CA* (Dearborn, MI: Society of Manufacturing Engineers, 1984).

16. Jens Rasmussen, "Models for Design of Computer Integrated Manufacturing Systems" (paper presented at First International Conference on Ergonomics of Advanced Manufacturing and Hybrid Automated Systems, Louisville, KY, 17 August 1988).

17. Jack Welch, Jr., "Managing for the Nineties" (presentation at the General Electric annual meeting of share owners, Waukeska, WI, 27 April 1988). See also Stratford P. Sherman, "The Mind of Jack Welch," *Fortune* (27 March 1989): 38–50.

Chapter 12. Managing Human Networking

1. Stephen Covey, *Principle-Centered Leadership* (New York: Simon & Schuster, 1992).

2. Tom Pryor, "Updating Cost Management: The CAM-I Cost Management System (CMS) Approach" (Arlington, TX: CAM-I, 1988 [unpublished]).

3. Robert N. Stauffer, "Converting Customers to Partners at Ingersoll," *Manufacturing Engineering* (September 1988): 41–44.

4. Ikujiro Nonaka and Hirotaka Takeuchi, *The Knowledge-Creating Company: How Japanese Companies Create the Dynamics of Innovation* (New York: Oxford University Press, 1995).

5. Donato Infante, "The Last Word: A Good Place to Work . . . Works for Everyone," *Manufacturing Engineering* (July 1989): 104.

REFERENCES

Abernathy, William J., Kim B. Clark, and Alan M. Kantrow. *Industrial Renaissance: Producing a Competitive Future for America.* New York: Basic Books, 1983.

Abraham, Richard G. *Computer-Integrated Manufacturing.* Edited by Warren Shrensker. Dearborn, MI: Computer and Automated Systems Association, Society of Manufacturing Engineers, 1986.

Ackoff, R. *Creating the Corporate Future.* New York: John Wiley & Sons, 1981.

Appleton, Dan. *Introducing the New CIM Enterprise Wheel.* Dearborn, MI: CASA/SME, 1986.

Argyris, Chris. "How Learning and Reasoning Processes Affect Organizational Change." In *Change in Organizations*, Paul S. Goodman and Associates. San Francisco: Jossey-Bass, 1982, 47–86.

———. *Integrating the Individual and the Organization.* New York: John Wiley & Sons, 1964.

———. "Single-Loop and Double-Loop Models in Research on Decision Making." *Administrative Science Quarterly* 21 (September 1976): 363–377.

———. *Knowledge for Action: A Guide to Overcoming Barriers to Organizational Change.* San Francisco: Jossey-Bass, 1993.

Aristotle. *The Basic Works of Aristotle.* Edited by Richard McKeon. New York: Random House, 1941.

———. *The Politics of Aristotle.* Edited and translated by Ernest Barker. New York: Oxford University Press, 1958.

Ashton, T. S. *The Industrial Revolution, 1760–1830.* New York: Oxford University Press, 1964.

Augustine, St. *Confessions.* Translated by R. S. Pine-Coffin. Baltimore: Penguin Books, 1961.

Babbage, Charles. *On the Economy of Machinery and Manufacturers.* 1832. Reprint, New York: Augustus M. Kelley, 1963.

Badaracco, J. L. *The Knowledge Link: How Firms Compete through Strategic Alliances.* Boston: Harvard University Press, 1991.

Bacon, Francis. *Selected Writings.* New York: The Modern Library, 1955.

Baker, Wayne. *Networking Smart: How to Build Relationships for Personal and Organizational Success.* New York: McGraw-Hill, 1994.

Barker, Joel A. *Future Edge: Discovering the New Paradigms of Success.* New York: William Morrow, 1992.

Barnard, Chester. *Functions of the Executive.* Cambridge, MA: Harvard University Press, 1938.

Barrentine, Pat, ed. *When the Canary Stops Singing: Women's Perspectives on Transforming Business.* San Francisco: Berrett-Koehler, 1993.

Bartlett, Christopher, and Sumantra Ghoshal. *Managing Across Borders: The Transnational Solution.* Boston: Harvard Business School Press, 1992.

Beer, Stafford. *The Brain of the Firm.* New York: Herder & Herder, 1972.

———. *The Heart of the Enterprise.* New York: John Wiley & Sons, 1979.

Bell, Daniel. *The Coming of Post-Industrial Society: A Venture in Social Forecasting.* New York: Basic Books, 1973.

Belasco, James, and Ralph Stayer. *Flight of the Buffalo: Soaring to Excellence: Learning to Let Employees Lead.* New York: Warner Books, 1993.

Bennett, Sherrin, and Juanita Brown. "Mindshift: Strategic Dialogue for Breakthrough Thinking." In *Learning Organizations: Developing Cultures for Tomorrow's Workplace.* Edited by Sarita Chawla and John Renesch. Portland, OR: Productivity Press, 1995.

Bergson, Henri. *Duration and Simultaneity.* Translated by Leon Jacobson. New York: Library of Liberal Arts, 1965.

Berle, Adolf A., and Gardiner C. Means. *The Modern Corporation and Private Property.* New York: Harcourt, Brace & World, 1932.

Block, Peter. *The Empowered Manager: Positive Political Skills at Work.* San Francisco: Jossey-Bass, 1991.

Bolman, Lee, and Terrence Deal. *Leading with Soul: An Uncommon Journey of Spirit.* New York: Jossey-Bass, 1995.

Bradford, D. L., and A. R. Cohen. *Managing for Excellence: The Guide to Developing High Performance in Contemporary Organizations.* New York: John Wiley & Sons, 1984.

Bradshaw, Pete. *The Management of Self-Esteem: How People Can Feel Good about Themselves & Better about Their Organizations.* Englewood Cliffs, NJ: Prentice-Hall, 1981.

Bridges, William. "The End of the Job." *Fortune,* 19 September 1994.

———. *Jobshift: How to Prosper in a Workplace without Jobs.* Reading, MA: Addison-Wesley, 1994.

Briggs, John, and F. David Peat. *Turbulent Mirror: An Illustrated Guide to Chaos Theory and the Science of Wholeness.* New York: Harper & Row, 1989.

Bucher, Karl. *Arbeit und Rhythmus* [Work and rhythm]. Leipzig, 1924.

Burckhardt, Werner, ed. *Schlank, intelligent und schnell* [Lean, intelligent and fast]. Wiesbaden, Gabler, 1992.

Burrus, Daniel, with Roger Gittines. *Technotrends: Twenty-four Technologies That Will Revolutionize Our Lives.* New York: Harper Business, 1993.

Carlson, Howard. "The Parallel Organization Structure at General Motors." *Personnel* (September–October 1978): 64–69.

Carlzon, Jan. *Moments of Truth.* Cambridge, MA: Ballinger, 1987.

Carse, James P. *Finite and Infinite Games: A Vision of Life as Play and Possibility.* New York: Free Press, 1986.

Chakraborty, S. K. *Managerial Effectiveness and the Quality of Worklife: Indian Insights.* New Delhi: Tata McGraw-Hill, 1990.

———. *Managerial Transformation by Values: A Corporate Pilgrimage.* London: Sage Publications, 1993.

———. *Ethics in Management: Vadantic Perspectives.* Delhi: Oxford University Press, 1995.

Chandler, Alfred D. *Strategy and Structure.* Cambridge, MA: MIT Press, 1962.

———. *The Visible Hand: The Managerial Revolution in American Business.* Cambridge, MA: Harvard University Press, 1977.

Chandler, Alfred D., and Herman Daems. *Managerial Hierarchies: Comparative Perspectives on the Rise of the Modern Industrial Enterprise.* Cambridge, MA: Harvard University Press, 1980.

Chawla, Sarita, and John Renesch, eds. *Learning Organizations: Developing Cultures for Tomorrow's Workplace.* Portland, OR: Productivity Press, 1995.

Chiantella, Nathan A., ed. *Management Guide for CIM.* Dearborn, MI: Society of Manufacturing Engineers, 1986.

Chrystal, Keith. "Holonic Management Systems." Alberta: Alberta Research Council, 1994. (Available at http://www.ncms.org).

Collins, James, and Jerry Porras. *Built to Last: Successful Habits of Visionary Companies.* New York: Harper Business, 1994.

Cousins, Steven A. *Integrating the Automated Factory.* Dearborn, MI: Society of Manufacturing Engineers, 1988.

Covey, Stephen. *The Seven Habits of Highly Effective People.* New York: Simon & Schuster, 1990.

———. *Principle-Centered Leadership.* New York: Simon & Schuster, 1992.

Crawford, Richard. *The Era of Human Capital: The Emergence of Talent, Intelligence, and Knowledge as the Worldwide Economic Force and What It Means to Managers and Investors.* New York: Harper Business, 1991.

Davidow, William, and Michael Malone. *The Virtual Corporation: Structuring and Revitalizing the Corporation for the 21st Century.* New York: Harper Collins, 1992.

Davis, Stanley M. *Future Perfect.* Reading, MA: Addison-Wesley, 1987.

Davis, Stanley M., and Paul R. Lawrence. *Matrix.* Reading, MA: Addison-Wesley, 1977.

Deal, Terrence E., and Allan A. Kennedy. *Corporate Cultures: The Rites and Rituals of Corporate Life.* Reading, MA: Addison-Wesley, 1982.

Deming, W. Edward. *Out of the Crisis.* Cambridge, MA: MIT Center for Advanced Engineering Study, 1986.

Dertouzos, Michael L., et al. *Made in America: Regaining the Productive Edge.* Cambridge, MA: MIT Press, 1988.

Drucker, Peter. "The Coming of the New Organization." *Harvard Business Review* 66, no. 1 (January–February 1988).

———. "Management and the World's Work." *Harvard Business Review* 66, no. 5 (September–October 1988): 65–76.

———. *The Frontiers of Management.* New York: Dutton, 1986.

———. *Managing in Turbulent Times.* New York: Harper & Row, 1980.

———. *The New Realities: In Government and Politics/In Economics and Business/In Society and World View.* New York: Harper & Row, 1989.

Durkheim, Emile. *The Division of Labor in Society.* Translated by G. Simpson. New York: The Free Press, 1969.

Easton, Loyd, and Kurt Guddat, eds. and trans. *Writings of the Young Marx on Philosophy and Society.* New York: Anchor Books, 1967.

Eccles, Robert G., and Dwight B. Crane. *Doing Deals: Investment Banks at Work.* Boston: Harvard Business School Press, 1988.

Eccles, Robert, and Nitin Nohria. *Beyond the Hype: Rediscovering the Essence of Management.* Boston: Harvard Business School Press, 1992.

Eliot, T. S. *The Complete Poems and Plays, 1909–1950.* New York: Harcourt, Brace & Co., 1952.

Emery, Fred, ed. *Systems Thinking.* New York: Penguin Books, 1969.

ESPRIT, Project No. 688, CIM/OSA. *A Primer on Key Concepts and Purpose.* Brussels, Belgium, 1987.

Etzioni, Amitai. *A Comparative Analysis of Complex Organizations.* New York: The Free Press of Glencoe, 1961.

———. *A Sociological Reader on Complex Organizations.* 2nd ed. New York: Holt, Rinehart and Winston, 1969.

Eureka, William, and Nancy Ryan. *The Customer-Driven Company: Managerial Perspectives on QFD* [Quality Function Deployment]. Dearborn, MI: ASI Press, 1988.

Fayol, Henri. *General and Industrial Management.* Translated by Constance Storrs. London: Pitman, 1949.

Feigenbaum, A. V. *Total Quality Control: Engineering and Management.* New York: McGraw-Hill, 1961.

Feigenbaum, Edward A., and Pamela McCorduck. *The Fifth Generation: Artificial Intelligence and Japan's Computer Challenge to the World.* Reading, MA: Addison-Wesley, 1983.

Fortuna, Raymond M. "A Primer on Quality Function Deployment." *CIM Review* (The Journal of Computer-Integrated Manufacturing Management) 5, no. 1 (fall 1988): 49–54.

Fritz, R. *The Path of Least Resistance.* Salem, MA: DMA, Inc., 1984.

Fukuda, Ryuji. *Managerial Engineering: Techniques for Improving Quality and Productivity in the Workplace.* Stamford, CT: Productivity, Inc., 1983.

Galbraith, Jay. *Designing Complex Organizations.* Reading, MA: Addison-Wesley, 1979.

———. *Designing Organizations: An Executive Briefing on Strategy, Structure, and Process.* New York: Jossey-Bass, 1995.

Galbraith, Jay, et al. *Organizing for the Future: The New Logic for Managing Complex Organizations.* San Francisco: Jossey-Bass, 1993.

Gale, Richard M., ed. *The Philosophy of Time: A Collection of Essays.* New York: Anchor Books, 1967.

Galloway, John J. "Revealing Organizational Networks." Annual Conference of Australian Communications Association, Sydney (July 1987).

Galloway, John J., and Anne Gorman. *Going Places: How to Network Your Way to Personal Success.* Sydney: Allen and Unwin, 1987.

Garfield, Charles. *Second to None: How Our Smartest Companies Put People First.* Homewood, IL: Business One Irwin, 1992.

George, Claude S., Jr. *The History of Management Thought.* 2nd ed. Englewood Cliffs, NJ: Prentice-Hall, 1972.

Gide, Charles, and Charles Rist. *A History of Economic Doctrines: From the Time of the Psyiocrates to the Present Day.* Translated by R. Richards. Boston: D. C. Heath, 1948.

Gilbreth, Frank B. *Motion Study: A Method for Increasing the Efficiency of the Workman.* New York: D. van Nostrand, 1910.

———. *Primer on Scientific Management.* New York: D. van Nostrand, 1912.

Gleick, James. *Chaos: Making a New Science.* New York: Viking Penguin, 1987.

Goldman, Steven, Roger Nagel, and Kenneth Preiss. *Agile Competitors and Virtual Organizations: Strategies for Enriching the Customer.* New York: Van Nostrand Reinhold, 1994.

Goldstein, Jeffrey. *The Unshackled Organization: Facing the Challenge of Unpredictability through Spontaneous Reorganization*. Portland, OR: Productivity Press, 1994.

Gouldner, Alvin. *Patterns of Industrial Bureaucracy*. Glencoe, IL: The Free Press, 1954.

Gozdz, Kazimierz, ed. *Community Building, Renewing Spirit & Learning*. San Francisco: New Leaders Press, 1995.

Grossberg, Stephen. "Nonlinear Neural Networks: Principles, Mechanisms and Architectures." *Neural Networks* 1, no. 1 (1988): 17–61.

———, ed. *Neural Networks and Natural Intelligence*. Cambridge, MA: MIT Press, 1988.

Guntern, Gottlieb. *Im Zeichen des Schmetterlings: Von powerplay zum sanften spiel der kräfte, leadership in der metamorphose* [Under the sign of the butterfly: from powerplay to the soft play of energy, leadership in the metamorphosis]. Bern: Scherz Verlag, 1993.

Gustavsson, Bengt. *The Transcendent Organization: A Treatise on Consciousness in Organizations, Theoretical Discussions, Conceptual Development and Empirical Studies*. Edsbruk, Sweden: Akademitryck AB, 1992.

Guterl, Fred V. "Goodbye, Old Matrix." *Business Month* (February 1989): 32–38.

Haglund, Thommy, and Leif Ögård. *Livs Långt Lärande: En Arbetsmodell för kompetensutveckling och för att Skapa en Lärande Organisation* [Life long learning: a working model for competency development and for creating a learning organization]. Uppsala: Konsultförtaget AB, 1995.

Hall, Robert, and the AIM Study Group on Functional Organization. "Organizational Renewal—Tearing Down the Functional Silos." AME (Association for Manufacturing Excellence) *Target* (AME's periodical news service) 4, no. 2 (summer 1988).

Hall, Robert W. *Attaining Manufacturing Excellence*. Homewood, IL: Dow Jones-Irwin, 1987.

———. *The Soul of the Enterprise: Creating a Dynamic Vision for American Manufacturing*. New York: Harper Business, 1993.

Hammer, Michael, and Steven Stanton. *The Reengineering Revolution: A Handbook*. New York: Harper Business, 1995.

Hampden-Turner, Charles, and Fons Trompernaars. *The Seven Cultures of Capitalism: Value Systems for Creating Wealth in the United States, Japan, Germany, France, Britain, Sweden, and the Netherlands*. New York: Doubleday Currency, 1993.

Handy, Charles. *The Age of Unreason*. Boston: Harvard Business School Press, 1989.

———. *The Age of Paradox*. Boston: Harvard Business School Press, 1994.

Haney, Lewis H. *History of Economic Thought: A Critical Account of the Origin and Development of the Economic Theories of the Leading Thinkers in the Leading Nations.* 4th ed. New York: Macmillan Co., 1949.

Harbison, F., and C. Myers. *Management in the Industrial World.* New York: McGraw-Hill, 1959.

Harrington, Joseph, Jr. *Computer Integrated Manufacturing.* 1973. Reprint, New York: Robert E. Krieger Publishing Co., 1979.

———. *Understanding the Manufacturing Process.* New York: Marcel Dekker, 1984.

Hayes, Robert H., and Ramchandran Jaikumar. "Manufacturing's Crisis: New Technologies, Obsolete Organizations." *Harvard Business Review* 66, no. 5 (September–October 1988): 77–85.

Hayes, Robert H., and Roger W. Schumenner. "How Should You Organize Manufacturing?" *Harvard Business Review* 57, no. 1 (January–February 1979): 105–118.

Hayes, Robert H., and Steven C. Wheelwright. *Restoring Our Competitive Edge: Competing Through Manufacturing.* New York: John Wiley & Sons, 1984.

Hayes, Robert H., Steven C. Wheelwright, and Kim B. Clark. *Dynamic Manufacturing: Creating the Learning Organization.* New York: The Free Press, 1988.

Hegel, G. W. F. *The Phenomenology of Mind.* Translated by J. B. Baillie. New York: Harper Torchbooks, 1967.

Helgesen, Sally. *The Female Advantage: Women's Ways of Leadership.* New York: Doubleday Currency, 1995.

———. *The Web of Inclusion: A New Architecture for Building Great Organizations.* New York: Doubleday Currency, 1995.

Hess, George J. "Computer Integrated Manufacturing—How to Get Started." Presentation at AUTOFACT Conference, Detroit, MI (November 1983) [unpublished].

———. "1982 Industrial LEAD Award Winner—Revisited in 1986." Presentation at AUTOFACT Conference (12 November 1986). Dearborn, MI: Society of Manufacturing Engineers, 1986.

Hirschorn, Larry. *Beyond Mechanization.* Cambridge, MA: MIT Press, 1984.

Hock, Dee W. "The Chaordic Organization: Out of Control and Into Order." In *World Business Academy Perspectives.* Washington, DC: World Business Academy, 1994.

Homans, George C. *The Human Group.* New York: Harcourt Brace Jovanovich, 1950.

Hopland, Jan, and Charles M. Savage. "Charting New Directions." *Digital Enterprise* 3, no. 1 (spring 1989): 8–12.

———. "Virtual Teams and Flexible Enterprises." *Digital Technical Management Education Program News* 3 (July 1989): 3–6.

Husserl, Edmund. *The Phenomenology of Internal Time-Consciousness*. Edited by M. Heidegger and translated by J. S. Churchill. Bloomington: Indiana University Press, 1969.

Imai, Masaaki. *Kaizen: The Key to Japan's Competitive Success*. New York: Random House, 1986.

Infante, Donato. "The Last Word: A Good Place to Work . . . Works for Everyone." *Manufacturing Engineering* (July 1989): 104.

Ishikawa, Akira. *Future Computer and Information Systems: The Uses of the Next Generation Computer and Information Systems*. New York: Praeger, 1986.

James, William. *Principles of Psychology*. 2 vols. New York: Dover Publications, 1950.

Janov, Jill. *The Inventive Organization: Hope and Daring at Work*. San Francisco: Jossey-Bass, 1994.

Jaques, Elliott. *Requisite Organization: The CEO's Guide to Creative Structure and Leadership*. New York: Cason Hall and Co., 1989.

Johansen, Bruce. *Forgotten Founders: How the American Indian Helped Shape Democracy*. Boston: The Harvard Common Press, 1982.

Johansen, Robert. *Groupware: Computer Support for Business Teams*. New York: The Free Press, 1988.

Johansen, Robert, and Rob Swigart. *Upsizing the Individual in the Downsized Organization: Managing in the Wake of Reengineering, Globalization, and Overwhelming Technological Change*. Reading, MA: Addison-Wesley, 1994.

Johnson, Barry. *Polarity Management: Identifying and Managing Unsolvable Problems*. Amherst, MA: HRD Press, 1992.

Johnson, H. Thomas, and Anders Broems. "The Spirit in the Walls: A Pattern for High Performance at Scania." AME (Association for Manufacturing Excellence) *Target* (AME's periodical news service), May/June 1995.

Johnson, H. Thomas, and Robert S. Kaplan. *Relevance Lost: The Rise and Fall of Management Accounting*. Boston: Harvard Business School Press, 1987.

Johnston, Russell, and Paul R. Lawrence. "Beyond Vertical Integration—The Rise of the Value-Adding Partnership." *Harvard Business Review* 66, no. 4 (July–August 1988): 94–101.

Joiner, Brian L. *Fourth Generation Management: The New Business Consciousness*. New York: McGraw-Hill, 1994.

"Kaiser Aluminum Flattens Its Layers of Brass." *Business Week* (24 February 1973): 8–14.

Kanter, Rosabeth Moss. *The Change Masters: Innovation and Entrepreneurship in the American Corporation*. New York: Simon & Schuster, 1983.

———. "How Strategic Partnerships Are Reshaping American Businesses." In *Business in the Contemporary World*. Edited by Herbert Sawyer. Washington, DC: University Press of America, 1988.

———. *When Giants Learn to Dance: Mastering the Challenges of Strategy Management, and Careers in the 1990s*. New York: Simon & Schuster, 1989.

Kanter, Rosabeth Moss, and Barry Stein. "Building the Parallel Organization: Toward Mechanisms for Permanent Quality of Work Life." *Journal of Applied Behavioral Science* 16 (summer 1980). Report on the "Chestnut Ridge" project.

Kaplan, Robert S. "Must CIM Be Justified by Faith Alone?" *Harvard Business Review* (March–April 1986).

Katz, Daniel, and Robert Kahn. *The Social Psychology of Organizations*. New York: John Wiley & Sons, 1978.

Keen, Peter G. W., and Michael S. Scott Morton. *Decision Support Systems: An Organizational Perspective*. Reading, MA: Addison-Wesley, 1978.

Kidd, Paul. "Technology and Engineering Design: Shaping a Better Future or Repeating the Mistakes of the Past?" *IEEE Proceedings* 135, no. 5 (May 1988): 297–302.

Kidd, Paul, and J. M. Corbett. "Towards the Joint Social and Technical Design of Advanced Manufacturing Systems." *International Journal of Industrial Ergonomics* 2 (Amsterdam: Elsevier Science Publishers, 1988): 305–313.

Kidd, Paul. *Agile Manufacturing: Forging New Frontiers*. London: Addison-Wesley, 1994.

Kiefer, Charles F., and Peter Stroh. "A New Paradigm for Developing Organizations." In *Transforming Work*. Edited by John D. Adams. Alexandria, VA: Miles River Press, 1984.

Koestenbaum, Peter. *The Heart of Business: Ethics, Power and Philosophy*. New York: Saybrook Publishing Co., 1987.

———. *Leadership: The Inner Side of Greatness*. San Francisco: Jossey-Bass, 1991.

Koestler, Arthur. *The Ghost in the Machine*. London: Hutchinson, 1967.

Kolind, Lars. "Thinking the Unthinkable: The Oticon Revolution." *Focus on Change Management* (April 1994).

Kotter, John P. *A Force for Change: How Leadership Differs from Management*. New York: The Free Press, 1990.

Kotter, John P., and James Heskett. *Corporate Culture and Performance*. New York: The Free Press, 1992.

Kouzes, James M., and Barry Posner. *The Leadership Challenge: How to Get Extraordinary Things Done in Organizations*. San Francisco: Jossey-Bass, 1991.

Kuhn, Thomas S. *The Structure of Scientific Revolutions*. 2nd ed. Chicago: University of Chicago Press, 1970.

La Barre, Polly. "The Dis-Organization of Oticon." *Industry Week* (18 July 1994): 22–28.

LaMarsh, Jeanenne. *Changing the Way We Change: Gaining Control of Major Operational Change*. Reading, MA: Addison-Wesley, 1995.

Lancourt, Joan. "Human Resource Leadership in Reengineering the Organizational Culture and Infrastructure." *Compensation and Benefits Management* (autumn 1994).

Lancourt, Joan, and Charles M. Savage. "Organizational Transformation and the Changing Role of the Human Resource Function." *Compensation and Benefits Management*, Volume 11, Number 4, Autumn, 1995.

Land, George, and Beth Jarman. *Breakpoint and Beyond: Mastering the Future Today*. New York: Harper Business, 1992.

Lardner, James. "Integration and Information in an Automated Factory." *Proceedings of the AUTOFACT 1984*, Anaheim, CA. Dearborn, MI: Society of Manufacturing Engineers, 1984.

Lawler, Edward E., III. *High-Involvement Management: Participative Strategies for Improving Organizational Performance*. San Francisco: Jossey-Bass, 1986.

Lawrence, Paul R., and Davis Dyer. *Renewing American Industry: Organizing for Efficiency and Innovation*. New York: The Free Press, 1983.

Lawrence, Paul R., and Jay Lorsch. *Organization and Its Environment*. Cambridge, MA: Harvard University Press, 1967.

Leavitt, Harold, ed. *Handbook of Organizations*. Chicago: Rand McNally, 1965.

Likert, Rensis. *New Patterns of Management*. New York: McGraw-Hill, 1961.

Lipnack, Jessica, and Jeffrey Stamps. *How Groups Think*. Waltham, MA: Networking Institute, 1988 [unpublished].

———. "A Network Model." *The Futurist* 21, no. 4 (July–August 1987).

———. *The Networking Book: People Connecting with People*. New York: Routledge & Kegan Paul, 1986.

———. *The Team Net Factor: Bringing the Power of Boundary-Crossing into the Heart of Your Business*. Essex Junction, VT: Oliver Wight, 1993.

———. *The Age of the Network: Organizing Principles for the 21st Century*. New York: John Wiley & Sons, 1994.

Livingston, Donald G., and Leslie J. Berkes. "Netmap: An Innovative Diagnostic Tool." *Journal of Managerial Psychology* 4, no. 4 (1989).

Lukas, Andreas. *Abschied von der Reparaturkultur: Selbsterneuerung durch ein neues Miteinanden* [Goodbye to the culture of repair: self-renewal through a new spirit of collaboration]. Wiesbaden: Gabler, 1995.

Majchrzak, Ann. *The Human Side of Factory Automation: Managerial and Human Resource Strategies for Making Automation Succeed*. San Francisco: Jossey-Bass, 1988.

Mandeville, Bernard. *The Fable of the Bees*. Edited by Phillip Harth. Baltimore, MD: Penguin Books, 1970.

Marca, David A., and Clement L. McGowan. *SADT: Structured Analysis and Design Technique.* With a foreword by Douglas T. Ross. New York: McGraw-Hill, 1988.

Marks, Peter, and Kathleen Riley. *Aligning Technology: A Guide for Selecting and Implementing Computer-aided Design and Manufacturing Tools.* Los Gatos, CA: Design Insight, 1995.

Marsh, James, ed. *Handbook of Organizations.* Chicago: Rand McNally, 1965.

Marshall, Edward. *Transforming the Way We Work: The Power of the Collaborative Workplace.* New York: American Management Association, 1995.

Maslow, Abraham. *Toward a Psychology of Being.* Princeton, NJ: D. van Nostrand, 1968.

Mason, Edward. *The Corporation in Modern Society.* New York: Atheneum, 1970.

Masuda, Yoneji. *The Information Society as Post-Industrial Society.* Tokyo: Institute for the Information Society, 1980. Reprint, World Future Society, Bethesda, MD, 1981.

Maturana, Humberto, and Francisco Varela. *The Tree of Knowledge: The Biological Roots of Human Understanding.* Boston: Shambhala Publications, 1987.

McGregor, Douglas. *The Human Side of Enterprise.* New York: McGraw-Hill, 1960.

McMaster, Michael D. *The Intelligence Advantage: Organising for Complexity.* Newton, MA: Butterworth-Heinemann, 1996.

Mellander, Klas. *Länge leve lärandet* [Long live learning]. Malmö, Sweden: Learning Methods International, 1991.

Miles, Raymond E., and Charles C. Snow. "Organizations: New Concepts for New Forms." *California Management Review* 28, no. 3 (spring 1986).

Mills, D. Quinn. *Rebirth of the Corporation.* New York: Wiley & Sons, 1991.

Minkowski, Eugene. *Lived Time: Phenomenological and Psychopathological Studies.* Translated by Nancy Metzel. Evanston, IL: Northwestern University Press, 1970.

Mintzberg, Henry. *The Nature of Managerial Work.* New York: Harper & Row, 1973.

Mohri, Shunji, and Kenji Tokunaga. "Holonic Manufacturing Systems." *Journal of Robotics and Mechantronics* 6, no. 6 (1994).

Monden, Yasuhiro. "Adaptable Kanban Systems Help Toyota Maintain Just-in-Time Production." *Industrial Engineering* (May 1981): 29–46.

Moody, Patricia. "Take Down the Walls! Building World-Class Customer, Supplier Partnerships." AME (Association for Manufacturing Excellence) *Target* (AME's periodical news service) (September 1992).

Mooney, James D., and Allen C. Reiley. *Onward Industry!* New York: Harper and Brothers, 1931.

Mohrman, Susan Albers, Susan Cohen, and Allan Mohrman. *Designing Team-Based Organizations: New Forms for Knowledge Work*. New York: Jossey-Bass, 1995.

Morgan, Gareth. *Ride the Waves of Change: Developing Managerial Competencies for a Turbulent World*. New York: Jossey-Bass, 1989.

Morton, Michael S. Scott. *The Corporation of the 1990s: Information Technology and Organizational Transformation*. New York: Oxford University Press, 1991.

Moto-oka, Tohru, ed. *Fifth Generation Computer Systems: Proceedings of the International Conference on Fifth Generation Computer Systems*. Amsterdam: North-Holland, 1982.

Moto-oka, Tohru, and Masaru Kitsuregawa. *The Fifth Generation Computer: The Japanese Challenge*. New York: John Wiley & Sons, 1985.

Mullin, Tom, ed. *The Nature of Chaos*. Oxford: Clarendon Press, 1993.

Naisbett, John. *Megatrends*. New York: Warner Books, 1982.

Nadler, Gerald, and Shozo Hibino. *Breakthrough Thinking: The Seven Principles of Creative Problem Solving*. Rocklin, CA: Prima Publishing, 1994.

Nolan, Richard, Alex J. Pollock, and James P. Ware. "Creating the 21st Century Organization." *Stage by Stage* 8, no. 4 (Lexington, MA: Nolan, Norton and Co., fall 1988): 1–11.

———. "Toward the Design of Network Organizations." *Stage by Stage* 9, no. 1 (Lexington, MA: Nolan, Norton and Co., fall 1988): 1–12.

Nolan, Richard, and David Croson. *Creative Destruction: A Six-Stage Process for Transforming the Organization*. Boston: Harvard Business School Press, 1995.

Nonaka, Ikujiro, and Hirotaka Takeuchi. *The Knowledge-Creating Company: How Japanese Companies Create the Dynamics of Innovation*. New York: Oxford University Press, 1995.

O'Connor, Dennis, and Wendy Wilkerson. *Guide to Expert Systems Program Management, Artificial Intelligence Guide Series*. Intelligent Systems Technologies Group. Maynard, MA: Digital Equipment Corp., 1985.

Ohmae, Kenichi. *The Mind of the Strategist*. New York: McGraw-Hill, 1982.

Olsen, Ken. "Presentation at the Annual Meeting of Digital Equipment Corporation, Boston, November 6, 1986." In *Digital Equipment Corporation Second Quarter Report 1987*. Maynard, MA: Digital Equipment Corp., 1987.

O'Toole, James. *Leading Change: Overcoming the Ideology of Comfort and the Tyranny of Custom*. New York: Jossey-Bass, 1995.

Ouchi, William G. *Theory Z: How American Business Can Meet the Japanese Challenge*. Reading, MA: Addison-Wesley, 1981.

Palgrave, R. H. I. *Dictionary of Political Economy*. 3 vols. London: Macmillan and Co., 1894.

Pascale, Richard T., and Anthony G. Athos. *The Art of Japanese Management: Applications for American Executives.* New York: Simon & Schuster, 1981.

Pedler, Mike, John Burgoyne, and Tom Boydell. *The Learning Company: A Strategy for Sustainable Development.* London: McGraw-Hill, 1991.

Peters, Tom. *Thriving on Chaos: Handbook for a Management Revolution.* New York: Alfred A. Knopf, 1987.

Peters, Tom, and Nancy Austin. *A Passion for Excellence.* New York: Random House, 1985.

Peters, Tom, and R. H. Waterman. *In Search of Excellence.* New York: Harper & Row, 1982.

Peters, Tom. *Liberation Management: Necessary Disorganization for the Nanosecond Nineties.* New York: Macmillan, 1992.

———. *The Tom Peters Seminar: Crazy Times Call for Crazy Organizations.* New York: Vintage Books, 1994.

———. *The Pursuit of Wow: Every Person's Guide to Topsy-Turvy Times.* New York: Vintage, 1994.

Pinchot, Gifford, and Elizabeth Pinchot. *The End of Bureaucracy and the Rise of the Intelligent Organization.* San Francisco: Berrett-Koehler, 1993.

Polanyi, Michael. *Personal Knowledge.* Chicago: University of Chicago Press, 1958.

Por, George. "The Quest for Collective Intelligence." In *Community Building: Renewing Spirit and Learning in Business.* Edited by Kazimierz Gozdz. San Francisco: New Leaders Press, 1995.

Porter, Michael E. *Competitive Advantage: Techniques for Analyzing Industries and Competitors.* New York: The Free Press, 1985.

Prahalad, C. K., and Gary Hamel. "The Core Competence of the Corporation." *Harvard Business Review* (May–June, 1991).

———. *Competing for the Future: Breakthrough Strategies for Seizing Control of Your Industry and Creating the Markets of Tomorrow.* Boston: Harvard Business School Press, 1994.

Prigogine, I., and I. Stengers. *Order Out of Chaos: Man's New Dialogue with Nature.* New York: Bantam Books, 1984.

Quinn, James Brian. *Intelligent Enterprises: A New Paradigm for a New Era.* New York: The Free Press, 1992.

Ranky, Paul G. *Computer Integrated Manufacturing: An Introduction with Case Studies.* Englewood Cliffs, NJ: Prentice-Hall International, 1986.

Rasmussen, Jens. "Models for Design of Computer Integrated Manufacturing Systems." Paper presented at First International Conference on Ergonomics of Advanced Manufacturing and Hybrid Automated Systems, Louisville, KY, 17 August 1988.

Ray, Michael, and John Renesch, eds. *The New Entrepreneurs: Business Visionaries for the 21st Century.* San Francisco: New Leaders Press, 1994.

Reich, Robert B. *The Next American Frontier.* New York: Times Books, 1983.

Renesch, John, ed. *The New Traditions in Business, Spirit and Leadership in the 21st Century.* San Francisco: New Leaders Press, 1991.

Rheingold, Howard. *Virtual Reality.* New York: Summit Books, 1991.

Richards, Dick. *Artful Work: Awakening Joy, Meaning and Commitment in the Workplace.* San Francisco: Berrett-Koehler, 1995.

Richta, Radovan. *Civilization of the Crossroads: Social and Human Implications of the Scientific and Technological Revolution.* Translated by Marian Slingova. Prague: International Arts and Sciences Press, 1968.

Rockart, John F., and Christine V. Bullen. *The Rise of Managerial Computing: The Best of the Center for Information Systems Research.* Homewood, IL: Dow Jones-Irwin, 1986.

Roitman, David B., and Manoj K. Sinha. "CIM as a Process of Organizational Change." Presentation at AUTOFACT Conference, 9 November 1987. Dearborn, MI: Society of Manufacturing Engineers, 1987.

Rothlisberger, Fritz J., and William J. Dickson. *Management and the Worker: An Account of Research Conducted by the Western Electric Company, Hawthorne Works, Chicago.* Cambridge, MA: Harvard University Press, 1967.

Rummler, Geary, and Alan Brache. *Improving Performance: How to Manage the White Space on the Organizational Chart.* 2nd ed. San Francisco: Jossey-Bass, 1995.

Sakaiya, Taichi. *The Knowledge-Value Revolution, or a History of the Future.* Tokyo: Kodansha International, 1991.

Savage, Charles M. "The Challenge of CIM: 80% Organizational?" *CIM Review* (The Journal of Computer-Integrated Manufacturing Management) 4, no. 2 (spring 1988).

———. "CIM and Fifth Generation Management." In *Tool & Manufacturing Engineer Handbook.* Vol. 5. Dearborn, MI: SME Press, 1988.

———. "Fifth Generation Management." Workshop at AUTOFACT 86, Detroit, MI, November 1986.

———. *Fifth Generation Management: 1986 Round Table Summary Document.* Dearborn, MI: Society of Manufacturing Engineers, 1987.

———. *Fifth Generation Management for Fifth Generation Technology.* Dearborn, MI: Society of Manufacturing Engineers, 1987.

———. "The Generation Gap: Between the Fifth Generation Technology and Second Generation Organizations." Yankee Group's Factory Systems Summit Conference, Chicago, 16 May 1984.

———. "Organizational Integration: Open Windows of Opportunity." *CIM Review* (The Journal of Computer-Integrated Manufacturing Management) 1, no. 1 (fall 1984).

————. "Organizational Integration: Renovating the Organizational Architecture." *CIM Review* (The Journal of Computer-Integrated Manufacturing Management) 1, no. 3 (spring 1985).

————. "Preparing for the Factory of the Future." *Modern Machine Shop* (January 1983).

————. *Work and Meaning: A Phenomenological Inquiry.* Unpublished Ph.D. thesis, Boston College, 1973.

————, ed. *A Program Guide for CIM Implementation.* Dearborn, MI: Society of Manufacturing Engineers, 1987.

————. "The Dawn of the Knowledge Era." *OR/MS Today* (December 1994).

Schein, Edgar. *Organizational Psychology.* Englewood Cliffs, NJ: Prentice-Hall, 1961.

————. *Process Consultation.* Reading, MA: Addison-Wesley, 1969.

Schrage, Michael. *Shared Minds: The New Technologies of Collaboration.* New York: Random House, 1990.

Scott-Morgan, Peter. *The Unwritten Rules of the Game: Master Them, Shatter Them, and Break Through the Barriers to Organizational Change.* New York: McGraw-Hill, 1994.

Semler, Ricardo. *Maverick: The Success Story Behind the World's Most Unusual Workplace.* New York: Warner Books, 1993.

————. "Why My Former Employees Still Work for Me." *Harvard Business Review* (January–February 1994).

Senge, Peter. *Fifth Discipline: The Art and Practice of the Learning Organization.* New York: Doubleday, 1990.

Shaiken, Harley. *Work Transformed: Automation and Labor in the Computer Age.* New York: Holt, Rinehart and Winston, 1984.

Sherman, Stratford P. "The Mind of Jack Welch." *Fortune* (27 March 1989): 38–50.

Shonberger, Richard J. *Japanese Manufacturing Techniques: Nine Hidden Lessons in Simplicity.* New York: The Free Press, 1982.

Shrensker, Warren. "Fifth Generation Management: Round Table Straw-Person Organization." In *Fifth Generation Management for Fifth Generation Technology.* Edited by Charles M. Savage. Dearborn, MI: Society of Manufacturing Engineers, 1987.

Simon, Herbert. *Administrative Behavior.* 3rd ed. New York: The Free Press, 1976.

————. *The New Science of Management Decision.* New York: Harper & Row, 1960.

Skirl, Stefan, and Ulrich Schwalb, eds. *Das Ende der Hierarchien: Wie Sie schnelllebige Organisationen erfolgreich managen* [The end of the hierarchy: how you can successfully manage fast and lively organizations]. Wiesbaden: Gabler, 1994.

Smith, Adam. *The Wealth of Nations.* London: Penguin Classics, 1987.

Stamps, Jeffrey. *Holonomy: A Human System Theory.* Seaside, CA: Intersystem Publications, 1980.

Stauffer, Robert N. "Converting Customers to Partners at Ingersoll." *Manufacturing Engineering* (September 1988): 41–44.

Stayer, Ralph, and James Belasco. *Flight of the Buffalo: Soaring to Excellence: Learning to Let Employees Lead.* New York: Warner Books, 1993.

Stevens, H. Chandler. *The Network Notebook.* Washington, DC: National Science Foundation, 1978.

Stewart, Thomas. "Your Company's Most Valuable Asset: Intellectual Capital: New Ways to Build It and Measure It." *Fortune* (3 October 1994).

Strassmann, Paul. *Information Payoff: The Transformation of Work in the Electronic Age.* New York: The Free Press, 1985.

Sveiby, Karl-Erik. *Toward a Knowledge Perspective on Organization.* Endsbruk, Sweden: Akademitryck AB, 1994.

Taguchi, Genichi. *On-Line Quality Control During Production.* Tokyo: Japanese Standards Association, 1981.

Tateisi, Kazuma. *The Eternal Venture Spirit: An Executive's Practical Philosophy.* Cambridge, MA: Productivity Press, 1989. (Contains an early reference to the "holonic Nineties.")

Taylor, David. *Business Engineering with Object Technology.* New York: John Wiley & Sons, 1995.

Taylor, Frederick Winslow. *Scientific Management* (comprising "Shop Management," "Principles of Scientific Management," and "Testimony Before the Special House Committee"). New York: Harper and Brothers, 1947.

Teicholz, Eric, and Joel N. Orr. *Computer Integrated Manufacturing Handbook.* New York: McGraw-Hill, 1987.

Thompson, J. *Organizations in Action.* New York: McGraw-Hill, 1967.

Tichy, Noel, and S. Stratford. *Control Your Destiny or Someone Else Will.* New York: Doubleday, 1993.

Tilgher, Adriano. *Homo Faber: Work through the Ages.* Translated by D. Fisher. Chicago: Regency, 1965.

Toffler, Alvin. *The Adaptive Corporation.* New York: McGraw-Hill, 1985.

———. *Powershift: Knowledge, Wealth, and Violence at the Edge of the Twenty-first Century.* New York: Bantam, 1990.

Togino, Kazuto. "A Global Programming Language and Orchestration of the Execution of Jobs and Tasks." National Research Council Canada, Symposium on Manufacturing Application Languages, June 20–21, 1988, Winnipeg, Manitoba.

Treacy, Michael, and Fred Wiersema. *The Discipline of Market Leaders: Choose Your Customers, Narrow Your Focus, Dominate Your Market.* Reading, MA: Addison-Wesley, 1995.

Trevor, Malcolm. *The Japanese Management Development System.* Wolfeboro, NH: Frances Printer Ltd., 1986.

Trist, Eric. "The Evolution of Sociotechnical Systems: A Conceptual Framework and an Action Research Program." Toronto: Ontario Quality of Working Life Center, Occasional Paper No. 2, June 1981.

Trompernaars, Fons. *Riding the Waves of Culture: Understanding Cultural Diversity in Business.* London: The Economist Books, 1993.

Ulich, Eberhard. *Arbeitspsychologie* [Work psychology]. Stuttgart: Schaeffer-Poeschel, 1992.

Urwick, Lyndall. *The Elements of Administration.* New York: Harper, 1943.

U.S. Air Force, Integrated Computer Aided Manufacturing. *ICAM Program Prospectus.* Dayton, OH: Air Force Materials Laboratory, Wright-Patterson Air Force Base, 1979.

Vaill, Peter B. *Managing as a Performing Art: New Ideas for a World of Chaotic Change.* San Francisco: Jossey-Bass, 1989.

Veltrop, Bill. "The Evolutionary Times: A Fable." In *The New Entrepreneuers: Business Visionaries for the 21st Century.* Edited by Michael Ray and John Renesch. San Francisco: New Leaders Press, 1994.

Vogel, Ezra F. *Japan as Number One: Lessons for America.* New York: Harper & Row, 1979.

Vogt, Eric Edwards. "Learning Out of Context." In *Learning Organizations: Developing Cultures for Tomorrow's Workplace.* Edited by Sarita Chawla and John Renesch. Portland, OR: Productivity Press, 1995.

von Neumann, John, and Oskar Morganstern. *The Theory of Games and Economic Behavior.* Princeton: Princeton University Press, 1944.

Waitley, Denis. *Empires of the Mind: Lessons to Lead and Succeed in a Knowledge-Based World.* London: Nicholas Brealey, 1995.

Waldrop, M. Mitchell. *Complexity: The Emerging Science at the Edge of Order and Chaos.* New York: Simon & Schuster, 1992.

Walton, Richard E. *Innovating to Compete.* San Francisco: Jossey-Bass, 1988.

———. *Up and Running: Integrative Information Technology and the Organization.* Boston: Harvard Business School Press, 1989.

Walz, Hartmut, and Thomas Bertels. *Das Intelligente Unternehmen: Schneller lernen als der Wettbewerb* [The intelligent enterprise: fast learning as a competitive advantage]. Landsberg: Verlag Moderne Industrie, 1995.

Ward, John T. *The Factory System.* 2 vols. New York: Barnes & Noble, 1970.

Warfield, John. *A Science of Generic Design: Managing Complexity through Systems Design.* Des Moines: Iowa State University Press, 1994.

Warnecke, Hans-Jürgen with Manfred Hüser. *The Fractal Company: A Revolution in Corporate Culture.* (Germany: 1992; reprint, New York: Springer-Verlag, 1993.)

Warnecke, Hans-Jürgen. *Aufbruch zum Fraktalen Unternehmen: Praxisbeispiele für neues Denken und Handeln* [Breakthrough to the fractal enterprise: practical examples for new thought and action]. Berlin: Springer-Verlag, 1995.

Waterman, Robert H. *The Renewal Factor: How the Best Get and Keep the Competitive Edge.* New York: Bantam Books, 1987.

Webber, Alan. "What's So New About the New Economy?" *Harvard Business Review* (January–February) 1993.

Weber, Max. *The Theory of Social and Economic Organization.* Translated by A. M. Henderson. New York: The Free Press, 1969.

Weick, Karl E. "Organization Design: Organizations as Self-Designing Systems." *Organizational Dynamics* (autumn 1977): 31–32.

———. *The Psychology of Organizing.* 2nd ed. Reading, MA: Addison-Wesley, 1979.

Weisbord, Marvin R. *Organizational Diagnosis: A Workbook of Theory and Practice.* Reading, MA: Addison-Wesley, 1978.

———. *Productive Workplaces: Organizing and Managing for Dignity, Meaning, and Community.* San Francisco: Jossey-Bass, 1987.

Weisbord, Marvin R., and Sandra Janoff. *Future Search: An Action Guide to Finding Common Ground in Organizations & Communities.* San Francisco: Berrett-Koehler, 1995.

Welch, Jack, Jr. "Managing for the Nineties." Presentation at the General Electric annual meeting of share owners, Waukeska, WI, 27 April 1988.

Wellins, Richard, William Byham, and Jeanne Wilson. *Empowered Teams: Creating Self-Directed Work Groups that Improve Quality, Productivity, and Participation.* San Francisco: Jossey-Bass, 1991.

Wheatley, Margaret. *Leadership and the New Science: Learning About Organization from an Orderly Universe.* San Francisco: Berrett-Koehler, 1992.

Whiteley, Richard. *The Customer Driven Company: Moving from Talk to Action.* Reading, MA: Addison-Wesley, 1991.

Whitney, John O. *The Trust Factor: Liberating Profits and Restoring Corporate Vitality.* New York: McGraw-Hill, 1994.

Wiener, Norbert. *God and Golem, Inc.: A Comment on Certain Points Where Cybernetics Impinges on Religion.* Cambridge, MA: MIT Press, 1964.

———. *The Human Use of Human Beings: Cybernetics and Society.* Garden City: Doubleday Anchor, 1954.

Wikstroem, Solveig, et al. *Knowledge and Value: A New Perspective on Corporate Transformation.* New York: Routledge, 1994.

Winograd, Terry, and Fernando Flores. *Understanding Computers and Cognition: A New Foundation for Design.* Reading, MA: Addison-Wesley, 1987.

Womack, James, Daniel Jones, and Daniel Roos. *The Machine That Changed the World.* New York: Rawson Associates, 1990.

Wycoff, Joyce. *Transformation Thinking: Tools and Techniques that Open the Door to Powerful New Thinking for Every Member of Your Organization.* New York: Berkley Books, 1995.

Zuboff, Shoshana. "Automate/Informate: The Two Faces of Intelligent Technology." *Organizational Dynamics* 14, no. 2 (autumn 1985): 5–18.

———. *In the Age of the Smart Machine: The Future of Work and Power.* New York: Basic Books, 1988.

INDEX